D0758145

A MODEST HARMONY

A MODEST HARMONY

Seven Summers in a
Scottish Glen

SHEILA GORDON

Seaview Books
NEW YORK

The author and publisher gratefully acknowledge permission to reprint excerpts from the following:

A History of Scotland by J. D. Mackie (Pelican Books, Revised edition, 1969), pp. 25, 285, 338. Copyright © J. D. Mackie, 1964. Reprinted by permission of Penguin Books Ltd.
Memories, Dreams, Reflections by C. G. Jung. Copyright © 1961 by Pantheon Books, a Division of Random House. Reprinted by permission.

Manufactured in the United States of America.

Second Printing

Seaview Books/A Division of PEI Books, Inc.

Library of Congress Cataloging in Publication Data
Gordon, Sheila.
     A modest harmony.

      1. Gordon, Sheila—Homes and haunts—Scotland.
2. Authors, American—20th century—Biography.
3. Scotland—Social life and customs—20th century.
I. Title.
PS3557.O687Z469   813'.54 [B]   81-84528
ISBN 0-87223-772-9   AACR2

Designed by Tere LoPrete

For my husband,
and for Helen and Bob Hunter

Author's Note

As this book is meant to be a portrait, rather than a literal account, real names of people and places are not used, and some of the characters and events are composites.

Contents

A MODEST HARMONY

CHAPTER
1

The Call

It is a story everyone likes to hear: how, without ever having seen it, we bought a small stone cottage beside a loch in Scotland, and spent our summers, year after year, in the fastness of those lonely hills, returning restored every fall to New York City.

It seems to stir up in the imagination of the listener some vaguely recognized longing, some submerged pastoral vision, idealized and beyond reach; and it is satisfying to hear that it has actually been done—a commonly held dream has been realized, and an accommodation made possible that gives privileged access to both the Old World and the New.

It begins with an unexpected phone call from a seventeenth-century Scottish farmhouse to a nineteenth-century brownstone row house in Brooklyn. A gray, dismal Sunday morning in January, our family morose around the breakfast table toast crumbs and coffee cups and who knows how much of a pine forest pulped, pressed, and printed into the Sunday edition of the *New York Times*. Someone scrapes the last of the marmalade from the jar, while our youngest stirs and stirs until the bottom must surely drop out of the cup. It seems that no one will respond to the telephone's insistence, so I bestir myself.

It is Bob Hunter, talking from the drafty hall of his ancient farmhouse in Fife, but sounding as near and clear as if he has dialed from the pay phone of Pepe's *bodega* at the corner of our block.

Scots, properly, do not, on a whim, make long-distance calls out of the depths of the damp chill and gloom of the Scottish Sabbath.

"Bob! Is everything alright?" At my exclamation the family looks up from the breakfast table.

"Everything's fine." He is always calm, unharried. "Fog—wind—rain lashing at every window, the house full of icy drafts, the beasts shivering out on the hillside waiting for me to go out into the dusk to feed them. . . . It's four o'clock in the afternoon and already pitch-dark, and Helen and I are contemplating death and futility in front of the gas fire. All quite normal for the time of the year. . . . Tell me," he goes on, "last summer, when you two were talking about wanting to buy a wee cottage in the hills, were you just blethering—or were you serious?"

Something takes place in my mind, like the first thin light that seeps in at dawn under the window shades and past the eyelids, disturbing the coziness of inertia with the new day's possibilities—imposing choice, and action. Were we serious? To this day I still do not know.

"Why do you ask?"

"Well"—his answer comes over the Atlantic Ocean in a leisurely, almost laconic fashion—"we saw a place today . . . so exactly like what you had in mind that we thought . . . well, this must be it. Lucky we both saw it, or I'd have been wondering if I'd taken too many sherries before my lunch."

I remain silent, winded momentarily, as if his news has butted the breath out of me. "Tell me about it," I ask. Four pairs of eyes are fixed on me as I listen.

"Helen saw it advertised in *The Scotsman* yesterday. So this afternoon—feeling a little stir-crazy, I think we were; the long, dark winter's beginning to get at us—Helen and I thought we'd take a run out to have a look at it. It's in the hills, in Perthshire, which we consider the bonniest county in all Scotland. It's a wee stone house—not old—built round 1870. It sits beside a loch; about half a mile long and a quarter-mile wide I'd say the loch is. There's plumbing, electricity—all mod. cons. It's tight and dry; there are good outbuildings, a garden. It was the reservoir keeper's cottage, but now the local Water Board is wanting rid of it. It's being sold by roup in two week's time."

"Roup?"

"That's an old Scottish word for auction. The upset price is three thousand pounds—that's where the bidding starts. Should we go along and bid for you, d'you think?" he inquires casually.

Swiftly, in the space of seconds, longings, apprehension, greed, anxiety, vie with each other, cutting crisscross through the mind; *yes, yes,* something clamors along with the uneasiness generated by the possibility that a dream is on the point of being made reality.

"Bob, can we talk about it and call you back? How soon must we let you know?"

"Och, there's no hurry. We have two weeks for the sober consideration of a foolhardy project. We'll post on all the details and description of the property we got from the wee Water Board mannie."

"Tell me one thing. Neighbors—how close are they?"

He laughs. "Neighbors! It's a right isolated spot; there's nothing around but hills and sheep. The nearest neighbor is a farmhouse about a mile down in the valley. There's not even a village or a postoffice. Just a few lonely farms and cottages dotted about the glen."

"Bob . . ." My sigh flutters, a homing pigeon, across the gray winter Atlantic, past his ear, to light on the chimney pot of that unseen cottage in the hills, where sheep crop patiently in the swift-fallen dusk. I know, before I hang up the phone, that it is all settled. I have read enough fairy tales in my life to know what our answer will be, after the mandatory discussion about the legal aspects, investment prospects, plumber's and surveyor's reports, problems of international currency exchange. "We'll call you back in a couple of days," I tell him.

It is a story everyone likes to hear: grown-ups, children, strangers encountered on the train chugging northward from

London to Edinburgh, my husband's barber, fellow-guests at dinner parties, the fishmonger in the village of Auchterbraehead, where in the summer we would buy our herrings and kippers. My butcher in Brooklyn took to calling me Lady G. after we became, in our small way, Scottish landed gentry, and never tired of questioning me, while trimming the chops, about the difference in flavor between Scottish lamb and American lamb, and was always intrigued by the mysteries of malt whiskey in relation to ordinary Scotch.

Back at the breakfast table, we pretended to discuss the impracticality of having a summer place three thousand miles away, presenting to each other the advantages and disadvantages in a serious responsible way, each of us knowing full well, as we argued and reasoned, that the conclusion was foregone.

By the end of the week the papers arrived from the Hunters, with two photographs that we assumed were black and white, and were dismayed to learn were actually color. They showed a white gate and a clump of blackish trees on a rise at the end of a snowy road; a gray house with dark windows and a chimney at either end lurked depressingly among the trees; beyond the house there was a faintly glimmering area that we took to be the loch. "An underexposed photo taken on a snowy, windy, freezing afternoon" we read on the back. But our faith in the Hunters' judgment never wavered in the face of the Wuthering Heights bleakness of the aspect—we merely doubted their competence as photographers.

We studied the description of the property drawn up for prospective purchasers by the Water Board: "a stone dwelling, hereinafter referred to as Glenauchen Waterman's Cottage, occupying an area of one acre of the property of Wester Glenauchen Farm, bordering Glenauchen Loch . . . consisting of kitchen, sitting room, two bedrooms, two dressing rooms and bathroom . . . spring-fed water supply . . . stable, carriage house, and sundry outbuildings . . . fishing rights . . . electricity supply . . . taxes. . . ." When we had read the papers through, to ourselves, to each other, picking out bits that particularly appealed, we called the Hunters. I am always astonished that I can lift up the phone in my kitchen, dial fourteen digits, wait a few seconds for the electronic disturbance I have initiated to make some mysterious connections, and in a remote farmhouse in another country, a telephone starts up its ringing. We asked them to go to the auction and bid whatever they considered reasonable.

"Leave it to me," Bob said.

We left it to him.

The week before the auction was to take place, the notion of the stone house in those unknown hills remained constantly in the family awareness; like a marvelous kite it hovered over us, and from time to time, each of us in our own way would tug at the string to bring it into mental range and contemplate its enchanting quality.

"We won't get it," our youngest, a natural pessimist, would declare.

"We will, we will," his older brother and sister reassured him with the careless confidence of youth.

The children had grown up in a house beside a canal that flowed into the Great South Bay of Long Island; with swimming, fishing, and sailing all available in the backyard, we had never needed a summer place. But that fall we had bought and renovated an old brownstone in the Cobble Hill section of Brooklyn, and our summers presented a problem that we barely had time to contemplate before the Hunters stepped in like fairy godmothers and presented us with undreamed-of possibilities.

At grade school, in South Africa, where Harl and I had been born, we had been made to learn much poetry by heart. There was a girl, Mavis, who sprang now into my mind although I had not thought about her for thirty years. Hand on heart, eye fixed on some distant point, she would declaim with much passion and no punctuation, "My heart's in the Highlands my heart is not here my heart's in the Highlands a'chasing the deer—Chasing the wild deer and following the roe my heart's in the Highlands where-ever I go." Pausing only long enough to draw breath to get her through the next stanza without turning blue, she would hurl herself through all sixteen lines of Robert Burns's poem before sinking, triumphant and anoxic, back in her seat.

"My heart's in the Highlands my heart is not here," I would inform the family during that week while we were waiting for the auction to take place. I would, at their repeated requests, do a rendering for them of Mavis's impassioned outpouring, all of us wondering why the girl, who had no Scottish ancestry and had probably never set foot out of our colonial backwater, should have invested that particular poem with such intensity of feeling.

On the Friday evening of the auction, Bob phoned. "We have it," he stated, complacent.

"We have it," I announced to the family.

The children looked jubilant, Harl bemused, at what we were letting ourselves in for.

"Five thousand pounds," Bob went on. "I had decided to go up to five and a half or six. The only other serious bidder was a clergyman chappie from Edinburgh; he told me afterward that he was wanting it in order to get away from the noise and pace of life in Edinburgh. *Edinburgh!* I said to him, 'I've been bidding for some folk who need to get away from the noise and pace of life in *New York!*'" Bob's mirth lasted for two expensive transatlantic minutes; it was obvious that he was enjoying the whole enterprise. "It was our good luck that the Water Board is so gormless. They held the auction in an un-heated milk-bar place, on a Friday morning in February! It was sleeting—there were gale-force winds tearing through the hills, and naturally no one came. There were only about four bidders willing to brave the foul weather; two of them soon dropped out, leaving us and the reverend gent. The rest of the audience were locals come to watch outsiders making fools of themselves. If those foolish bureaucrats had waited to hold the auction on a fine spring day, it would have fetched twice the price."

*   *   *

Later, Helen would describe the scene to us, and we could see how she and Bob would have appeared to the locals, both of them handsome and distinguished in their good tweeds. We could imagine Bob, his thick hair impressively silver with his face still young, bidding with nonchalance as he leaned on the shooting stick that he carried whenever he wanted to look the gentleman farmer. The flimsy milk-bar structure at the caravan site, shrouded that day in wind-driven rain and fog; the auctioneer, shivering, with a bad cold, Helen said, anxious to get the business quickly done; the locals then gathering around the Hunters, curious, but trying only in the most oblique manner to learn the identity of the purchasers of the old reservoir keeper's cottage; their astonishment on hearing that Bob had been bidding for "a certain party in New York who intends to use the place as a summer residence."

"Gave those wee glen folk something to gossip about over their fish and chips at teatime tonight," Bob went on, highly entertained by it all. After their triumph at the auction, they had stopped off at one of the local hostelries for a couple of whiskies to restore the circulation, and then had looked in on their bank manager to arrange a loan for us.

"But we have the money," I protested, reminding him of our unexpected inheritance, which had given us the notion of buying a place in the country.

He was horrified. "Don't you know that you must never pay cash for anything if you can get a good loan at a low interest? I see you are sadly lacking in business acumen. My lawyer is drawing up all the papers and documents for you; he'll be sending them along for your signatures."

It was done.

We found ourselves owners of a piece of Scottish hillside, with "a stone dwelling, stable, and sundry outbuildings thereupon." It would be another six months before we would see it.

Helen now took up the phone. "Wouldn't you like to know your Scottish address?" she asked. "Have you got a pencil?"

I jotted down as she spoke: "Glenauchen Cottage. Glencorrie (by Glenogle). Perthshire. Scotland."

"What does 'by Glenogle' mean?" I asked.

"That's the nearest village where there's a postoffice. There isn't even a postoffice in your glen; there's just two hotels and a couple of pubs. The nearest village is eight miles away."

When the phone call was done, each member of the family, in turn, studied the scrap of paper with the address scribbled on it, each reading it out loud, as if it were a poem or a piece of timeless wisdom.

CHAPTER 2

Explanations

I shall have to go back a little way and retrace the path leading across three continents that brought us to Glenauchen Cottage beside its still loch, where the brown trout, lurking in the depths, occasionally would stir the repose of a summer afternoon when they rose to the surface for air.

Harl and I were both born, raised, and educated in South Africa. Despairing of the problems that face that country, we chose early to leave. We married while still at the university, and soon after graduation went to live in Britain.

Harl, as a newly qualified doctor, was offered an internship at the Royal Hospital for Sick Children, in Edinburgh. Scotland has held great prestige as a medical center since the seventeenth century; we packed our baby, who had been born while we were in London, and our few possessions, and headed north. The city, medieval and Georgian, set among green hills, and the countryside, placid farmland surrounded by craggy glens and rivers and lochs, at once took hold of our imagination, and has kept it ever since.

One day Harl was asked by an acquaintance to give a talk on apartheid at a labor rally. The program included Scottish folk dancing and ballads. We were both taken by the singing

of a young woman with a clear, high voice, and tried to remember a little jouncing song she had sung:

> "Dance to your daddy,
> My bonny laddie ...
> Thou shalt have a fishie
> In a little dishie,
> Thou shalt have a fishie
> When the boat comes home."

The words and tune remained with us; we were charmed by
the singer, and the song.

Not long after this, on a bleak November evening, there
was a ring at our door. I went to open it, curious, as we knew
few people and seldom had visitors. On the doorstep stood an
uncommonly handsome young man, his looks made even more
striking by a shock of thick, bright, silver hair. His manner
awkward, reserved, he asked for Harl. I brought him into the
kitchen, where Harl was distributing spoonfuls of porridge
among the baby's hands, face, and high chair.

The young man introduced himself; he was Bob. He had
heard Harl's talk at the rally, had found that we lived around
the corner from him, and had called to ask us to tea.

We went. He had a wife, Helen, a classic, blue-eyed Scottish
beauty with a mass of russet brown hair and the fresh pink and
white complexion the climate is said to bestow on the women
of that damp, misty country; a graduate in English, an accomplished pianist with a good voice, she loved to sing religious
choral music though lapsed from the Congregationalist religion
in which she had been raised. Their baby, Tom, was the same
age as our David.

Bob, like Harl, had had his student days interrupted by the
war, and was now working for his doctorate in botany.

After tea, to soothe the baby, who was cranky, Helen
jounced him on her knee and sang:

> "Dance to your daddy,
> My bonny laddie,
> Dance to your daddy,
> My wee lamb."

We recognized her then as the young woman who had sung at the rally.

Our friendship took, and cemented, and has been one of the enduring and gratifying things of our lives. Their Scottish reserve, and Bob's fundamental unavailability to all but a chosen few, was breached, and the four of us and our babies went about everywhere together.

We moved, eventually, to New York, but our link with the Hunters held firm. Our second and third children were born within months of theirs, and we always kept in touch.

The summer before we bought the cottage, after not having seen the Hunters for some years, we made a visit to Scotland. They had given up the academic life and gone farming. We stayed with them in their 1680 farmhouse in Fife. Tom, their oldest, like our David, was now in his late teens; also like our David, and many of their generation at that time, he was dropping in and out of institutions of higher learning. The Hunters' middle child, also named David, and our daughter Philippa, in their mid-teens, were in high school; their daughter Elizabeth and our son Neil were not quite teenagers. The children all got along as amiably as their parents did.

On a drive through the nearby countryside one afternoon, we told them of an unexpected legacy we had received out of Africa. An elderly cousin of my mother's, much loved by all our family, had died childless, and left us some money; we had assumed that she was penniless, but it seemed that over the years, out of a modest salary, she had regularly put by small amounts in a savings account, and she had bequeathed her life's savings to my two sisters and myself. We felt that a gift of this nature should be put to extraordinary use, and had not yet been able to think of a way that would measure up to the meaning this legacy held for us.

We were driving through the ripe summer landscape; we passed a meadow on a hill slope where cows were drinking from a stream. Beside the stream stood a gray stone cottage, with a chimney at either end, smoke rising from one, and an open doorway with climbing roses; an old woman in a black dress came out and went walking down the path toward the cows.

Harl had been silent for a while. "That's what we should do with the money," he said now.

"What do you mean?"

"We should buy a little cottage—like that one—here, in Scotland." He is a practical, down-to-earth man, not given to flights of fancy. His suggestion left me breathless.

"Why not?" Bob remarked, unsurprised. "There are loads of nice wee country cottages to be bought."

"We could look one out for you," Helen said, matter-of-fact, "and you could come across every summer—get away from the heat of New York."

Bob then started to explain the difference between wheat and barley, pointing out the silken whiskers that grow on the ears of barley, and telling how the best of his barley crop went to the brewers for malt whiskey. We all forgot about the cottage, until the phone rang on that cold Sunday morning, the following January.

CHAPTER
3

To the North

There is no reason at all why my heart, like Mavis's in the fifth grade, should be in the Highlands. But there it is. I have been told that when my mother, having considered her family of four children complete, was taken unawares by my insistence on being born, followed not eighteen months later by my sister, she engaged a Scottish nanny for the two unanticipated infants. And I like to think that this Scottish lady, homesick in the dust and dry heat of Africa, must have whispered and crooned in my small ear of glens, and brimming rushing burns, and green hills concealing pewter-gray lochs, and ancient castles and keeps looking out over valleys where stone villages nestle and pinnacles of church spires draw the eye upward to vaulted skies.

The white sales were still on in the department stores by the time we had signed and sealed the deeds making us the unlikely owners of Glenauchen Cottage in Glencorrie (by Glenogle) in the county of Perthshire. I shopped for bed linens and towels and cutlery for a house that existed only in my imagination; the legal documents we had signed had no more power to impose a reality on our venture than the texture of the sheets and towels as I handled and packed them and mailed them off to the Hunters' farm to wait our arrival in the summer.

Helen, meanwhile, was finding a diversion from the winter gloom by attending sales in auction rooms in nearby country towns. Letters arrived describing the stove, tiny refrigerator, and vacuum cleaner she had bid for and obtained for a small sum; she had also bought a dozen pillows and one and a half dozen pure wool blankets at a boarding school whose effects were being sold off. "Why do we need so many blankets in a summer house?" the children wanted to know. "Don't ask," we answered cheerfully.

She sent the dimensions of Glenauchen's windows, and I sat at my sewing machine stitching curtains to hang at windows that looked out on an unknown landscape. "We've found excellent beds," Helen wrote, "and a very good Victorian mahogany chest of drawers, with inlaid mother-of-pearl, for only eight pounds. We're having the electrician install an immersion heater in the tank so that you won't need to light the kitchen fire whenever you need hot water. The people down at the farm have recommended a good house painter—what colors would you like? The walls are glum beige and dismal dun at present." "White," I wrote back, "all white," feeling dazed that the mere expression of my fancy was all that was needed for the cottage interior to be transformed.

"Nothing so enjoyable as spending other folks' money," Bob wrote. "We have all the pleasure of browsing and buying and choosing, and none of the discomfort of having to pay up."

We had opened an account at Bob's village bank, and given him our power of attorney so that he could sign our checks and pay our bills. The bank manager, Mr. Baillie, wrote, informing us of his pleasure in handling our affairs and assuring us of his cooperation at all times; I doubt if we ever had much more than five or six hundred dollars in our checking account, but we were treated always, by Mr. Baillie and his assistant manager and the tellers, with an Old World courtesy and consideration, as though, Bob said, we were Andrew Carnegie himself.

* * *

"Your nearest neighbours," Helen wrote, "are the Camerons. Mr. Cameron is long dead, and his wife, a spry old farmer body who looks to be in her sixties but apparently is nearer eighty, runs the place with the help of two grandsons who are reputed to be *wild*. The acre on which your home stands was part of the Camerons' farm; they sold it to the Water Board a hundred years ago so that the reservoir keeper's cottage could be built beside the loch. The loch belongs to the Water Board, but the Camerons retained the fishing rights.

"Our source of information is one Donny MacIver. He is the reservoir keeper of the other loch in the glen, but since the Water Board has sold off Glenauchen, he's now in charge of both reservoirs. You're bound to get to know him well, as he visits your loch daily to check water level and pressure, etc. He is a deacon of Glenauchen Kirk, a classic specimen of Scottish Calvinism, but with a quick eye and a sharp turn of phrase for what goes on in the glen. 'We look forward to welcoming the Gordons to our congregation at Glenauchen Kirk,' he said to us. I soon put a stop to that nonsense. 'Neither the Hunters nor the Gordons are churchgoers,' I informed him."

Our place, *our* neighbors, *our* glen, *our* loch. . . . We read the letters, becoming increasingly bemused at all this life that was accumulating around us in an unknown range of Scottish hills, with only a few signatures on documents, and the Hunters' letters, to vouch for the reality.

"Although the glen looks as if it consists of a few far-lying cottages and farmhouses," Bob wrote, "you'll learn when you get here that it is a veritable Mafia of connections—feuds and scandals and cliques and spheres and domains; subtle overtones and undertones at a pitch so rare that you'd need to have lived here since the rebellion of 1745 to be tuned in to their implications. I have no doubt that on the windowsill of each cottage and farmhouse there lies a spyglass that they employ to bring each other's activities into range close enough for inspection and dissection and speculation. Amongst all the apparent isolatedness, these places teem with plot and gossip and intrigue. Your Brooklyn Mafia is nothing compared to the Scottish Mafia in a glen like this."

* * *

As the spring drew on, Helen reported that the interior of
the cottage was looking much improved in its coat of fresh
white paint; they enjoyed going out to inspect the progress on
a fine Sunday, and their encounters with Donny MacIver were
always rewarding. MacIver's latest story was gossip that assumed legendary dimensions, Bob wrote. It concerned a local
farmer named Geordie McCaskie, a curmudgeonly character
notorious in the glen for his wealth, parsimoniousness, and mis-
anthropy, owner of the fishing rights at Glenshinnoch Loch,
the other reservoir. "Anyone wanting to fish there," Bob's
letter explained, "is required to stop by at McCaskie's farmhouse and pay fifty pence for a permit, but fishers often slip
by without paying. Some years ago, three men were fishing
illegally on the shore of Glenshinnoch Loch when one of them
fell dead of a heart attack. His two cronies carried him up to
the old curmudgeon's farmhouse and knocked on the door.
McCaskie appeared, glowering, and they explained their predicament and asked for help. 'And what aboot yer fishin'
permit?' the old man growled. Abashed, the two men reached
into their pockets and forked up their fifty pence each. Stone-
faced, McCaskie pocketed the money, and then, pointing to the
deceased lying stiffening on his doorstep, demanded, 'And what
aboot *his* fifty pence?' Bob commented, "Sounds apocryphal,
but it's too good not to be true. You're in for an interesting
time when you come to this glen."

The letters brushed in the local color on the gray and white
of the wintry photograph of Glenauchen Cottage which we
had stuck on the kitchen wall and contemplated in our different
ways as the winter turned to spring. "The slope of your front
lawn is covered in snowdrops . . . crocuses . . . daffodils," Helen
reported. "What a pity they'll be over by the time you get
here—the glen looks so bonny with the new lambs gamboling
about on the green hills."

I wondered if we would ever get to see the glen in the
springtime.

We began to feel impatient for the summer. "We must buy
floppy hats," I wrote to Helen, "and long, baggy cardigan
sweaters and shoes with pointed toes, and all sit about in basket
chairs taking tea on the front lawn, like Virginia and Vanessa
and Clive and Lytton and Morgan Forster, and someone must

photograph us looking, languidly, as if we know some profound truths of which the *others* will always remain in abysmal ignorance."

I was to go on ahead of the family to complete the furnishing and equip the cottage so that it would be ready when they all arrived in early July.

In the middle of June, I set off; in my luggage were stowed items of cutlery, a garlic press, a pepper mill, a bag of garlic, a hard lump of Parmesan cheese, a good corkscrew, herbs and spices, and various other staples without which one would not venture into the remote reaches of the wild Scottish countryside. Helping me pack, Harl said I was like those nineteenth-century British explorers of the source of the Nile who hacked their way through the jungle, confident that in the boxes carried by their native bearers was an adequate supply of Twinings Tea and Bath Oliver Biscuits and Frank Cooper's Oxford Marmalade, purchased at Fortnum & Mason to sustain them on their danger-fraught expeditions.

I flew first to London. From there I was to make my way north by British Railways, stopping over for a visit with old friends in Nottinghamshire, whose house in Sherwood Forest has a woodland path that leads to Newstead Abbey, Lord Byron's home.

At St. Pancras station, where porters—like many of life's amenities—have become scarce, I struggled with my luggage, trying to secure it on a trolley I had been quick enough to grab. As a suitcase tumbled off for the third time, a quiet voice, speaking in English public school accents, said, "Here, let me do this for you." Soon my possessions were ranged in an orderly pile on the cart; the voice belonged to a middle-aged man, a distinguished-looking executive type in a well-tailored gray suit, who placed his own leather attaché case on top of my luggage and asked which train I was taking. "Nottingham? Good. That's where I'm going. Come along, then." I accompanied him obediently as if he were a courier sent to escort me by some All-Knowing travel bureau that had anticipated my tiredness and jet lag. He soon had me settled in a compartment, with my cases stowed neatly up on the rack. The train chugged out of the glass-domed station, past rows of narrow backyards where washing hung and cabbages grew in the clouded coolness of the summer day. We had the compartment to ourselves. He seated himself opposite me. "I assumed by your clothes and luggage that you were American, but now I confess that your accent has got me confused."

As the grimy urban back gardens changed to industrial suburbs and then to green farmland, we chatted amiably, I surmising that he very likely would not have engaged in conversation with me if he had thought I was a fellow Briton. I explained to him my mixed background, and told him of the place we had bought in Scotland. Like everyone else who heard the story, he was much taken with it, especially liking the idea that we had not even seen it. "It will probably turn out to be damp and drafty and cold," I said, gloomy suddenly, and expressing some of the doubts that were assailing me as my journey brought me nearer to the reality of what now appeared to be an irresponsible impulse. "And we'll end up huddling around the smoky fireplace gazing glumly at each other and wondering how we ever came to engage in such folly."

"I think not," he assured me. He puffed at a pipe he had asked my permission to light up. "I think not. I suspect that you will never regret it. I have been in New York in the summer; you will find Perthshire very agreeable by comparison."

"It's possible that it will rain incessantly every summer. Seven wet years—like the seven lean years in the Bible—"

"It won't." He was pleasant and serious; the *Financial Times* was folded neatly in the pocket of the raincoat he had hung up; his suit was West-of-England woolen cloth, his shirt and tie conservative, his shoes of excellent leather, his hair graying at the temple; the impression he gave was one of ease and self-assurance in the world. "You will never regret buying that place," he told me. "You'll see—the summers will be pleasant and dry, seven warm summers." He performed some small ritual with a silver implement, and the smoldering glow in the bowl of his briar pipe flared up with heat and brightness. "You'll have . . . a unique experience . . . it's a wise thing you have done."

"It's our Scottish friends, really, who've done it."

"Then you are felicitous in the friends you have."

A steward beating out a tune on a brass gong popped his head round the door to announce lunch, and my courier invited me to join him. In spite of the fact that the food on British trains is, these days, mostly unpalatable, the overcooked meat, soggy vegetables, and doughy puddings are served with skill and aplomb by a crew of such amiable characters that, with the country landscape streaming past the windows, the dining car is always a pleasure. There is generally a decent selection of French wines, the whites properly chilled; and the reconstituted powdered soup, limp green beans, floury gravy, and thick blob of custard over steamed pudding cannot quite dispel the childhood association of glamour and excitement that dining on trains still evokes.

Back in the compartment, as we neared Nottingham, he brought my luggage down from the rack. When the train slowed and halted for a crossing signal, he reached into his breast pocket and handed me a card; without looking at it I slipped it into my purse. Inside the station, he carried my bags off the train. At the far end of the platform I saw one of my friends approaching. My fellow traveler shook my hand, assuring me once more that we would have many happy summers with fine weather in Scotland; we exchanged the appropriate civilities, and he disappeared into the crowd.

At the house in Sherwood Forest, over dinner, my hosts were intrigued by my encounter on the train.

"Did he tell you his name?" they asked.

I fished his card out of my purse. "Arthur Greenleaf," I read. "Barleycroft House, Lower Papplewick, Nottinghamshire."

The telephone directory was fetched and leafed through; but we could find no one with that name and address.

"Strange . . . I saw him helping you with the luggage—though I must say he made off pretty hastily when he saw me approaching. . . . The mysterious Mr. Greenleaf, making predictions and forecasting the Scottish climate—I wonder who he really is."

*　　*　　*

The word "Midlands" starts up visions of dark Satanic mills, with row upon row of squalid factory workers' houses huddled beneath their pall; it is a true vision, but it exists among some of England's most beautiful countryside. In mining villages just like Eastwood, where D. H. Lawrence was born, apart from the cars parked in the streets and television antennae on the rooftops, little seems to have changed; the miners, in heavy boots, shuffle with bowed shoulders about the narrow cobbled streets, caps pulled well forward over pale faces, dressed in shabby suits, their neckerchiefs knotted at collarless throats. The meat hanging in the butchers' windows is lean and stringy, and miners' wives in headscarves park their babies' prams on the narrow strips of pavement while they shop or gossip in low regional accents. But where the village ends and the slag heaps fall away, cows graze under oak and beech in great quiet meadows, and farmers tend acres that roll greenly away to the horizon.

For a few days, my friends took me about through the gently ripening landscape of Nottinghamshire and Derbyshire, where a distant church spire pinpoints a village or market town drowsing in the sun, tiny cottages sport nosegays of bright-colored flowers in miniature gardens, and old gaffers dream away their declining days in benign warmth of benches outside inns with quaint names: The Bird and Bottle, The King's Arms, The Bull. In the distance, outlined against the sky, the stolid oblong of a Norman tower or the romantic ruins of an ancient castle— its ramparts fallen like giant children's blocks on the brilliance of the grass—confer a timelessness and serenity on adjacent villages. We looked at a couple of stately homes now thrown open to the public by an aristocracy impoverished by high taxation and the loss of an empire—houses and landscaping on so grand a scale that the imagination quails on contemplating how noble a conception of themselves and their destinies these people must have had. Smaller Elizabethan manor houses seem more appealing, more modestly conceived, their huge hearths and low-ceilinged chambers giving a feeling of bustling domestic life—a less overbearing view of man in relation to the rest of the universe.

*   *   *

They put me on the train at Doncaster, a four-hour run to Edinburgh. It became the custom, every year, on my way from New York to Perthshire, to break the journey in Nottinghamshire, to stroll along the path through the trees of Sherwood Forest to Newstead Abbey and walk on the banks of the lake in Lord Byron's garden; to be with our old friends, and to become acclimatized to the geographical and spiritual change, before heading north to Glenauchen.

CHAPTER
4

The Cottage

The rhythm of the pistons turning the train wheels northward sang out in my ears: *Glenauchen Cottage, Glencorrie (by Glenogle), Perthshire, Scotland.* From way back, Mavis's voice in the chalk-dusty schoolroom declaimed, *My heart's in the Highlands my heart is not here my heart's in the Highlands a'chasing the deer.* . . . In my mind's eye, a picture of a bleak stone house set on a barren hillside, its surrounding trees bending to the wind's thrust. But it was impossible to connect the purpose of my journey with an unknown reality that lay waiting in the hills, and the train carried me through a limbo, a space between what my logical mind knew and an actuality that my imagination could not grasp.

As the train pulled into Waverley Station in Edinburgh, the thick silver of Bob's hair stood out from the mass crowding the platform; beside him I spotted Helen looking excited and anxious, her cheeks flushed pink.

When our greetings were over, Bob asked if I had had lunch. I had eaten on the train.

"Good. Then we can drive straight out to Glenauchen." He was excited too, in his phlegmatic way, impatient to be showing off what they had wrought for us, confident of its rightness.

It was a gray day. We drove up Princes Street, overlooked by its medieval skyline, where tourists thronged and stared and shopped; along Queensferry past rows of stone mansions converted into small genteel hotels; through suburban streets where the bright-polished windows of staid houses reflected rose gardens flourishing alongside immaculate sidewalks. We crossed the Firth of Forth bridge and sped away into the Fifeshire countryside.

"My mother has been making me very nervous," Helen told me after we had exchanged family news, "and Kate the dairymaid too—going on at me, the two of them, girning away about how buying a house for someone else is the surest way of ruining a friendship."

"Your mother. Old battleax," Bob countered comfortably. "There's never a thing you've done that the old girl has approved of . . . including marrying me."

"*Especially* marrying you."

"Dinna' fash, Helen, my dear. The old battleax is wrong once again; the Gordons are going to like Glenauchen fine."

We chatted in a commonplace way, as if this were no extraordinary expedition, while my eyes took in details as if the landscape had to be learned, instantly, committed at once to memory and filed permanently away for future reference.

The motorway skirted Loch Leven; the Hunters pointed out the castle in the middle of the loch where Mary, Queen of Scots had been imprisoned by the lords who rose up against her liaison with Bothwell. "Fed up with her they were," Bob remarked, "having Darnley strangled, and then having the cheek to marry Bothwell. Shocked everyone—more by the marriage than the murder."

Around the island and its fifteenth-century castle, where Queen Mary had languished, with Mary Douglas, her father's mistress, as her jailer, anglers, motionless in rowboats on the still dark water of the loch, waited with endless patience for the fish to bite.

Loch Leven fell behind; we passed whiskey distilleries and knitting mills whose brand-name products were familiar from sophisticated advertisements on the glossy paper of magazines. We left the motorway for minor roads that went through a string of neat, joyless mining villages, where pubs and fish-and-chips shops did not open till late afternoon, and loutish youths and heavily made-up girls stood about bored, aimless, outside the Woolworth's and the Boot's Chemists and the Cooperative chain stores that operate wherever there is commercial life in Britain. Behind the villages lay the desolation of dark peaty moorland, mining machinery, slag heaps.

Expectant, making no judgment, my mind clicked away like a camera, recording details of the scenery.

"We're coming into Kinross-shire," Bob announced. "It's the next-door county to Perthshire."

Quite suddenly, then, we were in a different world. We had turned onto a broad country road lined by magnificent trees—oak, chestnut, and beech, winding through green pastures where cows and sheep browsed. On the left a river coursed, gleaming darkly in the gray clouded afternoon.

"And there . . . there are the Blairrossie Hills," Bob said, "*your hills*"—presenting them to me with a broad sweep of his arm.

Our hills. At that instant the sun broke through the leaden canopy of cloud and flooded the green flanks of the range of hills that lay to the east, the radiance overflowing, spilling and running into every grassy declivity; the clouds moved swiftly aside; oblique rays of brilliant sunlight, like a Blake illustration, slanted down out of an increasing patch of pure blue sky.

"Well, now," Bob said, satisfied with the celestial arrangements, "that Great Old Realtor in the sky Himself is certainly putting on a good show for your benefit—displaying the Almighty Real Estate in its best light."

We were all silent in the face of what so obviously appeared to be a good omen; we had received the affirmation we had been wanting, all of us having been able to ignore any possibility of ill-omen in the clouded grayness of the day up till that moment.

The transfiguring change in the weather made it seem as if one had awakened from a dream of wanting to enter a place, to find that access had been granted and the vision was not to

be snatched rudely away. There was a sign, ENTERING PERTH-
SHIRE; we turned right, onto a narrow road where the hills
reared up on either side. A smaller signpost in the shape of an
arrow said TO GLENCORRIE, 2 MILES.

"This road goes right through your glen," Helen explained,
a little nervous over my speechlessness.

"*Glen*: A mountain valley, usually narrow and forming the
course of a stream," says the *Oxford English Dictionary*. "At
first applied to the narrow valleys of the mountain districts of
Scotland." In Scotland, streams are known as "burns"; in our
glen, Glenauchen Burn springs silver out of the hillside to
tumble downhill and feed into the River Corrie—about fifteen
feet across at its widest—that meanders along the floor of the
glen to pour itself eventually into the waters of the River Forth
on its journey to the sea.

In future summers we would trace out Glenauchen Burn to
its source. But at the moment we were driving against the
direction of the flow of the river, paralleling it on the narrow
road scarcely wide enough for two cars, as it wound and
twisted its way out of the hills. On the sides of the hills around
us was a scattering of farmsteads, and we passed an occasional
stone wall or glimpsed a cottage chimney or garden beside the
road. We crossed a bridge that forded a deep ravine, and
around a hairpin bend came upon a great pile of a castellated
building. THE CORRIE HOTEL a sign over the arched stone
gateway proclaimed. ACCOMMODATIONS—MORNING COFFEE—
LUNCHES—AFTERNOON TEAS—HIGH TEAS—DINNER. Over the
years, the Corrie Hotel would serve to accommodate an overflow of our guests: friends and relatives who found their way
from different parts of the globe to our hideaway in those
hills.

Further along the road was another hotel, the Bencleish,
small, trim in its whitewashed walls and black woodwork, an
old posting-inn where coaches would have stopped to refresh
travelers and horses in the eighteenth century. On a bench
outside the bar, a few hikers drank tankards of beer, hotels
being exempted from the drinking regulations that close pubs
between three and five. A log-cabin youth hostel, half a mile
later, explained the hikers' presence.

The road ran close beside the burn now; the water could be seen flowing clear over rounded boulders, pebble beds, and dark pools; green pastures sloped gently from the banks, and black-faced white sheep grazed in the calm radiance of the afternoon. The sun's heat had massed monumental cloud formations against the blue density of the sky. There was a primal, Old Testament element in the serenity.

"The Lord is my shepherd, I shall not want," Helen sang in her high, clear soprano voice. "He maketh me to lie down in green pastures. . . ."

Then, as if it were time for a lesson in humility, she broke off the hymn singing and said, "Here it is, the eyesore."

A range of low green hills descended to a grassy meadow; the turret of a medieval castle emerged above the trees of a small forest. The meadow was bright-colored with closely ranged caravans, campers, and parked cars; in the center of a tarmac parking ground stood a flimsy, sky-blue, barracks-like structure beneath a huge billboard: MILK BAR.

"The caravan site," she apologized.

On washlines strung up between the caravans, baby clothes, shirts, and diapers danced in the fresh hill air, along with swim suits, tea-towels, socks, and underwear. A few white-skinned girls in bikinis lay about, sunning themselves on towels of garish shades that clashed with the more muted tones of the landscape. Blue-jeaned youths had stripped off their shirts, and fished in the running water of the burn; the pallor of their skin, and their narrow shoulders, told of cramped housing in factory towns where the sun rarely poked through the sooty air. Elderly men and women sat at folding tables set up beside the burn, brewing pots of tea as complacently as if they were in their own parlors. Children romped with dogs and balls and cricket bats, and transistor radios babbled.

Bob had pulled up for us to survey the scene. "According to Donny MacIver," he said, "the villain of the piece, the architect of this rural pillage, is Gavin MacFadyen, a scion of the local "big house"—a once well-to-do family rapidly going to seed, according to all reports. See that fine medieval castle on the hill? Actually it's more likely a keep, built as a fortress by the feuding clans. Now, look at those imposing gateposts—do you see a sign? It says LOCKUP PUB. He's got a bar and disco flourishing in the ancient dungeons of his castle, to keep the caravan folk happy and tipsy at night."

"His goings-on are a scandal in the glen, according to Tottie MacIver," Helen added.

"It's awful," I said. It looked like a pastel plastic shantytown. "All the same, it must make a pleasant change for Glasgow slum people—even cramped with Granny and Grandpa and all the kids in one caravan."

"Come now," Bob teased me, "if you're going to play the part of landed gentry you have to choose sides; we can't have any of this shilly-shallying."

We continued on our way. Instead of nymphs and shepherds disporting themselves on the greensward, we had encountered youths and maidens with transistor radios and cans of beer and packets of potato chips. I gazed uneasily out of the rear window until the caravan site fell out of view.

Without warning, Bob made a sharp left turn at a single beech tree with a huge, spreading leaf-canopy that hid the entrance to a private road. There was a signpost: GLENAUCHEN LOCH. NO UNAUTHORISED ADMITTANCE. NO PARKING. NO PIC-NICKING. NO CAMPING.

"We're authorized. This is the private road that leads to your house—it's almost a mile. How d'you like this wee humpback bridge?"

They had not mentioned, in their letters, a gracefully arching stone bridge fording the river whose waters washed over a stony bed into swirling rock pools. Dragonflies hung motion-less, their wings shimmering in suspension over the flux of sliding water. On either side of the bridge, fields, planted with light green hay, spattered blue and yellow and white with wild flowers, lay placid in the afternoon sunlight.

Beyond the bridge, the road plunged into deep woods where the light fell mottled through the branches; then, rising steeply out of the trees, it made a sharp bend to the right and led past a farmyard with a crowstepped stone barn and a tall white-washed farmhouse. Hens, pecking briskly in the grass under a copse of chestnut trees, were the only sign of life. A stillness lay over everything—for a few moments holding life suspended, like an insect congealed in a lump of amber, immobilizing what ordinarily shifts and slides over consciousness.

"That's the Cameron farm—Wester Glenauchen—your closest neighbor." Helen's words restored the time flow to the afternoon. "Mrs. Cameron's a nice old body. She keeps a spare key to your house, which she's been handing out to the painters and the electric and whoever needs to get in."

"Should we stop and introduce me?"

"No, no—you must see your house first."

We rattled over the bars of a cattle grid and started to climb into the hills we had seen from the main road. Where was the house concealed? I wondered, seeing all about us only uninhabited landscape. Bob slowed down and pointed: "See that clump of trees up there on the horizon? Those are your trees. The house is amongst them; you can just about make out the chimney pots if you know they're there."

After another quarter of a mile uphill in low gear, the road ended abruptly in front of a white-painted gate on the crest of the rise. Ahead, beyond the house, the waters of the loch dazzled the eyes. Helen was out of the car in a moment, swinging the gate open, and we drove down a gentle incline into a broad courtyard formed by an ell where the back wall of the house joined the gray stone outbuildings.

We stood in the yard, bemused at what had come about from an idly mentioned wish. The air that I breathed was piercingly clear as though sharpened by its purity.

"That's your carriage house—your garage now," Helen pointed out, "and that's your stable." She was attempting to make it all ordinary, but each sweep of her hand increased my sense of incredulity. Helen and Bob escorted me along a slate-paved path between the side of the house and the hedge of a kitchen garden, turning left onto a narrow terrace. The back and sides of the property were sheltered by a belt of trees: mostly pine, spruce, wild cherry, and mountain ash, with a few splendid larches. A lawn sloped down away from the house front toward the loch that glimmered beyond, roughly triangular in form, merging at its apex into the receding declivity of the hills.

I turned to face the house; it regarded me from its windows, one at each side of the front door, and, upstairs, a row of three. The front door was set in a stone portico with a small, carved stone pinnacle at its gabled peak; a flowerless rose clambered up the wall, its leafiness softening the plain angularity of the gray granite house front. "A late bloomer," Helen commented.

"You're about a thousand feet or more up in the hills here," Bob said. "You'll be lucky if this rose blooms by the end of July."

It turned out to be a creamy pink rose, heavily perfumed, and it bloomed, we were to discover, only in August. Meanwhile my eye went past the climbing rose to the rooftop, which was patterned with black slate tiles as snugly and regularly laid down as the scales on a fish. "Hand-hewn Welsh tiles," Bob explained with the satisfaction everything about Glenauchen Cottage afforded his sense of rightness and solidity.

From each end of the roof a chimney rose up, the functional simplicity of the shape like a child's drawing of a house that embodies what is fundamental in shelter and security from whatever lurks in the world outside. Like a place once glimpsed and not forgotten, I remembered it all, recognized it; it was what I had had in mind.

We remained silent, contemplating the house front; the Hunters, familiar with it, considering it from my viewpoint. Bob placed something in my hand—a large key of black iron, its weight and size symbolizing impregnability. I fitted it into the keyhole; the tongue of the lock swung heavily and smoothly out of its chamber and the door opened. A narrow window set in each side of the tiny portico let long slabs of sunlight across the stone floor. It was the only time I was ever to see the little antechamber bare—its hooks were always to be hung with raincoats, jackets, and sweaters, and the floor lined with hiking boots, sneakers, and damp socks. Wild flowers, branches, and berries would be deposited there, and interesting bits of rock; pieces of agate, which occur naturally in the region, would be ranged in a collection on the windowsills, along with an owl's pouch and birds' feathers; fishing-rods against the wall, and even a sheep's skull, which Neil found and wanted to bring back to New York—deterred from doing so by our threats and the horror stories his brother and sister told of what would happen to both his skull and the sheep's at the hands of the U. S. Customs authorities.

I opened the inner door. We stood in a stone-floored center hall of modest, welcoming proportions; ahead, a stone staircase with pine newelposts and bannisters marched up, angling back on itself under a window that filled the upper wall and let the sunlight wavering in through panes of irregular glass. Beneath the stairs was a storeroom.

On each side of the hall a door stood open. The lefthand one led into the kitchen: a large room with a stone floor and an old-fashioned sink and cupboard set in under the window overlooking the garden and loch. There was a tiled fireplace, a built-in china closet with windowpanes of embossed glass, and a large pantry where Helen had had the small electric stove and refrigerator installed to form a small kitchenette that left the rest of the room as a living-dining room.

To the right of the hall was a bedroom with a plain pine mantel and pine shutters that folded back into angled recessed niches; all the woodwork displayed a high standard of craftsmanship. A small room opened off from the bedroom, with a window looking out over the valley. "The dressing room?" I said. "We were all wondering, when we read the description of the house, whether dressing rooms weren't a little unusual for a humble reservoir keeper's cottage."

"Real-estate broker's language," Bob said, "designed to catch the attention of the middle-class. Too big for a cupboard, too small for a bedroom, so they called it a dressing room."

Helen had put a single bed in it. "For one of the children—"

"Or the children of the many houseguests you will be having," Bob suggested.

"No guests," I stated firmly. "This is our eyrie, our hideaway."

"There's no eyrie remote enough not to be discovered by the determined and the persevering," he said.

We went upstairs. "I've defined the architectural style of the house," Bob said. "It's Victorian Municipal—ordained by the gentlemen who sat a hundred years ago on the Water Board, with their solid gold watch-chains draped across their solid tweed paunches, to be built in solid enduring style, with dignity, as befits a municipal body; the walls are at least three foot thick." Everything was constructed of good material with a handsome sobriety; somehow the proportions were just right, so that with the strong personality of the carpenter—who was obviously an artisan who loved his trade—an unintended charm displaced the Victorian stuffiness.

The windows on the staircase landing overlooked the court-yard and stable; a short flight up the turn of the stairs brought us to a small hall with three doors leading off. The middle door opened into a bathroom larger than any we had in New York, with old-fashioned fittings and white-painted walls and floor; the sink was set under the sash window, which had a splendid view of the loch. "Best view in the house," Bob commented. The righthand door opened into the sitting room, with high windows looking out both on the loch and the kitchen garden; a handsome pine mantelpiece was built around the fire-place, and a delicately fashioned plaster molding of grapes and vine leaves embellished the ceiling cornice.

"This room is more grand than the rest of the place, because it was most likely used by the municipal stuffed-shirts to hold their board meetings," was Bob's conjecture.

Across the hall, the bedroom and dressing room matched the one below, the window entirely filled by the aspect of loch and hills.

That was the whole house. It was all that a house should be.

In the bedrooms there were the beds, blankets, and pillows that Helen had got for us, and in the sitting room was a large, handsome chest of drawers she had bought: Victorian, mahog-any, with inlaid mother-of-pearl and a cunningly concealed secret drawer. "You paid eight pounds for this! It would cost a packet in New York." She pointed out the six-paneled pine doors throughout the house, considered, she said, a rare archi-tectural feature.

Clear bright light filled the house—it was a stone box brim-ming with light; in every window, green hills, water, sky. The proportions of the house—something about the relation of ceiling height to room dimension, the scale and balance of the windows—were mysteriously felicitous, so that, as in a Shaker dwelling, there was a sense of adequacy, modesty, and tranquillity, a sense of grace.

"It's just how it should be," I said to Helen and Bob. I kissed them. There were no words to acknowledge how I felt about what they had done for us; what can one say to friends who transform an idea, a longing, a sense of place, into thick walls of stone, rooms of grace and modesty, windows filled with broad views? "I can't believe it's ours."

Helen looked relieved. Bob continued as satisfied as he had been from the start of the whole unlikely project, when he had recognized the particular quality of Glenauchen Cottage on that bleak February day. "The white paint is an improvement," was all he was prepared to say. "It was all dim browns when we first saw it. Come and view the outside of your piece of *real estate* now."

He enjoys using American idiom, separating it off, with marked irony, from the flow of his conversation. He is amused by what he calls the American version of the English language, finding it lively and expressive, but would never use it without clearly denoting quotation marks, fore and aft, by an ironic pause and a certain gleam in his eye; recounting how a neighboring farmer had made an absurdly low offer on a load of hay, he says, "The old bugger thought he could *rip me off*."

We went out to inspect the rest of our real estate: the carriage house, now the garage, with its cobbled floor and massive roof-beams, opened into the stable, where the stalls for three horses were divided by charmingly carved and ornamented wooden partitions. There was a workbench in the stable, and a window that looked out over the back garden, which sloped away down the natural incline of the hill, and a tall hand-built ladder leading up to the hayloft. Further down the back slope was a byre for a cow, the top half of the door standing open as if the spirit of departed cows remained waiting for a handful of remembered hay; adjoining was a washhouse, with a great copper cauldron set in a hearth with a chimney, and a heavy old mangle clamped to a stone trough.

"That's how we did the washing when I was a girl," Helen said. "A fire would be lit under the cauldron, and the wash would be boiled up with grated soap until it was antiseptically clean."

"There was nae a germ would have had nerve enough to confront your mother," Bob interposed. "If I know her she was probably chanting spells over it as it boiled and bubbled."

"And then it would be rinsed out in a tub like this one, rinsed and mangled till the water ran clear. Och, it was murder turning the handle of the mangle; your back would break. And then it had to be carted in a laundry basket out to the drying green, and pegged up to blow sweet and dry in the wind— when the weather was dry. . . . But in this climate, the kitchen was nearly always draped in damp laundry."

Outside there was a drying green with four poles connected by a clothesline. "But you'll probably find a launderette in one of the nearby villages," Helen assured me. "You'll be wanting a taste of the simple joys of country life, but you won't want to have to go entirely primitive."

"Just load the dirty washing into the machine," was Bob's advice, "and then go and wait in the nearest pub with a few foaming pints, remaining sober enough to remember when it's time again to go and pop another sixpence into the drying machine. That's the only way to enjoy the simple rural life."

The place had been unoccupied for over a year, since the death of the last reservoir keeper, and the garden was sadly neglected. The grass needed cutting; weeds and nettles had sprung up everywhere. Small white picket gates opened into the various sections of the garden, as if they led to outdoor chambers; over each gateway a pair of tall trees had been planted so that the overhead branches intertwined to form an archway. "Rowan trees," Bob said. "In the autumn they'll have bright red berries."

"They look just like mountain ash."

"That's what they are—same tree; it must have been some kind of Victorian landscaping idea to train them to form arches like this, though I've never seen it anywhere else."

In the kitchen garden they pointed out a flourishing rhubarb patch, raspberry canes, and currant bushes, neglected and over-grown. A path led through the garden to a further rowan-arched picket gate, which opened onto the banks of the loch.

We stood on the grassy slope; it was thick with wild flowers that in subsequent summers would become as familiar to us as old friends. By now the day had cleared and the sky was the cerulean blue that one sees in Venetian paintings, with here and there a small puff of white cloud intensifying the blue, just as the whiteness of the sheep dotting the landscape made the hillsides appear more vividly green. The water of the loch gave back the blueness of the sky, the high hills around it running greenly into the still depths below. Even the grazing sheep could be seen, upside-down, in the hilly slopes reflected in the loch; it was as if all of life was replicated under the clear water, suspended in secret, silent, tranquil form—beauty and stillness without pain, or joy, or judgment.

Occasional plops on the water's surface were trout coming up for air, sending widening rings radiating out to dissolve in silence. To our left, from the near bank of the loch, a path ran up the hill through gorse, heather, and bracken, leading to a road cut like a gash into the hillside, girdling the hill and continuing in a southerly direction till it disappeared where the loch ended, far off in the distant hills. Above the cut of the road, the hillside had been planted with thousand upon thousand of young conifers.

"The enterprising Gavin MacFadyen again," Bob said. "According to Donny, he sold all that parcel of land where formerly sheep had safely grazed to the Forestry Commission, for a very tidy sum, which he needed in order to fit out the Lockup Pub in that rock-pop-medieval decor which sends the caravaners wild with delight. They're in the process of planting a million pine trees; that road has been cut along the hill for the forestry tractors and workmen to get through."

"It's impossible to escape from progress." Helen swept a disapproving eye across the broad side of the hill. "Look at it— it must be three or four thousand feet high, and they've planted every inch of it. Still, a pine forest's a pine forest, and at least preferable to a caravan site. Once the wild flowers and bracken spring up and start to spread, the gash of the road will be concealed, and it will come in handy for taking walks."

"In time, it will be like Norway—dense pine forest covering the hills around the loch," Bob said.

"In our grandchildren's time?" I wondered.

"Och, long before that," Bob said. "Pine grows fast; it's a cash crop. Fifteen years and it's ready to harvest—that's why the Forestry Commission plants conifers instead of deciduous forest; oak and beech take about a hundred years to mature. There's a battle waging between the conservationists and the Forestry."

"I'd have thought conservationists would have approved of forestation."

"Not this sort—too homogeneous. Planting conifers limits the variety of flora and fauna that occur in mixed forests. But the softwoods are a quick return on your investment, so to hell with the ecological balance, they say."

"It's a shame; deciduous forests are so bonny," Helen lamented.

"Who has the time to wait a century for the fruits of one's investment?" Bob went on. "There's one thing to be grateful to the landed aristocracy for: each generation accepted the responsibility of maintaining the land, so that it could be handed intact to succeeding generations. Remember Levin, in *Anna Karenina*—how he felt he was only the custodian of his property during his lifetime? It's a sort of long-term self-interest that we'll all need to cultivate now, if we aren't bent on self-extinction. Now, there's only enough vision for the time it takes to grow a box of matchsticks."

"Leave off your doom-saying on Sheila's first day here; I'm sure she gets enough of it in the States. . . . That's heather covering that slope that leads up to the road. By the end of August it will be purple and bonny."

"And judging by the number of rings on the water," Bob observed, "there must be a fair quantity of trout in the loch. With a bit of arm twisting I might allow myself to be persuaded to come and sit here on the bank, contemplating the absurdity of life, and pulling out a few wee fishies for our dinner."

"Done in oatmeal and butter, they're quite tasty," Helen added.

New York . . . our narrow brownstone house with its spiral staircase curving upward through its four storeys like the in-

terior of a conch shell . . . another world . . . unreal. Where we
stood, talking, on the shore of a dark blue loch hidden among
high hills—here was an enchanted reality.

Ever practical, Helen suggested we'd best be getting back.
"There's a lot needs doing before Harl and the children get
here. Tomorrow we'll have to go round to Mr. Menzies's saleroom in Kirkcaldy to see if we can pick out the rest of the
furniture—you've got a busy time ahead of you."

We locked the front door, took one more lingering look at
the house front, and drove away out of the hills over the
humpbacked bridge. "From the window of every dwelling in
the hills"—Bob elaborated his favorite theme—"from each wee
humble farm laborer's cottage, or farmhouse, or mansion, I'll
guarantee there's someone peering through a spyglass to try and
catch the first glimpse of the Yanks who've bought the old
waterman's house."

"Don't exaggerate, Bob."

"Don't forget, my dear, my grandfather's place, where I
spent all my summers as a boy, was in a glen like this. I know
how these glen Mafias work." He pronounced the word with
a short *a*—*maffia*—obviously relishing the term. "Now, before
we go home, I want to show you the bonniest view in all
Scotland."

Instead of turning right to go back through the hamlet of
Glencorrie, he turned westward. "The glen road continues
through the hills for about five miles," he explained, "then
joins up with the main road that goes one way to Stirling and
the other way to Perth."

The hills curved, high and grassy with rocky outcroppings,
on each side of the road—impressive enough to be mountains,
I thought. We passed an occasional farmhouse or roadside
cottage, grazing sheep, cows, the road twisting mile after mile,
until, suddenly, the hills fell away into a broad flat plain, patterned with rich farmland in large variegated rectangles of
green and pale gold lying in the steady sunshine. Far off, the
houses of a gray stone village clustered in the shelter of the
valley, a church spire pinning it to the landscape. A toy-like
train chugged its way through the afternoon, and in the stillness of the countryside we could hear the regular throb and

rumble of piston turning wheel, the reassuring toot of its whistle as it busily made its way to where its punctuality was confidently anticipated.

"Strathmuir." Bob pulled up into a lay-by. "It means 'the valley of the River Muir.' It's amongst the best agricultural land in the country. That train is on its way to Gleneagles Station, which British Railways maintains specially for access to its Gleneagles Hotel—where all the rich Yanks and Japs and Germans and Arabs come and play golf, and disport themselves in great luxury, with uniformed flunkeys falling about all over the place to do their bidding. See yon great pile of a building . . . gray stone . . . way over to the left of that village?"

"That huge castle?"

"That's no castle; it's Gleneagles Hotel. Very posh, very dear. There are three golf courses that are the Mecca of golfers."

Golf, the Scottish national pastime, "a game of considerable antiquity in Scotland . . . first recorded in 1452," according to the *Oxford English Dictionary*, is played now by everyone: schoolboys in kneesocks, tweed-skirted matrons, grocers, and retired admirals.

As the Hunters had presented me with the house, they offered me now that glorious landscape.

"Let's be getting back now, Bob; I must get dinner on the stove."

"Dinner is it tonight then, instead of tea!" Bob teased her. "We kulaks are accustomed to dinnertime being twelve midday."

We drove back out of the hills into broad farmland, through the little mining villages, into Fife, where the land is cultivated right up to the edge of the cliffs and beaches of the seacoast. I felt as I had in childhood, on occasions when one was securely aware of benign forces sustaining one in the form of family affection, kindness, warm regard, and safety, the consciousness that benevolent and responsible adults were in control, and concerned with one's well-being.

But then I began to feel apprehensive. Life is not supposed to be like this, all my experience warned me.

"I'm starting to feel uneasy," I confessed. "Perhaps there's a kind of spiritual arrogance . . . I mean . . . living the way we do in New York, and now all this. . . ." My arm swept out over a swathe of green barley-fields in a crescent of blue sea, past an old man stooping to pluck a lettuce in the garden of a cottage where smoke puffed from the chimney.

"Och, just try letting go of all that guilt and nonsense," Bob suggested, "or you might end up like my mother-in-law, who believes our unworthy presence upon this earth can be justified only by grim restraint, hard work, clean living, and regular worship—God help us all. Start asking what you've done to deserve that idyllic place, and you'll just have to hand it all back again. You *don't* deserve it. But now that you have it, you might as well enjoy it for all you're worth. Try being just a wee bittie pagan for a change—do you the world of good."

CHAPTER

5

Moving In

I have no desire to visit Illiers, the original of Proust's Combray; no wish to see Tante Leonie's house or the pastry cook's shop, nor to smell the bittersweet almond fragrance of the hawthorn that still blooms in Swann's park. In the center of Illiers, I am told, there is a map, prominently displayed, to enable those who make the pilgrimage to guide themselves to landmarks of the place that inspired Proust's genius. But it is sufficient to open *Swann's Way* and read "Now and then, crushed by the burden of idleness, a carp would heave up out of the water, with an anxious gasp" for me to be transported among the irises on the bank of the little river with the churchbells sounding in the heat of the summer day.

Why, that first evening in the guest room of the Hunters' farmhouse, was I considering Proust? Outside my window, the soft light of early evening lay over a field enclosed by a stone wall; beside three ancient broad-limbed chestnut trees a calf suckled, while its mother placidly munched. Downstairs Helen was preparing dinner, and I had been instructed to take a rest. But my sense of pleasure and excitement about Glenauchen Cottage, now that I had had a solitary moment to contemplate its apparent perfection, was disturbed by apprehension. Proust writes of "people who set out on a journey to see with their own eyes some city that they have always longed to visit, and imagine that they can taste in reality what has charmed their fancy." Might not this be the nature of our folly? I wondered; could one purchase for a round twelve thousand dollars the stone substance of what perhaps should remain only the furnishings of the imagination? I remembered how, as a small child, I would indulge in temper tantrums when denied something I badly wanted; generally I would be punished or ignored, but sometimes I would be given what I had screamed and cried for—and then I would feel wicked. Is it human perversity, I pondered, or just my own, to feel a sense of obliquity when a wish is granted, when one receives what one has desired? Perhaps it is better to wake up and find the requital has occurred in a dream.

The cow moved on to a fresh patch of sorrel; its calf, roused from drowsy nuzzling contentment, looked startled and then hurried long-legged after, to attach itself once again to the bounty of the engorged udder.

I was called down to dinner. Among some excellent cooks we know, Helen is one of the finest, her vegetables always cooked to the right degree of crispness, her sauces full-bodied and speckled with chive or parsley, her tart crusts light and her puddings substantial; she fries fish golden dry on the outside, moist and succulent within, and no one's French fries can surpass hers. There is always on her table a wholemeal loaf delivered daily by the village baker, Scottish butter, and cream from the Hunters' own dairy, so rich and thick that it must be spooned up. From Helen's kitchen garden the summer's supply of raspberries, rhubarb, strawberries, gooseberries, and black currants is transformed into tarts and fools and flans, and jellies and jams and chutneys that glow in an array of deep color on her larder shelves.

Bob appreciates his wife's cooking. "Very good, Helen," he compliments her as each emptied plate is cleared away, and he leans back, his contentment evident, in anticipation of the next course.

Over dinner at the huge kitchen table, I told them about the encounter with my traveling companion, the mysterious Mr. Greenleaf. "A celestial messenger," Bob stated with conviction, "that's who he was." He scooped cream over his rhubarb tart. "Said the summers would be dry and hot, did he? Obviously the chap's been sent along to announce that the climate of Scotland is about to undergo a change. About time. . . . Last couple of years' harvests were ruined by bad weather—never a fine day for weeks on end. We can do with some of your Mr. Greenleaf's dry weather. A celestial messenger on the 9:55 to Nottingham; that's just where you'd expect to run into one." Helen was gazing at him as he poured the last of a second bottle of wine into our glasses. "Don't look at me like that, Helen, my dear; it's not the claret—you mark my words. One must be receptive to the irrational. Och, just wait and see how we'll all be getting our suntans on the banks of Glenauchen Loch. Let the hoi-polloi go to the French Riviera—*we* have been given a signal."

"If you're done with the cream, pass it over to me" was Helen's response.

We drank our coffee in the comfortable, shabby living room whose French windows look out on the walled garden; farm records from Victorian times show that it took two full-time gardeners to maintain the garden and orchard, but Helen does it all now, with the aid of a power mower and her passion for flowers. The billiard room next door, these days, contains only a Ping-Pong table among the Victorian glory of paneled walls and scoreboard and elaborate lighting. For formal occasions, there is, on the third floor of the farmhouse, which was built in 1680 and added to over the centuries, a formal drawing room, furnished with family antiques and the Persian rugs and Scottish watercolors that are Bob's delight to collect. Outside the long windows, the lawn, herbaceous borders, orchard, and greenhouses seemed suspended in the watercolor wash of the midsummer twilight, the color altering without diminishing the light. Beyond the farm and village we could see across the Firth of Forth, where the lights of Edinburgh pricked the blue translucence with points of orange and yellow.

"The celestial Mr. Greenleaf notwithstanding," Helen said, "I'll turn on the gas fire; it's chilly in this room."

Bob poured malt whiskey into small glasses. "Drink this neat; no need to adulterate it with ice-cubes. It's 'Glenmorangie.' Better than any of those fancy cognacs . . . pure, unblended malt whiskey, brewed from the highest-grade barley and untainted spring water. You'll never drink blended whiskey again if you can get your hands on this stuff."

It has a dark, peaty aroma, a golden lightness on the palate, a mellow heating power; regular Scotch seems lacking in soul and substance once one acquires the taste for malt whiskey. Over the years we tried many of them—all splendid in varying degrees—but Glenmorangie remained the standard by which we judged all the others.

Bob raised his glass: "To many happy years at Glenauchen. And to the mysterious Mr. Greenleaf."

Who are we to estimate the vagaries of the climate and the powers of a stranger encountered on a train? All I can say is that for the next seven summers our part of Scotland experienced an extraordinary amount of sunshine, and high-yielding harvests. There were even a few record-breaking heat waves.

We drank. The gas fire spluttered and hissed. On the gravel path we watched a hedgehog make its leisurely way until it disappeared into a clump of lupins. "The hedgehog moves about the world with confidence because it has no natural enemies . . . fortunate little bugger," Bob observed.

"If your skin were covered with sharp bristles neither would you have any," Helen offered. "We'll need to rise early." She stood up and gathered coffee cups and glasses onto a tray. "There's a lot to be done if we're to have Glenauchen Cottage ready for Harl and the kids. I'll knock you up at eight, Sheila— is that alright?"

"Och, let her lie a little. It's just a few more sticks of furniture you're wanting still, and some pots and pans," Bob murmured from the depths of his armchair.

"No, no. Call me early. I want to move in as soon as I can. I won't believe it's really our place until I do."

I lay awake for a long time in the blue and white guest room I was to occupy on the first night of the annual return to the glen. Behind my closed eyelids the landscapes of green hills unreeled on an endless ribbon. When I fell asleep, long past midnight, the western sky still cupped the glow of the departed sun, and though the curtains were drawn it never got dark in the room all night; in just a few hours the sun would be rising again, here in this northern midsummer.

It took us a week and a couple of hundred pounds—roughly four hundred dollars—to complete the furnishing of Glenauchen Cottage.

Tucked away on a steep side street of Kirkcaldy, the Hunters' nearest market town, is Mr. Menzies's saleroom; *Menzies*, I was warned, is pronounced *Mingus*. From the crowded, bustling High Street of Kirkcaldy, narrow little streets run downhill to the sea, so that at every corner there is a tantalizing view of sky and sea and ships, which never failed to delight and surprise when I stepped out of Woolworth's or Boot's Chemists and stood among rumbling lorries and lines of traffic waiting for the lights to turn. A plaque on the wall of a quaint old house wedged in between the ubiquitous chain stores announces that Adam Smith lived there, in 1767, when he wrote *The Wealth of Nations*. Mr. Menzies looks more like a lawyer or doctor than an auctioneer: well-tailored, handsome, and at ease with himself, courteous and exerting no pressure on his customers, who instantly have confidence in his honesty and judgment. In three warehouses, household goods of every sort are stored roughly according to function.

It took us three or four forays through the stacked chambers to find all that we needed: a gateleg oak table, bentwood chairs, room-size Axminster and Wilton carpets, thick and unworn.

"Young people don't even look at these good wool carpets anymore," Mr. Menzies told us. "They all go for that bright cheap synthetic stuff they're selling in the High Street. It wears out in a couple of years." Helen told him that the hall and stair carpeting at the farm had been laid down after the Great War and was still not quite worn out yet, and we all shook our heads at the waste and profligacy of the times. "They don't go for wood furniture either," he went on. "They prefair plastic, that they can just wipe over with a rag, so they can get back to sitting gormless in front of the telly; they wouldn't know what to do with a tin of furniture polish if you handed it to them. That's why all this stuff you're getting is dirt-cheap—no demand for it."

A date was set for Mr. Menzies to deliver our household goods.

Helen has never learned to drive, and when Bob was not with us it was I who negotiated the Hunters' car through narrow, crowded streets of towns and villages, unaccustomed, then, to driving on the left. Helen was rather nervous about my driving, warning me constantly that I was about to run into the curb and unsuspecting citizens on the left, where she sat; once she even gasped and declared so convincingly that I had driven over the toe of a large policeman that I slowed down and waited to be apprehended and taken in custody. But he stolidly continued directing the traffic, his face immobile. "He must have iron toe-caps in his boots, then," Helen conceded, and we went on our way.

Back at the farm, Bob's dung-covered Wellington boots stood outside the kitchen door; he was sprawled with a pre-lunch sherry in his leather armchair beside the kitchen hearth, where the slow-burning-anthracite stove gave off its low, steady heat winter and summer.

"We've got a car for you," he told me. "Some chap from Kinghorn left his wee Singer station wagon at Henderson's garage for a tuneup; he's wanting it running smoothly so he can sell it. 'Any good?' I asked George. 'No' bad,' he said. 'What's he asking?' I said. 'A hundred quid,' he said. 'Tell him we'll take it for eighty,' I said."

We got it for ninety pounds, our small, dark green station wagon, and it gave us good service for many summers, in its benign way malfunctioning only before we set out on trips, so that we never once found ourselves stranded when we were far from home. Once though, the brakes failed as we were driving out of the stable at midnight to pick up a hitchhiking nephew at Gleneagles Station; there was no phone at the station, no way of contacting the boy, so we set off through black night, through eight winding, treacherous miles of hill roads, and by the judicious use of low gears and prayer that the hand-brake would not fail us, made the nerve-racking journey without the hideous accident I anticipated at every twist of the road. At the end of each summer we would leave the car parked in a small barn at the Hunters' farm; Bob would take it out for a run over the winter to keep the battery charged, and every year, on our return, it would be covered with starling droppings and cobwebs and feathers, but would cough obligingly back to life and we would go bowling off to the glen.

"I've asked Jessie and her sister if they'd like to drive out to Glenauchen with you to get the place properly cleaned up before the furniture comes," Helen said. "It will cost you a pound an hour each, but they're strong and very thorough, so it's well worth it."

Jessie and her sister lived in the council housing development that abutted on the Elizabethan stone wall of the farmhouse garden. They worked for the Hunters, helping with the house-cleaning, and with the milk bottling in the dairy; in summer, they joined with other of the village women at roguing the rows of barley, pulling up the wild oats—rogue plants that would choke the crops and could only be effectively controlled by hand-weeding. Strong, red-cheeked women who contended daily with high prices, meager incomes, feckless husbands, and delinquent children, they remained tough and cheerful, forgetting their troubles at the bingo games that provided excitement and offered the hope of unearned riches three or four nights each week.

They very rarely left the purlieus of their village, except once, when they splurged a big win at bingo on a trip to Belgium. Why Belgium? Helen had no idea. Bob thought perhaps a special bargain excursion was being advertised that week at the travel agent on the High Street. Even Edinburgh, a half-hour's bus ride away, lay beyond the boundary of their existence. They were delighted at the prospect of a day's outing to Glenauchen, some twenty miles off; they had never been into Perthshire, they told me. Helen packed a lunch basket for the three of us, supplied us with rags and dusters

and pails and scouring powder and detergent and a vacuum
cleaner, and away we went in the little green Singer, the two
of them exclaiming with childlike wonder at every new vista
each turn in the road brought into view. They brought to
mind characters out of a Thomas Hardy novel who regard a
ten-mile walk away from their own village as a journey to
another country. What they thought of someone from America buying a summer cottage in Perthshire, I did not care to
contemplate; if Glenauchen seemed exotic to them, America
was probably some fantasy of television where anything at
all was possible.

We drove into the stableyard. They took in the rolling
hills, the loch, the stone house sitting beside it. "Aye, it's
bonny, just like Mrs. Hunter said," Jessie commented, and in
no time their jackets were off, their aprons on, pots and kettles
were set to boil until the immersion heater had warmed up,
and one was down on her knees scrubbing the kitchen floor
(they scorn mops) while the other set to washing the windows.
I have never seen anyone clean house like these two sisters,
buxom, vigorous women in their late forties; it was as though
every speck of dust and dirt was an outrage to some sense of
order in that limited sphere of existence where order is possible. In their daily lives, the scrimping and frugality and
making do, the contending with drunken husbands, chronic
unemployment, and illegitimate grandchildren—these they accepted as something to be endured (*tholed* is the Scottish word
for putting up with what one has no control over). But in the
house, there was no reason to submit to the chaos of life; here
was one area where order could be imposed. In Scottish villages the brass doorknobs and doorplates are rubbed and
polished to a burnished shine; window glass clearly reflects sky
and passers-by and gardens; the walls of the rooms are washed
down every spring in a frenzy of cleaning that must contain
some remnant of a pagan rite that rids the household of dark
demons of winters; the tiny front gardens are as neat as parlors,
an unkempt house being spoken of in shocked whispers as a
sign of unmitigated depravity. All this proclaims that godliness, so hard to come near in the hurly-burly of living, is accessible, at least, in cleanliness.

While they worked, I lined drawers and the shelves of the built-in closets, and unpacked what I could, and the physical contact with the little house began to transform it into a place where one might live, rather than an idea for the imagination to entertain.

My chores done, I left the two women with the thermos flask and sandwiches, went through the white-painted gate that led out of the stableyard to the start (or end) of the private road, and struck off downhill, to introduce myself to our neighbors at the farm, about a mile out of our hills toward the main glen road.

That first walk down the hill road is so firmly set in my mind that all subsequent recollections refer back to its freshness and quietness, a sense of solitude I had never before encountered. On the left rose the green slopes of Ben Shawe, a high, conical hill where sheep browsed among bracken and heather; to the right ran a gentle grassy valley that we came to know as the Home Park—enclosed fields surrounding a farmhouse are called "parks." We were to learn that this one, sheltered from the wind, its grass lush, was reserved for the ewes that had mothered twins and required more nourishment than was available on the scrubbier hills. Each black-faced ewe, with her shaggy woolen pelt and thin black legs, was, I saw, accompanied at every move she made by a pair of lambs whose coats were still short, curly, and creamy white. The field that adjoined our property was called Monroe's Park, but it was several years before we learned the reason for its name. The burn, after being released from the confines of the loch that dammed it up in front of our house, ran along the bottom of the Home Park, past Wester Glenauchen Farm, to join up eventually with the River Corrie on its way down to the sea.

There was not a person to be seen. At first the silence had only a negative quality: it was an absence of sound. As I continued down the road a variety of sounds began to distinguish themselves in the quiet; between the lambs' bleating and the ewes' hoarse reassurances there emerged the purling of running water as it sprang out of the ground and ran sparkling downhill in narrow rills of silver into a ditch dug alongside the road. On the banks of the ditch grew a profusion of leafy plants starred with small blue flowers, which were to become familiar to us as forget-me-nots, and, as if my sight grew more sharp in that clear light, I saw that each tiny flower of sky blue was centered with a yellow eye as exquisitely rendered as an Elizabethan lady's embroidery. Another noise separated itself from its serene background: the tearing of grass as the sheeps' teeth wrenched it, clump by clump, from the ground; then a diversity of birds' calls, which took many summers for us to learn, since our ears were attuned only to loud, coarse sounds of city living; further along I became aware of the hum and buzz of insects at work in the sunshine—the silence was alive with natural music.

The Camerons' farm came into view as a cluster of buildings known as the "steading." Approaching, I could make out a white farmhouse overlooking the burn; behind it, a stone barn with crowstepped gables—crowstepping being the only architectural ornamentation that austere Scottish design grudgingly indulged in. I crossed the cattle grid that forded the road, then passed some stone sheep pens, a few sheds, and a farm laborer's cottage. On a gatepost a hand-lettered sign was posted: FISHING PERMITS AT HOUSE. FLY FISHING ONLY. OFFENDERS WILL BE BANISHED FROM THE LOCH.

In the farmyard hens scratched and clucked, and an old black and white sheepdog lay asleep in the sunshine at the back door. It opened its eyes and watched me without stirring as I rang the bell. Mrs. Cameron opened the door—a sturdily built woman in a long, plain dress and stout shoes, with a plain no-nonsense face, her iron gray hair pulled back in a tight knot. She looked to be in her middle sixties.

"You're Mrs. Gordon," she said, and took my hand. "Now, come away in. Is everything alright up at the loch? What fine weather you're having for moving in. Sit down now and I'll make a fly cup of tea. The boys will be in for their dinner at twelve, but it's all ready for them. . . . Sit down, now." She led me through a stone-floored back kitchen with stone sinks and a pulley for drying laundry; rows of boots and Wellingtons were lined against the wall; raincoats and jackets hung from hooks, as well as fishing gear, creel baskets, and a rack of guns. I followed her as she talked on in lilting, low-voiced Scottish speech; we passed through a kitchen where pots hissed on the stove and there was evidence of an attempt at modernization, the plastic and fake wood and other synthetic materials ill at ease with the original red-tiled floor and the great open stone hearth that had an old-fashioned mahogany radiophonograph on it. I was left in the sitting room while she made the tea. It was crowded with shabby furniture; carpets and upholstery were worn and faded; an electric heater burned with red imitation coals. The walls were hung with a number of pictures of slender, jodhpurred young women mounted on horses; the mantelpiece was festooned with riding trophies. A large color television set skulked under a window with a splendid outlook into the hills.

Over a pot of strong tea and a plate of drop scones I thanked her for keeping the keys to hand to all the workmen who had been fixing up our place. "Och, we were glad to do it. It will be nice to see the lights shining up the hill again; Glenauchen Cottage has been standing empty for too long. It must be nearly two years since Mr. Cunningham died, poor mannie. His wife's moved to Dunfermline to be near her sister. . . . No sugar? No milk?" She did not consider me a true tea drinker. They take it dark-brewed and strong in Scotland, with plenty of sugar and creamy milk. In all our summers I never once crossed that threshold without being sat down in front of the lurid glow of the electric fire and served tea and home-baked cakes. People who have traveled in the Sinai desert tell how the humblest Bedouin will not allow the traveler to pass the tent he has struck in the wilderness without pressing upon him tiny cupfuls of syrupy black coffee; it occurs to me that the Scots are imbued with the same primitive sense of hospitality, so fundamental in its ordering of human intercourse that it would be taboo for the guest to decline what has been offered.

Curious to learn about us, our family, and our intentions in the glen, Mrs. Cameron couched her inquiries in an elliptical form, without direct questioning—as though uninquisitive spaces were being shaped that one found oneself filling in with the desired information. I, on the other hand, never tired of asking questions—as if I would rattle around this new, unknown environment until firmly wedged in with information, names, customs, histories, and geographies. We had lived in so many places, in three different countries—no two of our children was born in the same place—and for me, there was unending interest in a life that had been rooted for many generations in an area bounded by a few square miles. Over the years Mrs. Cameron would fill in the landscape for me with reminiscence, gossip, and legend, availing me of the spirit of the place, so that it would become to me as known and familiar as each bend of the burn, as the changing light over a day and a season, the habits of the shepherd and the flock, and the scent of the honeysuckle and the rose that clambered over the front of Glenauchen Cottage.

That first day I learned that Mrs. Cameron had been born on a farm on the opposite slope of the hill, about half a mile down the glen road. Her grandfather had given up his ministry in the Kirk of Scotland to become a farmer. Her unmarried sister, Kirstie Aird, still ran the family farm. Marrying a neighboring farmer, John Cameron, she had moved across the glen road almost half a century earlier, and had had three daughters, one of whom had not married and lived at home with her still. Mrs. Cameron had been running the farm singlehanded since her husband had died fifteen years ago; now two grandsons worked the place under her supervision. The two wild grandsons I recalled from a letter of Bob's, and I wondered in what way the wildness manifested itself. Most of the farmers in the glen were tenants of the Laird of Glenauchen, whose own estate lay about four miles along from there, but John Cameron's father had bought their farm from the old Laird —the grandfather of the present Laird—and every acre of it was their own, she said with satisfaction. She told how her late husband's grandfather had sold off an acre of land adjoining the loch to the Water Board more than a hundred years ago for the waterman's house—*our house*—to be built up there. Though the loch now belonged to the Water Board, the Camerons had retained, in the deeds, the fishing rights, and we were to feel at liberty to fish there whenever we wanted. She told me that our property was surrounded by the four thousand acres of Wester Glenauchen Farm.

She looked forward to meeting the rest of the family when they arrived from New York, she said when I rose to go, and I must be sure to stop by for anything I was needing. As she walked me across the yard, I noticed that a gateway leading into her garden was arched over with a pair of mountain ash trees. "We have those in our garden too," I remarked.

"Rowan trees," she said. "Aye, you'll see them wherever you go; they're planted to keep the witches away."

"Witches? And do they keep them away?"

"They say they do. The glen was a place that was famous in the old days for witches. There's even a book about it. Jessie MacFadyen up at Glencorrie House gave a talk on the witches to the Rural Women's Institute last winter."

"Well, I'm glad we have so many rowan trees in our garden," I said. "I'm going to be staying there on my own for a while, and I didn't know about the witches."

Crossing the cattle grid, I read the faintly lunatic signpost about fly-fishing, and decided it must be the work of one of the wild grandsons. My apprehension about the response summering Americans might receive in a self-enclosed Scottish community had been allayed by the warmth of Mrs. Cameron's hospitality. I walked back up the hill, my mind alight with curiosity about our neighbors and about the landscape that was going to reveal itself to us; the sense of anticipation was similar to that almost voluptuous feeling in childhood at the moment of opening a large, thick storybook. Everything my neighbor had told me invested the hills with more meaning.

Often I had passed through beguiling areas of countryside, glimpsing—in a woman taking washing off a line, or a man pruning an orchard, or a wagon stacked with hay bales lumbering along a country lane, or a tweeded person closing ornate gates set in mossy walls of an old estate—a mysterious fragment of an unknown way of life. Now, here was opportunity to penetrate a little of that mystery. In half an hour, over a cup of tea, the curtain had been slightly lifted. She didn't go about much, Mrs. Cameron had told me; she was a homebody. She had been to Edinburgh (some forty miles off) only a few times in her life, and found it too crowded and noisy. She had never been to England; went to Perth, the local county town, only for the sheep sales, or if she needed something not available in Auchterbraehead, the nearest village. Every year she and her daughter Meg took a week's holiday at Largo, a small seaside village on the east coast of Fife, an hour's drive from the farm. Later we discovered that Largo was the birthplace of Alexander Selkirk, the original of Robinson Crusoe—a bit of information that had no relevance to Mrs. Cameron's annual vacation.

She told me which tradesmen she patronized in the village, and that the baker's van and grocer's van came once a week to the glen. "Aye, it's quite handy," she said of a service that brought fresh staples, including fish and poultry, fruit and vegetables, to the back doors of remote outlying farmsteads. I contemplated the narrow perimeters of a life deep-rooted in the soil of this lonely glen, in which I surprisingly found myself walking toward *our place* . . . *our place*, as I kept repeating to myself without much conviction. On the brow of the hill a thicket of trees appeared with our two chimneys emerging from the green. Stopping to pick a stalk of forget-me-not, I thought that Mrs. Cameron was as native to this glen as the modest blue flower.

At Glenauchen Cottage, Jessie and her sister had wrung out their swabbing cloths and stowed the pails and paraphernalia in the car; they were sitting side by side on the bed in the downstairs room, smoking and chatting in a dialect so broad and rapid and fraught with glottal stops that I could catch only an occasional word. When I came in, they switched back to their Fife-accented English, jerky, sharp, without the musical lilt of other regional accents. They had opened the windows, and the house was fresh with the hill air. All surfaces gleamed with the cleanliness of a hospital, and the old glass in the windowpanes wavered with the brightness the sun threw off the glimmering water of the loch. The house stood ready to receive its occupants.

We closed up and left. In the years that followed, each summer started off with Jessie and her sister's ritual house-cleaning; they would push all the furniture to the center of the rooms, wash walls, swab floors, drag the carpets out onto the lawn, and beat them savagely with sticks, going at the cleaning with a kind of dementia that subsided, with tea and cigarettes, only when every offending trace of dirt had been vanquished. They enjoyed coming out to Glenauchen—it was always a treat for them.

The cattle grid rattled noisily under the wheels as we drove past the Camerons' steading. On the doorstep of the laborer's cottage a young woman sat, looking absolutely blank, smoking in the sunshine, while a baby and a kitten tumbled about on the garden path. Mrs. Cameron appeared in the doorway of the farmhouse and waved as we passed, and a cock crowed in the stillness of the afternoon.

Mr. Menzies had delivered the furniture; the curtains hung in the windows; the telephone was installed with a number that described the smoothness of the move: Glenauchen 1–2–3. On the kitchen wall was a botanical poster of kitchen herbs from the Brooklyn Museum. The front hall looked mini-baronial, with rush matting on the floor, and a pair of splendid oak armchairs that Helen had requisitioned when she came upon the son of Kate, the dairymaid, hauling them off to throw in the rubbish-tip because his mother had acquired new chrome and plastic chairs.

There were four days still before the family would be arriving from New York, but I was moving in.

"Won't you feel nervous," Helen worried, "all alone here? It's such an isolated spot."

"I don't know; ask me tomorrow."

We were drinking Glenmorangie in the upstairs living room; beyond the windows the far bank of the loch dissolved, merging with hill and sky in the distance.

"Tomorrow morning," Bob said, "when we open the back door to take in the milk, there will be Sheila, in her wee goonie, waiting to slink in with the cat and the newspaper."

"It's highly likely." I agreed. "I've never been alone—all on my own—anywhere."

"I'll phone first thing in the morning," Helen called from

the car as I stood waving to them at the white gate. Watching
them disappear, I stroked the carved thistles that decorated the
top of each gatepost, my tactile sense familiarizing itself with
the surfaces and textures.

I came into the house. It was past ten, and still, in late June,
broad daylight. I locked the stout front door with an iron key
longer than my hand and secured the inner hall door. All the
locks and bolts were of strong black iron and swung heavily
into their grooves and chambers; the door hinges and hooks
and latches throughout the house were all handsomely hand-
crafted by some bygone Victorian blacksmith. I went from
room to room, the palms of my hands and my fingertips learning the feel of doorknobs, mantels, lintels, bannisters, the
swing and smooth fit of the pine shutters in all the windows.
I moved from window to window to take in the different
aspects they afforded, hardly believing that each view would
become as familiar to me as the street and sidewalks outside our
house in New York. As dusk thickened toward midnight, I
made out, from an upstairs window, a handful of lights down in
the valley which must be the Cameron steading. Far off, on a
hill, the light of a solitary house twinkled. All the rest was
gray-green hills with milky mists gathering in their folds, the
sky the transparent green of seawater. Though I drew the
bedroom curtains, it never grew dark all night; the twilight
glow was dimmed only by the rising sun.

My toothbrush suspended in a rack in the bathroom, slippers
familiar beside the bed, robe on a hook behind the door, combs
and jars and bottles on the dressing table—none of these well-
known tokens of habit were able to dispel, even as I handled
them, a feeling of dreamlike unreality. Even sleep, when it
came at last, was tattered and veiled with the mists the glen
floated in, stirring with images of the new impressions the eyes
had taken in but the system had yet to absorb. In half-sleep, I
wondered about the unknown occupants of the house, the
living and the dying that had gone on here in the last hundred
years, with the particular quality the splendid isolation must
have imposed. It was reassuring to know that the arches of
rowan trees over all the gateways into the garden were sentinels against the witches. . . . In New York now, I calculated,

it was late afternoon; the subways were rushing people on subterranean journeys home to dinners cooking on stoves. I was aware of the little house surrounding me like a mollusk shell in the inscrutability of the range of ancient green hills that had been thrown up in some convulsion of the planet's core before the ice age.

Waking in that hushed moment just preceding the dawn, I had no idea where I was, finding myself in a limbo, unable to place myself in any recognizable space. When one is drowning, one's past life is said to whirl through the mind; in the small panic that overtook me, I clutched out at the memory of all the rooms I had ever slept in—childhood bedrooms, our first apartment, various houses in different countries—unable to locate myself in any one of them. Around me was only unknown silence. If I could recall which room it was, I could reach out for a light switch, know which side of the bed to step out of . . . the guest room at the Hunters' farm? Then the link was made, and in the cobwebby transparence of the curtains at the window the shape of the bedroom at Glenauchen reasserted itself and everything fell into place. I knew where I was. I reached out and turned on the light, looked out of windows into impenetrable gray mist, and returned to bed still shaken by having been so profoundly lost. But the bed was warm and comfortable, and I fell back into sleep in the unknown house with the hills all around, and the witches swooping about trying to get in where there were gardens without rowan trees.

I was awakened by a continuous raucous din—a bunch of rowdy youngsters walking up the street with transistor radios blaring, was my thought, until I saw the yellow and white print of the curtains lit up with sunshine. I sprang out of bed to look out of the window. The loch lay peaceful and still as glass in the fresh morning. I crossed the hall to the living room, where one window looked out on a rutted sheep trail that ran alongside the hedge of the kitchen garden. Streaming along the trail were the undulating backs of hundreds of sheep and lambs, all of them bleating and protesting as they were channeled off the hillside into a white and black quivering mass. Two sheep dogs ran up and down barking and bullying the sheep into line. A voice calling out strange sounds came from a young man striding along with a shepherd's crook. Shirtless, he wore flared denim jeans held below his flat stomach by a broad leather belt, and his black hair curled about his shoulders. The shepherd . . . a wild grandson? He looked no different from any fellow of his generation one has seen in summer in Greenwich Village or on Hampstead High Street. His torso was smooth-skinned, well-muscled, and the sheep and dogs responded briskly to his authority; some image of a shepherd lad in smock and round-brimmed hat, a yokel of bucolic innocence, was banished from the mind, as much by his garb as by the cocksure set of his gait and the insolent glance he flung as he looked up at the house and saw me watching him— not that I had anticipated any tugging of the forelock. The bleating, pushing mass coursed in a stream past our gate onto the hill road; shepherd, dogs, and flock all moved down the hill and out of sight, the clamor growing fainter as they went.

I brewed coffee in the filter pot I had brought from New York and drank it staring out at the loch and hills that lay outside the window. I never learned to take the view for granted; every time I looked was the first time.

The telephone rang.

"How was it?" Helen wanted to know.

"Well, I got through the night. . . ."

She sensed my doubt. "Come back to the farm and stay till the family gets here," she urged me.

"No—no. Here I am and here I'll stay."

Bob came on the line. "Made it alright, did you?"

"Did you know that the rowan trees in the garden are to keep witches away?" I asked.

"Did you see any witches during the night?"

"Not one."

"Then the rowans must work, obviously."

CHAPTER
6

Come Away In

In late June, on a bright windy day of sunshine and scudding shadow, I drove to the station at Gleneagles to pick up the family. They had flown from New York to Glasgow, from where it was an hour's run by train to Gleneagles.

They all had the dazed, buffeted air that we brought each year along with our luggage, and that a few days of the space and silence in the glen would dispel.

"How is it?" the children called from the train's window as it slowed down.

"Wait and see," I told them, out of my tranquillity.

Whatever they had expected, the reality exceeded it: the broad cultivated fields of the valley of Strathmuir lying placid beneath monumental cloud formations, the road twisting around the high green hills of the glen, the river flowing under the humpbacked bridge as we turned onto our road. They gave up exclaiming, and fell silent. They could only stare, and wonder.

At the cottage, Neil was first out of the car, and rode the gate open for us. Then everyone was everywhere: in and out of the stable and the byre, through the little gates into the green chambers of the garden, out onto the banks of the loch, in and out of the rooms of the house.

In the living room, Harl and I stood at the window looking at the loch. "It's the perfect place," he said. He moved over to the side window. "Come and see." The three children, released from the confines of plane and train, were already halfway up Ben Shawe, freed by the great sweep of landscape opening to them outside the gates. We watched them scramble through bracken and heather, until they all stood, outlined, triumphant against the sky.

When they came down off the hill, faces bright and cheeks flushed, a change in their demeanor was already evident. The hill air was beginning to work on them.

Every morning at nine, and every afternoon at four, a small blue van belonging to the Water Board would toil up the hill and turn off just before our gate. It would head down to a small pump-house at the bottom of a shallow gorge that sloped down from the far end of our garden. A man in gum boots would step out, disappear into the pump-house for about fifteen minutes, lock up, and drive off.

He was Donny MacIver, the waterman; he lived over at Glenshinnoch, the other loch, and was in charge of the operation of both. He would take readings of pressure gauges, adjust valves and water flow, and tend the pots of geraniums he grew on a sunny windowsill to make the place a little "homey." Like the housewives of Königsberg who set their clocks when they saw their local philosopher, Kant, passing up the street, we knew the exact time of day when Donny made his appearance. He became the daily link between our isolation and the world of the glen.

On the third day after the family's arrival, we were all at breakfast. There had been little time for exploring, as each day brought jobs to be done that required a ladder or a hammer or a piece of wire or a box of nails, and we had come to know the ironmonger in the village after making the eight-mile trip several times for urgently needed twine, picture hooks, electric plugs, lightbulbs, a shovel. But we went about our chores in a state like intoxication at the wildness, beauty, and quiet surrounding us.

We heard the sound of the blue van coming up the hill in low gear. "There he is," I told Harl. "Dash out and catch him and bring him in for a cup of tea."

So we met Donny. A neatly built, hatchet-faced man, he was always nattily turned out in hand-knitted sweaters of pink, puce, or lavender, work-pants tucked tidily into gum boots; he had a ruddy outdoors complexion, and the features of the dour schoolmasters, or *dominies*, of Scottish literature— "the rigidly righteous" Robert Burns called them.

He knew all about everyone—their histories, circumstances, and peculiarities, their faults and follies—and he entertained us and educated us in the ways of the glen. Just below his pious exterior there twinkled a sharp wit and a dry humor. When he was relaxed, as he generally was with us—as if he considered us interested observers who did not fall within the range of his criticizing judgment—the dominie expression would dissolve in a wide toothy smile and a shrewd, ironic gleam of the eye. He had the storyteller's gift and enjoyment of an appreciative audience. He was a deacon of the kirk, and active in parish affairs, but he had been warned by Helen that we were an ungodly lot and made no attempt to save us.

He came in and shook hands, and sat down for a cup of tea, his curious eye taking in all details. He had known the house in its former days, had been in charge of the sale when it went on the market, and was interested to see what we had made of it. As he drank his tea I guessed he was making mental notes so that he could bear the news around the glen of how the waterman's house had been transformed into a pleasure dome.

He knew all the mechanical details of the house, and was able to describe to us the exact spot, halfway up the slope of Ben Shawe, where we could locate the source of the spring whose water had fed Glenauchen Cottage for over a century. "Everyone else in the glen gets their water from the reservoir, chemically purified," he said, "but you're fortunate to receive only the purest, finest spring water straight out of the ground." And indeed, we have never drunk such water; it ran icy cold, fresh, sweet, the water in other places tasting heavy and metallic by comparison.

The two wild grandsons down at the farm were a constant

source of outrage and righteous wrath to Donny. "Have you met them yet?" he asked. He shook his head. "Wait and see . . . a bad lot they are. What they're wanting is a good thrashing; their granny's too soft with them, and they get away with murder. Just this morning I met Dougal down by the loch with a gun—and it's illegal to hunt, you ken, before the twelfth of August. 'You're oot poachin' airly today,' I says to him. 'Poachin'?' he says. 'I'm going fishin'. I'm after a few of those brown trout for my dinner. I wait for them to pop up for air and then I take a shot at them. There's nothing illegal about hunting fish before the glorious twelfth, is there?' he asks, all innocent-like. Och, but my hand was itching to strike the young *skellum*."

In that first summer a friendship formed between us and the MacIvers. Tottie, his wife, would write to us in the winter; gifts would be exchanged at Christmas; and each year they welcomed us back to the glen in a way that made us feel we were not considered intruders. A factor that may have eased our acceptance by the glen folk was that they considered our colonial background British; our accents—though not those of our children—were British, and Harl had done his internship in Edinburgh. And our now being American added a certain glamour to all this. Though the British, generally, have a patronizing attitude toward Americans and things American, underlying it there is a deep admiration for the country: its technology and efficiency, its openness and flexibility, its sense of possibilities. Their scorn is part astonishment; their patronization, part envy. Also, word had got around the glen that we intended to retire to Glenauchen in our old age: a logical supposition, based on the fact that it is the ideal of both the British wanderer and the townsman to retire, one day, to the country, to spend the declining years pottering about in a picturesque cottage. We found that our mixed background endowed us with a sort of classlessness, which protected us from social categorization and allowed us to cut across the class divisions that kept the various groups socially apart from one another. We were invited into the homes of agricultural workers, the farmers who form a sort of yeoman class, the reservoirkeeper and the forestryman, as well as the so-called gentry, who would not all be on visiting terms with one another.

Tottie MacIver, a small stout woman, must once have been a pretty girl but now had a washed-out appearance that made her look older than Donny, and older than she probably was. Scottish working-class women seem to fade early; their flowering period is brief—certainly when compared with their American counterparts. Tottie's brown-gray hair was frizzed, her eyes a faded blue, but she retained her pink cheeks and her skin was like fine creased silk. She wore long, flowered, shapeless dresses and a woolen cardigan, except on Sundays, when she, and all the glen women, changed into their "good tweeds" for church. She fluttered and twittered and talked unceasingly in soft, musical accents, each line of thought giving rise to a branch line, which in turn led to a subbranch until we were led far from the original subject. In the countryside, people have more curiosity about their neighbors than city folk do, and go into great detail about the antecedents, the rise and fall of fortunes, the scandals, tragedies, and health of the people they stand on line with at the fishmonger or pass the time of day with outside the church gate after Sunday services.

Tottie's soul is filled with kindliness and hospitality: she would call us up to remind us to do our marketing in the morning on early closing day, or to warn that rain was forecast when she knew we had planned a long hike; she would snip interesting items of news or information out of the local newspapers and send them along with Donny.

Donny offered to drop off the newspaper for us each morning, a service he performed for several of the neighbors as he made his rounds. The world being too much with us the rest of the year, we had decided to forswear radio, television, and newspapers at our country retreat, but his offer was too much of a temptation for me, and I succumbed in spite of the family's protests. Though they berated me for my addiction to newsprint, none of them failed to read the paper once it was there.

We had received an inkling of Donny's political leanings when, on his first visit, he denounced the staid, conservative *Scotsman* for its "leftist" views. Subsequently, he never missed an opportunity to flay the trade union movement for being "communistic." "Ruining the country, they are," he declared. "Tea's too cold—out on strike; not enough sugar—tools down. We're all at the mercy of that lot of red yobs!" So we were a little apprehensive when we placed our order for the liberal *Guardian*. Whatever he thought, he never commented; perhaps our agnosticism put us beyond the limits.

Unless he was coming in for a cup of tea, Donny would leave the paper just inside the stable door, and it became a delicious morning ritual, while the coffee brewed, to step out into the fresh day to the glimmer of the loch, walk around the house to the stableyard, lift the heavy iron latch of the door, and find the paper lying on the round cobblestones of the floor. Often, on top of the folded paper, there lay a gift: a bowl of strawberries, a cabbage, or a lettuce; sometimes a long cucumber from the MacIvers' hothouse, or some of Tottie's baking, or a shovel or scythe or whetstone we had called up the night before to ask to borrow.

Our first social call in the glen was a visit to the MacIvers for after-dinner coffee—at least it was after dinner for us; the glen folk have their main meal of the day at midday, followed by high tea at five, with a light snack around nine in the evening that they call "supper." Lunch is neither in their vocabulary nor their custom. We drove down our private road, past Wester Glenauchen farm, where the only sign of life was the eerie glow of the television from a downstairs window; about two miles along the glen road we turned off onto a side road that ran another three miles into the hills, passing only one farmhouse: the property of the infamous Geordie McCaskie, who had demanded fifty pence from the dead fisherman.

The road ended at Glenshinnoch Reservoir House. Donny came out to unlock the gate, and we drove into a garden laid out like a municipal park. In its precision and rectilinear regularity, Donny's nature was evident: asphalt paths, close-clipped weedless lawns, neat bright flowerbeds, a regimented vegetable plot, strawberry beds set out like a well-trained corps de ballet, the hothouse controlled like a laboratory. There was no view of their loch, as a high retaining grassy bank had been constructed between them and the water. Their house was only about forty years old, characterless, built in a period when the local municipality perhaps regarded itself with less dignity than the Victorian board that was responsible for our place.

There were other guests: Robbie and Jenny Kirkbride, the local forestryman and his wife. We were entertained in a formal sitting room with shiny furniture, embroidered cushions, doilies and mats, and many ornaments of china and cut glass, with amateur watercolor scenes of highland cattle and antlered deer gazing, pensive, over lochs and mountain scenery. An electric fire did little to dispel the chill.

We never saw that room again, subsequent visits taking place in a cozy living room–dining room off the kitchen. Shabby, homely, and kept overwarm by a grate in which red coals glowed all year, it was dominated by a large color television with a framed photograph of a brown and white collie on it.

On the mantel in the sitting room was another picture of the same dog. The MacIvers were childless, and we had barely sat down, after the introductions were made, before Tottie handed us the picture and was telling us about Hamish, their collie, who had died the previous winter at the age of eighteen. Her eyes welled up with tears, and Donny blew his nose and sternly replaced the picture on the shelf. Would they not think of getting another dog? we asked. Tottie shook her head and said they could never replace Hamish, then told us stories of his intelligence and devotion until Donny observed that the kettle must by now have boiled dry, and she went out to see to supper.

While Tottie was preparing the food, we were inducted further into the ways of the glen. No drinks were offered, Donny being a strict teetotaler. The Kirkbrides, a little shy to begin with, came out more and more in their eagerness to acquaint us with what went on in their small community. They were a charming couple. Jenny, plump, bonny, and blue-eyed, gave off a sense of soundness that one gets from a good apple: tart, crisp, firm-skinned, not too sweet but with excellent flavor; she combined an air of competence with placidity. Robbie, small, compact, and muscular, with strong capable hands and a handsome face of much sweetness, was reserved, leaving his wife to answer our questions. The son of a forestryman, he had been raised in these hills, and was part of the work force that was presently planting a million trees on the hills that rose from the east bank of our loch. With their two children, a girl and a boy, they lived in a small cottage owned by the Forestry Commission, which stood alone on the forestry road girdling Dalrioch, the highest hill above the loch. Originally a shepherd's cottage, built in 1680 on the bare hillside, it had been very bleak when they moved in two years previously, they told us, but they fixed it up, made it quite cheery inside, and were building up the garden. "Och, you should see it—they've done wonders," Donny said. "They've transformed the place. It was all stones and thistles when they moved in, and now it's like a picture out of a calendar."

"It will be quite nice when we've done," Jenny said. "You must come and see us; you have to pass right by our gate if you're walking over the hill to the main road or the caravan site."

We were called in to supper, and received another lesson in glen etiquette: eat every crumb of whatever is offered; never refuse a single dish; the moment your plate is empty, expect to be coaxed to more food; allow your cup to be filled and refilled until oceans of beverage swirl about inside you, and only then will your by-now-feeble excuses about repletion be accepted with reluctance. It is your *duty* to eat, you begin to understand, and you are expected to do your duty. We ate platefuls of crisp hot sausage rolls and small triangular sandwiches, and girdle scones with butter and jam, followed by an assortment of fruitcake and jam tarts and biscuits, all home-baked by Tottie, all excellent, but an assault on the system an hour after one had eaten. We would know in the future to skip a meal before one of Tottie's spreads. Not eating one's fill constituted an insult to the hosts and a grave breach of the laws of hospitality.

Robbie and Jenny Kirkbride were our only neighbors within walking distance, apart from the Camerons down at the farm, and we came to know them well. To reach their place we would leave our garden by the small picket gate that opened on the bank of the loch, go along the near bank till we reached a steep heather slope that would turn purple in August, and scramble up the slope and over a fence onto the forestry road, where a half-mile's walk would bring us to their cottage.

Over the years they wrought a transformation that turned the bleak, neglected little shepherd's dwelling into a place of charm and prettiness. They whitewashed the gray stone exterior and trained old-fashioned roses, honeysuckle, and clematis around doors and windows. With his bare hands Robbie lugged boulders to build rockeries into the hillside, which Jenny filled with varieties of brilliant perennial rock-plants; she was always on the lookout for cuttings, which rooted and flourished with her tending. Robbie mowed the sides of the hill until it turned into a thick lawn, and around the house set flowerbeds that bloomed from the earliest snowdrops, hyacinths, and daffodils, through the lupins, stocks, sweet williams, and daisies of summer, until the shaggy brilliant chrysanthemums, dahlias, and zinnias of autumn. "I love flowers," Jenny said; "I couldn't live without them." The sunny south side of the acreage that they had enclosed off the hillside was like a small market-garden, and made them almost self-sustaining in summer: huge beds of potatoes; rows of beets, turnips, carrots, cabbages, and brussels sprouts; runner beans clambering up poles; peas and onions; a strawberry patch; and alongside the south wall of the stone barn, raspberries, gooseberries, and black currants flourished. The burn ran from our place right through the middle of their garden, its banks bright with yellow mimulus that they called "monkey flowers," and to reach their front door one crossed the stream by a tiny wooden bridge over which Robbie had built a pergola embowered by climbing roses.

If we came by their cottage in the evening, after they had had their tea, we would watch Jenny as she filled a dish with dry chicken-feed, mixed it with water that she lifted in an old tin saucepan out of the clear-running burn, and went over the lawn to the henhouse, murmuring soothing noises to the chickens, who raised a clucking clamor as she approached. Every morning the six hens delivered six brown eggs, and we became fortunate recipients of their bounty, rarely needing to

buy eggs at the store. The Kirkbrides waved off all our offers
to purchase their eggs with an "Och, no; you're doing us a
favor taking them off our hands. We hardly know what to do
with all the eggs they keep laying; we can't keep up with them,
and it would be a sin to let them go to waste. But never eat
them before they are twenty-four hours old—when they're
new-laid the white is still too runny."

To crack the top off a fresh, brown-shelled, four-minute
boiled egg from a free-ranging hen, and taste the sweet deep
yellow yolk and delicate white, is to evoke the morning freshness and the anticipation of the delight of another day of the
hill air and the grassy quiet in those green hills.

In this country there seemed to be a natural genius for
gardens. It was interesting to see how restrained these Scottish
people were in their dress and the interior of their homes,
while outdoors, something let loose and exploded into color,
in the way the sober Amish, in their plain dark clothes, allowed
some simmering vibrant energy to discharge in the brilliant
pink, purple, and orange fabrics they stitched into the patchwork quilts that covered them at night. Inside the houses of
our glen neighbors, grays, fawns, and browns predominated,
and there was little evidence of the development of taste or
aesthetic sensibility—ornament tending toward calendars with
kittens or robins, the ubiquitous muddy-colored Highland
scenes, and Disneyesque china artifacts from Woolworth's
squatting on crocheted doilies on sideboard and mantel. It is
depressing to contemplate how the sentimentality and cuteness
of Walt Disney has swept all before it—its evidence in shop
windows and cottage parlors in village and hamlet in remote
regions of the country; perhaps it merely fell on receptive
ground.

But in landscaping, there is a shift to another level. The
gardens are massed, composed, laid out with an understanding
of color, perspective, form, contrast, and harmony that leads
the eye from texture and mass to vista, with a true sense of
artistry, and the color that is eschewed indoors riots in the
flowerbeds. Is it some deep-bred racial impulse brooded and
formed through millennia of dark wet winters and damp gray

summers, some reaching out toward warmth by color-starved souls in their fundamental need for the consolation of beauty— an adaptation toward survival, perhaps? Whatever it is, the most modest cottage is never without its small embroidery of color; wonders are done with little alternating posies of white alyssum and blue lobelia with a dazzle of orange nasturtium as a foil, flourishing in strips of garden, in window boxes, or suspended from hanging baskets; and no bungalow or manor house is without its bed of mixed roses. Scots take their flower gardens as seriously as primitive agriculturists cultivating yams for subsistence; they talk of flowers and exchange cuttings and horticultural advice with the same earnestness as we discuss traffic jams and crowded subways in New York. Eavesdrop on a conversation between two old gaffers sunning themselves on a bench outside the public library, or two housewives in the queue at the butcher's shop, and from their murmurings phrases will rise up: "The cuttings rooted very quickly." "A good way of getting rid of greenfly . . . sprinkle tea leaves around the roots." "The best time to prune it. . . ." "The lupins are coming along lovely but stocks aren't flowering at all yet." Beyond the flowerbeds, everyone seems to have a vegetable patch, and the neat rows of sprouting produce flanked by regiments of fruit-bushes have the satisfying pattern and orderliness of American folk paintings.

Both Robbie's and Jenny's families had lived for generations in these hills, Robbie's father and grandfather forestrymen before him. In summer, Jenny worked at the local hotel supervising the cleaning of the rooms, and though making ends meet could not have been easy, the Kirkbrides were self-sufficient and imbued with a sense of their own worth that endowed everything they did with dignity. They put one in mind of some of George Eliot's rural people, drawing their sense of self from the quality of their life, which kept them in contact with nature; and in spite of their television set and the posters of American pop heroes on the walls in their children's rooms, they remained, in some fundamental way, unspoiled by contemporary life.

Their love of the countryside, their harmony with the seasons and weather, the birds and beasts of the hills, the wild flowers, the agricultural cycles, have formed their natures through generations. Their knowledge of the environment came direct to them; one never met them tramping through the hills with a guide to wild flowers or birds in their pockets, but they knew the common names of the flora, or could identify a birdcall, or explain why the sheep were behaving as they did, or what those mists rolling down the slopes of Ben Shawe betokened. There were few books in their house—or in any of the houses of the agricultural folk where we went. Jenny read; once I met her coming from the library and noticed the titles of the books she had taken: a couple of light romances, an autobiography of a rural Scottish minister, and a book about deep-freezing home-grown produce. A freezer that took up much space in her cramped kitchen was her pride and delight.

We would pass the Kirkbrides' cottage whenever we walked along the forestry road to the caravan site, where we went to buy milk, which was sold in plastic envelopes—like cold square udders, almost impossible to transfer into a jug without drenching one's hands and sink and floor in milk. "Come away in," they would call if they saw us, and tea and biscuits would be served in front of the log fire (which they call a "stick fire") that always burned in the low-ceilinged, cluttered living room. The stone-built, three-hundred-year-old cottage was so chilly in summer that we were filled with admiration for constitutions that could survive there, with only that fireplace for warmth, through the grip of the Scottish winter. The children, Gladys and Keith, both as bonny and sound as their parents, would sit, shy and polite, trying to restrain Spot, their maniacal little Jack Russell terrier—an energetic breed raised for hunting hare and rabbit. A gray cat dozed, unconcerned, in front of the fire. On the hill two pet lambs, hand-raised, nibbled; their butchering for the freezer was postponed season after season by the children's protests at the idea of stewing or roasting family pets. We rarely came away from their cottage without the gift of new-laid eggs or a pot of jam or some fresh-picked garden produce.

When I was alone at Glenauchen Cottage at the beginning of each summer, as I preceded the family to the glen, Jenny would phone sometimes, after tea, to ask if I would like to take a walk. Depending on which way we went, one of us would pick up the other. She was always dressed in the clothes she had worn to work that day at the hotel: a short, neat skirt; a blouse and cardigan, or "twin-set"; nylon stockings and medium-heeled dress shoes. I, the city-dweller roughing it in the country, would be in dungarees and stout hiking boots. We would set out, over fences and barbed wire, stone walls, ditches and streams, clambering over rocks and sliding down stony slopes, all of which she maneuvered as if she were tripping down the High Street with a shopping basket on her arm, never stumbling nor snagging her sweater nor laddering a stocking. Leading the way, she would warn me when we reached boggy ground or thistles or nettles. I am slimmer than Jenny, and fit, and could take ten- and twelve-mile hikes easily in stride, but when we got back from those evening rambles, my boots and trouser bottoms would be encrusted with mud, my face flushed, burrs and leaves clinging to my clothes, while her neat shoes, stockings, and clothes remained unsullied, and her person unruffled.

She took me on walks our family would never have discovered on our own, so that when the others came, I, in turn, could lead them alongside the secret burns where copses of hazel and ash flourished on steep banks thick with bluebells, where small cataracts tumbled over rocks into unexpected pools where waterlilies floated. She showed me new shortcuts and back paths that would reveal sudden familiar views, places where wild raspberries ripened early, a pond with a rotted wooden jetty, used, when frozen over in winter, by the locals for curling—an old Scottish sport involving heavy stones cut into flat rounds and sent spinning over the ice. She tried to explain the intricacies of the game played in winter weather. "Och, the glen is bonny when there's a good snowfall," she said; "you should just see it, all white and sparkling." Perhaps we might, sometime, I told her.

As we went along, she would stop to pick a wild flower I had not noticed and identify it for me, or stop suddenly so we could listen to a birdcall. "Ssh . . . d'you hear that sound? Like two stones being rolled together, then a chirp; two stones, then a chirp . . . that's a stone-chat."

I always wanted to hear a skylark. "Is that a skylark, Jenny?"

I'd ask whenever some lyrical flight of birdsong caught my ear. But it never was. "You hear them quite a lot in the spring," she said. "They make quite a commotion—it's bonny to hear."

On an evening when the sky was as blue as Bristol glass, she stopped and whispered, "Stand quite still, don't move. Look—down there—an owl." In the hushed valley below us, an owl, early abroad, curved in silent flight, a slow soaring swoop, its unmoving wings supported by the substance of the still blue air, to disappear, soundless, behind a knoll. My first owl; I had beheld a miracle. "Their wings are designed so that they are noiseless," Jenny explained, matter-of-fact. "They catch an air current and glide along with it. They're so silent in flight it makes it easy for them to swoop down on their prey without being heard."

As we walked we would discuss our children, recipes, gossip of the glen. She told me about the Rural Women's Institute, which in winter organized classes and lectures for the benefit of women who otherwise would remain isolated on outlying farms and remote cottages; there were classes in baking, cake decorating, sewing, and Scottish country dancing, with guest lecturers who would talk about history, archeology, and folklore. "The R.W.I. meetings give us a chance to get together—the weather has to be pretty bad to keep us from attending. The winter evenings can be very long and lonely in the hills."

One evening we returned from a long walk to find Robbie in conversation with a man who had just stepped out of a small battered Morris Minor. I was introduced to the Reverend Mr. Alexander Scroggie, minister of Glenauchen Parish as well as two adjoining parishes. A well-spoken, jovial young man, he chatted a while but appeared impatient to be off. "What about the lantern now, Robbie?" he asked. "Aye, it's in the barn," Robbie answered, and the two of them went off across the yard. Jenny explained that the Reverend Mr. Scroggie was an ardent collector of moths, and was after a couple of rare specimens said to inhabit our glen. With the lantern and some honey for bait, he was off to spend the darkening hours lurking on the hill in hope of a find.

"It's his way of relaxing," Jenny said over a cup of tea. "It's a hard job taking care of three parishes, but the Kirk of Scotland can no longer afford a minister at each kirk. In fact, there are quite a few churches standing unused, and they are being put up for sale and people are making them over into houses. It's a shame. And poor Mr. Scroggie is overworked; he has to preach the sermon here at Glenauchen Kirk at eleven on Sundays, then he hurries off to take the service over at Skelmorlie Kirk at twelve-fifteen, and there's a rotating student minister who gives the sermon at Ladybank. There's rarely more than a couple of dozen people in each congregation, though in summer a few trippers drop in. But he has to cope with the pastoral duties of three parishes, and the pay isn't much, and they have four children, so Mrs. Scroggie has had to take a job as a secretary at a private girls' school. They live in a huge, cold old manse that she hardly ever has a moment to clean, what with her job and all the bairns. So the poor minister has to do a lot of the housework and he doesn't often find the time for his precious moths, poor mannie."

"Does he live in that black and white manse beside Glenauchen Kirk?"

"Och, no. The Balfour-Kinnears bought the Manse about five years back. Mr. Balfour-Kinnear is a quantity surveyor. They were out in Africa or Arabia or somewhere for a long time; then they came back so that their boys could get a proper education. Glenauchen is famous for having a very large manse and a wee kirk. They say the ministers here always had big families and small congregations. The Scroggies live in the manse over at Ladybank. We go to church every Sunday— Robbie and me and the bairns—winter and summer; we never miss a service. And Robbie does a lot of repairs and fixing there, in his spare time."

Robbie came in, always having to overcome initial shyness, but becoming more relaxed with us over the years. "He's away hiding up on Dalrioch waiting for this very rare specimen with black spots on its wings," he reported. "I've asked him to step in for a wee taste when he gets back."

In the glen, the offer of a "wee taste" always meant sherry for the women, whiskey for the men. Though my preference is for whiskey, I accepted the glass of sherry he placed in my hand.

* * *

Neil came dashing into the kitchen, where we lingered with the newspaper at the breakfast table. "They've brought all the sheep in from the hill to the farm—let's go down there and see what's happening!" Early in the morning we had been awakened by the sounds of the sheep bleating and protesting, the dog's yelping, the shepherds' sharp cry of command.

As we walked down the hill road we could see the gathered flock, its living flow dammed up in a white quivering mass in the basin of the valley. At the steading, the two wild grandsons, yelling and prodding in a rage at the sheep for their stupidity, were penning the herd inside interleading stone-walled sheepfolds, and the anxious cries of lambs and mothers unable to locate each other in the crush filled the air, which smelled strongly of disinfectant. Mrs. Cameron stood by with her shepherd's crook upright, and beckoned to us to come and stand beside her; we watched as the sheep were forced through a small opening into single file, then pushed and harried one by one into a dipping tank, from which they stumbled out like distraught bundles of sodden laundry, to be released into the Home Park, where families ran about like refugees trying to reunite with one another.

"How will they find one another?" Philippa asked, upset by the distress of the ewes and lambs as they thrust and butted, the anguished bleating of the lambs and hoarse responses of the mothers creating a din so that we had to shout to be heard.

"Och," offered Angus, the younger grandson, rough and offhand, "they'll find each other alright; they recognize one another by smell. The stink of the disinfectant's confusing them for a bit—that's what all the bloody noise is about—they're too damn stupid anyway to have feelings."

Angus and his brother, Dougal, swarthy handsome youths with curly shoulder-length hair, looked as if they could have ridden with Prince Charlie or even taken part in some of the more brutal atrocities to which the primitive warring Highland clans were prone; they wore their surliness like a kilt and plaid that proclaimed they despised their fellows and would kowtow to no one. Friday was pay day, and on Saturdays the glen was often abuzz with mutters about what the two of them had been up to the previous night at one of the local hostelries.

They smashed cars and knuckles and noses, and as often as not they would be seen at the ploughing or mowing sporting a black eye or swollen nose, or bedecked with plaster patches and bandages. One Saturday morning, Harl pulled off the road to allow Dougal to bring the tractor through a gate out of a field; he waved thanks with a bandaged fist, grinned, explained that he had hurt his hand when he accidentally drove the tractor into a wall, winked broadly, and drove off.

But Donny MacIver had other explanations for all their injuries. "They're coarse tinks—that's all they are," he invariably complained when he dropped off the Saturday morning paper. "A guid skelpin' is what they desairve . . . soakin' their brains in whiskey and getting into brawls every Friday night at the Lockup Pub, then drivin' home drunk as lords and endangering everyone on the roads. They'll be lucky if they don't kill themselves one day. Have you haird what Angus got up to last night . . . ?"

Dougal, the older grandson, was always announcing his engagement to a succession of "fiancees," who, whenever we met one, turned out to be pretty, modest, and charming, nearly always a university student conscientiously pursuing a laudable career. Donny was always astonished, as he doubted even the literacy of the two brothers. Whenever the news spread through the glen that the "engagement" had been broken off, he would nod in his sage way and remark, "I knew the gairl was too good for that unruly yob."

Meanwhile, the sheep re-formed themselves into family groups and started drying out, the ewes cropping the grass while the lambs nuzzled them for milk and reassurance. "You'll all come away in now for a cup of tea," Mrs. Cameron said. "Meg has just baked a tin of her famous shortbread."

Meg, the unmarried daughter, flushed from the oven's heat and flustered by the unexpected company, greeted us in a voice strangely high-pitched and schoolgirlish for a woman in her forties. Her hair was jet-black and her face matted with pancake makeup; she had about her the air of a hearty hockey-playing schoolgirl anxious to please. "Now, you just sit down by the fire with the Gordons, Mummy," she instructed the vigorous old farmer lady, "and I'll bring in the tea." She was justly famous for her shortbread, which was crisp and rich with a dark, nutty butteriness, and it was pressed upon us with an insistence we were unable to withstand, so that none of us was able to eat lunch afterward.

She had a part-time job in a small boutique in the village High Street. "It's no' bad," she told us. "I get to meet some quite interesting people. We get quite a few Yanks coming in to buy souvenirs—golfing people from Gleneagles; very friendly they are. Yesterday there were even a few of those *Ayrabs*. Mrs. Taggart of the teashop peeked out and saw they had come in a great blue Rolls-Royce, and there were some women dressed in veils inside the motorcar, and the number-plate was in those Arabic letters. 'I thought I'd seen everything till I saw that,' she told me when I dropped in for morning coffee. You never know what next you'll see in the High Street nowadays. Still, I enjoy having a little job; it makes a nice change from the farm. In the afternoons I go across to Stonebyres—that's my auntie's farm—it's where Mummy was born. I give Auntie Kirstie a hand with the ironing and the baking. There's always so much to do—I'll never catch up. Now, you must have another wee shortbread. Don't be shy, now, children, there's heaps more in the kitchen. Come on, now, have another; I know the guid hill air gives you a healthy appetite. Let me fill your cup for you . . . why are the dogs barking like that?" She peered out of the window. "Oh, talk of the devil—there's Aunt Kirstie just driven up. I'll go and get another cup."

Aunt Kirstie, known in the glen as Miss Kirstie Aird, came in, followed by two Corgi dogs. She ran the old family farm with the help of a shepherd; in later summers, when our ears had become attuned to the nuances and signals emitted by the glen "Mafia," is appeared that there was a long-time "understanding" between Meg and her auntie's shepherd. Speculation abounded in the glen about what would happen to Stonebyres Farm when Miss Kirstie Aird "went." The farm was part of the Glenshinnoch Estate, whose tenants the Airds had been for generations; the tenure, however, could be passed on only to direct descendants of the original tenant, and as Miss Kirstie Aird was without issue, no one knew who would succeed to her tenancy. A pretty woman, with curly white hair and lively blue eyes, she seemed to be in her sixties, and swooped about the countryside, a menace to all in her small blue car, which she only knew how to drive in forward gear. "I never lairned how to revairse," she would say, laughing and throwing up her hands when we met, hood to hood, on the narrow hill road; either we would have to back up to the nearest layby to allow her to pass or we would have to get into her car and reverse it for her. She bred Corgi dogs, and had been a famous horsewoman in her youth. Meg pointed out that many of the Cameron pictures of a slender, good-looking young woman, well-mounted on a prancing horse, were of Aunt Kirstie, and many of the silver cups and now-faded blue satin rosettes were trophies of her horsemanship.

Miss Kirstie Aird took a great fancy to Harl. "And where is your handsome husband this morning?" she would ask if we met on the High Street or in the library. Or "I just saw the handsome doctor buying stamps at the postoffice. He tells me you all did the hike to Skelmorlie yesterday—it's a bonny walk. I used to ride there when I was a gairl."

In the same way that the Hunters took vicarious pleasure in our enjoyment of Glenauchen, so were the glen folk pleased at the way we liked their hills and came to know them so well. They always wanted to hear where we had walked and what views we had come upon, and they would tell one another about our expeditions. "I haird from Tottie MacIver that you all climbed Ben Auchen," Mr. McKenzie, the butcher, might mention while he was cutting lambchops off a carcass of a sheep suspended from a hook in the shop window. "Your visitors from the States must have enjoyed the view of the castle from up there. . . ." Our activities were buzzed along the glen grapevine.

Now, the dish of shortbread well depleted, the quantity we had been prevailed upon to consume awash in the tea we had drunk, we stood up to leave. "Before you go, now"—Miss Kirstie Aird opened her handbag and took out a book of pink coupons—"I'm sure you'll be wanting to buy a few tickets for my coffee morning at Glencorrie House. It's in aid of the League of Pity—for the prevention of cruelty to children."

We bought four pink tickets at ten pence each, and she was delighted. "It's Auntie Kirstie's pet charity," Meg caroled. "I remember her coffee mornings at Glencorrie House when I was a wee gairl."

"Now, mind you're all there next Thursday," Miss Aird said. "Mrs. MacFadyen is looking forward to meeting all of you. She very kindly lends us the use of her house, and her housekeeper, Mrs. Darroch, makes lots of delicious cakes and sandwiches. You'll love Glencorrie House, I know. It was built in 1766, and they say it's one of the few Georgian bungalows in the whole of Scotland."

Mrs. MacFadyen . . . Mrs. MacFadyen . . . the name was already familiar to us. Everyone spoke it in the special tone—hushed and awed—the British use when referring to the "upper class," even in Scotland, where, because of the fiercely independent spirit of the Scots, the class system doesn't have the same hold it does in England. From all accounts she sounded like an imperious, formidable old woman, and it was understood that we were expected to pay her homage. "Oh, we'll certainly be there," we told Miss Kirstie Aird.

As we walked back home up the hill, the flock was now placidly dispersed. One of the children pointed up to the forestry road and said, "There they go, as usual," and we saw what had by now become a daily event: a tall woman, dressed in tweeds and brogues, striding purposefully along with a pack of small dogs at her heels. If a single one lagged or strayed, she would blow a peremptory note on a silver whistle that hung from her neck, bringing the miscreant sharply to heel. Just above the heather slope beside our loch, she turned smartly about with a piercing toot of the whistle, and she and her yapping brood marched back and disappeared over the hill behind the Kirkbrides' cottage. We had not yet established her identity, and speculated, as we walked, who she might be.

On the day of the coffee morning, everybody bowed out; Neil, because he had been learning from Bob the art of fly-fishing, and was off to the loch to try his luck with the brown trout; Harl and David and Philippa, because they planned to climb up Innerdownie, from which, they had been told, they would have a fine view of the River Forth. I was deputed to represent Glenauchen Cottage at the League of Pity's annual fund-raising. Discarding hiking boots and blue denim, I dressed appropriately in matronly clothes, and drove the four miles to Glencorrie House, which still represented, in the folk view of the glen, the grand-house status of the original landed gentry who had built it.

Donny and Tottie had briefed us about the MacFadyens. The late Mr. MacFadyen's parents had been poor crofters who had emigrated to Perthshire from one of the outer Hebridean Islands. When the family found itself unable to eke out a living, the wife had started to supplement their income by selling home-baked shortbread and oatcakes to the workers employed in a local textile mill. The demand increased, their operations expanded, and after a few years the MacFadyen Biscuit Factory was employing much local labor; their product, wrapped in bright tartan paper, was being sold all over Scotland, and Mr. MacFadyen was on his way to becoming an industrial tycoon. With his profits he had bought up large tracts of farmland in the glen, including the eighteenth-century mansion and the medieval castle owned by the Honeymans, an old, once wealthy glen family who could no longer afford to keep up the estate. But there was a "weakness" in old MacFadyen's son and heir, Donny told us, looking his most rigidly righteous and raising his elbow to indicate the exact nature of the sin. "Drank himself right into the grave," he pronounced sternly, making me hope that from where he sat at our kitchen table he could not see the bottles of whiskey and sherry on the pantry shelf.

He drank himself into the grave, leaving the bankrupt biscuit factory and the country estates to his only son, Gavin: "a ne'er-do-well, spoiled rotten," according to Donny. "You'll pass the abandoned biscuit factory when you drive into Perth," Tottie told us, and over the years the blank face, shuttered windows, and faded lettering of the factory became a familiar landmark to us. Gavin had tried to sustain what was left of the family fortune by sheep-farming, for which he had neither the bent nor the energy. In need of ready cash, he had sold off thousands of acres to the Forestry Commission, which accounted for all the young pine forests on the hills above our loch.

His old mother lived on in the grand house to which she had come as a bride, while Gavin and his wife, the daughter of a local shepherd, made their home at Glencorrie Castle, the small fortalice that had been built as a fortification overlooking the approach to the glen in medieval times. Their flocks and fortunes on the decline, a spark of his grandparents' business acumen had flared up in Gavin; breaching the ire and opposition of the inhabitants of the glen, he had somehow managed to get a zoning permit that allowed him to set up a caravan park beside the burn, in one of his pastures that skirted the main road of the glen.

Caravaning seems to be one way the British working class can get away from the soot and grime of crowded industrial urban life to spend their annual two weeks' vacation in the countryside; in the caravan parks they are still cheek by jowl with other folk, but hills and streams and fresh air are all around instead of factory chimneys. They string their washing up on makeshift lines to dry, play transistor radios, set up folding tables, and brew pots of dark strong tea; if the sun should, by some happy chance, shine, they expose as much bare skin as decently possible to its scant charity, and if a misty rain envelops the glen, they huddle within, the children's faces showing wistfully at the windows.

Once we drove past the caravan site as a gloomy drizzle swept down the hills, no sign of life visible apart from the damp washing limp on the lines. "Headline in tomorrow's newspapers," Bob forecast: "Father Murders Wife and Seven Children after Thirty-ninth Game of Monopoly in Caravan." In fine weather—and in all our summers there, the weather, as predicted by the celestial messenger, was unusually dry— the caravaners fished and paddled in the burn, and sunbathed, their white skins, unaccustomed to the sun's rays, quickly turning a painful red. Over the years, we came to notice a pattern in the way they took their vacations that made us wonder about the truth of the sociologists' theories on the demise of the extended family; it seemed that each caravan held three generations of family: one or both old parents, the young couple, and the grandchildren. At the caravan site we heard a great variety of English and Scottish regional accents and dialects, and once there were three exquisite little Oriental children chattering away in Glasgow accents so broad that they were barely intelligible to us.

Gavin MacFadyen cornered the market on tourist trade in the glen, his grocery shop and milk-bar the only place for miles around where caravaners could buy milk, bread, eggs, canned goods, soft drinks, and candy, with a couple of pinball machines to divert the simmering boredom of adolescent youths bridling at the constraint of three generations confined in one caravan. He then transformed the dungeons of his castle into a bar and disco. Dim, lurid lighting was installed beneath the massive stone ceilings; imitation leather upholstery and synthetic carpeting filled the cavern-like interior; the nine-foot-thick walls with their inset arrow slits echoed and rang with the din of a jukebox and itinerant rock-and-roll groups; and liquor was stacked high behind the ancient iron gates of cells where once prisoners of feuding barons had languished until they were tortured or murdered.

All that went on in the Lockup Pub outraged Donny's Calvinist sensibilities. "It's a pit of iniquity," he said. "And they don't even stick to legal pub hours. They're supposed to stop dispensing their alcoholic beverages at ten o'clock sharp. But what they do is carry on regardless, but send one of their bairns out to keep watch at the telephone booth near the castle gates; and if the wee gairl sees the polis coming, she smartly pops two pence in the slot and phones Daddy to warn him; and by the time the polis get there the lights are out, doors shut, and it's quiet as the tomb. He's a disgrace to the parish!"

Curious, now, to meet the mother of the ill-famed Gavin, the widow of the bibulous biscuit baker, I turned off the main road; then I crossed a humpbacked stone bridge, similar to ours, that forded the river and led past a small gatehouse onto a rhododendron-lined drive that twisted its way for half a mile through the hills, ending in a broad graveled terrace at the front of the house. The small, gracious mansion, with Gothic windows and doorway set into walls of mellow golden stone, surrounded by landscaped lawns, shrubbery, and trees, was set like a modest jewel against the green of the hills, and radiated the sense of grace and ease, the harmony of man with his surroundings, that Georgian domestic architecture accomplished so satisfyingly.

The front door stood wide open to the sunny morning; an oblong anteroom led into a spacious stone-flagged central hall from which all the rooms of the house radiated. There was a great stone hearth, worn rugs, shabby chintz armchairs and sofas, dark paintings, a mixture of ugly Victorian furniture and fine eighteenth-century pieces, the ubiquitous china knick-knacks, and piles of dog-eared *Country Life* magazines. It was all familiar—recognizable from the pages of Jane Austen and Anthony Trollope, all the way through the English novel to Henry Green, Evelyn Waugh, and the flourishing industry of writings about Bloomsbury—that unconscious arrogance displayed in the combination of tradition, past splendors, present shabbiness, and except for the intuitive rightness of the flower arrangement, an absence of taste and personal intention; the country house seems to impose its own character, and there is little evidence of individual distinctiveness.

I followed the sound of voices through a small library lined with leather-bound volumes, the brilliance of the sunlit walls flooding the tall Gothic windows. Miss Kirstie Aird appeared and took me in tow. I was presented to Mrs. MacFadyen, who presided, straight-backed, in an ornately carved Jacobean chair, and was placed beside her on a sofa with a cup of coffee in my hand, and a plate of tiny, crustless sandwiches on my lap. The large, handsome, shabby sitting room hummed with a murmur of conversation, the decibel level considerably lower than in an equivalent gathering of Americans.

Mrs. MacFadyen was a small, stout woman, in her early seventies, I guessed, with auburn hair set in tight curls, large protuberant blue eyes, and a complexion of pink and white porcelain, remarkably fine; she was carefully made up, and, like most of the women there, dressed in heathery tweeds. She summed me up with a shrewd eye while subjecting me to a round of brisk questioning about myself, my family, our reasons for coming to the glen. "Well," she observed, "we're glad to have Americans in the glen. Puts us on the map, doesn't it, Kirstie? Kirstie and her sister, Ella Cameron, who's your neighbor up at Glenauchen, and I—we all grew up together; did you know that? We all went to the little one-roomed schoolhouse near the kirk, though it's a schoolhouse no longer, I'm sorry to say; it's only two years since that it's become a private house, and the glen children have to be taken by bus into the village school now. And the Manse, alas, is a manse no longer; the Balfour-Kinnears live there now.

"Shuna," she called out to a tall, elegant woman who leaned against the marble mantel and was separating the two halves of a sandwich to examine what lay within. "Shuna, come over here and meet the new people up at the loch. . . . This is Shuna Balfour-Kinnear. She lives at the Manse."

A languid hand was placed briefly in mine as though I might be the carrier of some insalubrious organism. The woman's red hair, plain bony features, and fine-grained faintly freckled skin, with her lean, long-legged stance, all added up to an impression of thoroughbred horsiness. "How evah," she inquired, in fruity upper-class English accents that jarred among the soft Scottish burr all around, "did you get to hear about our glen in New York—when no one in *Edinburgh* is aware of its existence?"

So, once again, I told the story: the story of our having lived in Edinburgh, of Harl's internship at the children's hospital, of our friendship with the Hunters, the casually dropped remark, the telephone call, the auction . . . the group around me all listening, much taken by the story—which is, as I have said, one that people like to hear.

"I come by your place every day," Shuna Balfour-Kinnear said, "though I've never actually been inside. I go along the forestry road all the way to the top end of the loch—exercising the dogs, you know." She snapped up a sandwich in one quick neat bite.

"So it's you we see with all those little dogs. We were wondering who it could be."

"The dogs must have a good run every day. I breed 'em. Jack Russell terriers. Husband breeds Arab horses and a few head of Charolais cattle, but he's away all day in Stirling, so everything's left to me. I'm tied down to the place. Shouldn't even be *here* this morning—so much to do—but one simply must get away sometimes." Her pale, milky complexion became for a moment suffused with blood, as if some deep rage had risen to the surface. "One more spot of coffee and I must be getting back." She strode off to pour coffee from a Georgian silver coffee service.

Miss Kirstie Aird presented me to a solidly built man with fresh ruddy cheeks and black hair: "Now, I want you to meet Alistair Kirkland."

His long sideburns, reserved yet courteous manner, and the old-fashioned cut of his tweed clothes gave him the look of a rural character out of Thomas Hardy. "And are ye likin' it up at the loch?"

"Oh, very much."

"Must make quite a change from New York," he suggested. "At least, from what we see of it on the television: all those gangsters and skyscrapers and subways." Everyone laughed.

"Alistair farms over at Knockinlaw," said Miss Aird. "You'll see his place up on the hill across from the wee bridge when you leave here. His family has been farming in the glen as long as mine."

"Aye, Miss Aird," he said. "I mind when I was a wee lad," he told me, "Miss Kirstie Aird would come riding on her horse up to our house; selling sprigs of white heather, she was, for the League of Pity."

"Aye, Alistair, it's a good few years I've been doing my bit for the League. I won't confess *just* how long I've been at it."

"What a fine sight she was upon her horse," he recalled. "She was a famous horsewoman in the district—took all the prizes."

"And nowadays," she said, her manner amused and vivacious, "it's all I can do to keep my wee car on the road. I was morr . . . tified yesterday; I met your handsome husband head-on as I was rounding that *terrible* curve on the loch road, and he had to get out of his car and revairse my car for me, for I'm always afraid I might go over the edge like Dougal did with the tractor last spring." Everyone laughed again.

"Pay no heed to the motorcar, Miss Aird," Alistair Kirkland said gallantly. "To this day there's still no one in the glen can match you when it comes to sitting on a horse."

Tottie MacIver was at the coffee morning, bundled up in a tweed suit, and she introduced me to her cronies, who were curious to see one of the "people from America up at the loch." The only time the local agricultural people, tradespeople, artisans, and shopkeepers ever came into Glencorrie House was on this sort of public occasion, and they talked among themselves, and examined the furnishings, silver, and plate with intense interest. I learned later that one of Tottie's favorite pastimes was to visit the great houses and castles of Scotland, and she could chat knowledgeably about the contents of the Earl of Inchcape's banqueting hall and Lord Mungo's bedchamber, and there was no better guide to the gardens of the grand houses that were open to the public. She was, as well, a sort of Burke's *Peerage* to the Scottish aristocracy, and while pouring tea would explain that old Lady Glachan, who lived with her housekeeper and epileptic son in that gray mansion on the hill above the village, was sister-in-law to the Earl of Auchendoon, who carried one of the ceremonial objects at the coronation of the Queen; and the honorable Donald Tainsh, who was in the glen to buy a load of hay from that old miser Geordie McCaskie, was second cousin on his wife's side to the Marquis of Brenochlie.

Mrs. MacFadyen introduced me to a harried-looking woman who scurried about in a floral smock, clearing away used crockery and replenishing the cakes and sandwiches. "I want you to meet my *precious* Mrs. Darroch, without whom I would be *quite* unable to maintain Glencorrie House. Were it not for her, I would have had to shut up the place and move into Glencorrie Castle with my son Gavin and his family." Mrs. Darroch gave me an exhausted smile and staggered out with a huge silver tray laden with cups and saucers. Mrs. Mac-Fadyen fitted a cigarette into a long onyx cigarette-holder, lit up, inhaled luxuriously, and continued, "She is an absolute treasure, that dear woman—been with me since Gavin was a bairn. I could not carry on for a single day without her." Her accent was Scottish, but more clipped and authoritative than that of the other glen folk. There was no evidence of cooks, butlers, housemaids, gardeners; later we would learn that all of these functions were served by the indefatigable Mrs. Darroch,

who even helped out as barmaid on busy nights at the Lockup
Pub.

Mrs. MacFadyen walked me out to the car when I left.
"Now, you must come for a proper visit. Bring the doctor; I
would like to talk to him about your American president and
his foreign policy. And I know you'd like to see around the
house—it has a grand history. We even have a ghost."

We got to meet the lady of the Manse, the red-headed
Shuna Kinnear-Balfour, by chance, on a day when we had decided to explore the church and its graveyard, which nestled
in a bend of the river a few miles to the west of us. We followed the burn from where it flowed out of the loch, ambling
along its banks through the Camerons' pasture, until it broad-
ened out into the river. It led, purling and eddying over its
rocky bed, into the thick woods bordering on the MacFadyen
estate; from here, a small private footpath led to a bridge that
the grand folk from Glencorrie House had, for centuries, used
as a shortcut to the church.

The wooden bridge, fallen now into disuse, was rickety and
gapped with missing and rotten planks, precariously fording
the dark rushing water under an overhang of low-branching
trees. We crossed, stepping cautiously, and followed a path out
of the woods into the graveyard.

What a place to lie forever, this country churchyard, a
green pillow rising gently above the river bank, the gray head-
stones embedded in lush mown grass, the sound of flowing
water, the hills banked in a ring all around. What must it feel
like, we wondered, to be born in the glen and live out the
measure of one's days knowing the final resting place will be
such a setting as this?

The earliest gravestone we could decipher dated from 1769;
the engraving on the older ones had been erased by time and
weather. We recognized family names of people we had already
got to know: Cameron, Aird, and Kirkland, MacFadyen and
McWhirter, as well as the families of the butcher, baker, and
ironmonger, going back three and four generations. There
were memorial stones to young men killed in colonial wars in

Africa and India, and, even in such a tiny burial place, to many who fell in World War I. There is hardly a hamlet, village, or town in Scotland that does not have its marble column raised in memory of its men who died in the trenches of the first of the terrible wars of our time. In these small country graveyards one gets a sense of the cost, in pathetic human terms of sons and fathers and brothers, of the awful glory of the British Empire.

The church is old, but no one seems to know just how old. The earliest references are from the sixteenth century, but it is believed that a church has stood on this site since time immemorial; perhaps it was originally a site where standing stones for some pagan rites were once raised. Though it has been restored and repaired many times, the present building is thought to be at least five hundred years old. It is a low, modest structure, of whitewashed stone, with the same hand-hewn slate roof-tiles as at our house; only a small bell-tower on the roof over the apse marks it as an ecclesiastical structure; there is no architectural ornament, no spire, to draw the eye heavenward. It is a low church, physically and ritually. Its manse rises three times larger beside it. One enters by a small porch, with memorial tablets set in the walls and a bulletin board hung with parish news. In recent years, the inside has been paneled in rich wood. There are pleasant stained-glass windows, and the buttressed arched ceiling is whitewashed plaster. The ladies of the parish see to it that there are always fresh-cut flowers for the altar, and there is the serene atmosphere of a modest country church.

The gateposts at the entrance to the burial ground are carved stones on which a slab, now crumbled, once rested: a memorial to the victims of the plague, the Black Death, which had reached from England into Scotland in the late fourteenth century. We strolled among the graves, reading names from around the district, until we came to an odd gap in the ancient wall; it was neither broken nor crumbled, but had been opened up to give access to a grassy rectangle with one impressive marble tomb at its center. The area lay just outside the church wall, and was bounded on three sides by a clipped hedge with four tall yews standing sentinel in the corners. The stone was

engraved in memory of Jane Honeyman of Glencorrie House:
born 1797, died 1894 in the ninety-seventh year of her life.
"The keep, Glencorrie Castle," I had read in the old records,
"has been in the possession of the Honeyman family since
1776." The Honeymans were the family who had built Glencorrie House, and we were curious to find out why this one
descendant of theirs—for there were no other Honeymans
lying under the green sod beside the river—was buried here,
outside the precincts of the walls of the graveyard.

Opposite the small gates of the church stood the high-walled
garden of the Manse, its immaculately tended grounds laid out
in smooth lawns and formal flowerbeds, visible through a pair
of high, wrought-iron gates; beyond the garden was a vista of
green pastures at the foot of the hills, where some horses and
a small herd of creamy Charolais cattle grazed. The Manse,
an oblong, four-storied house, whitewashed, with black painted
woodwork, windowpanes reflecting the sunshine, stood with its
back close to the main road and its front facing out over the
hills. We followed the lane that led out to the main road. Keeping to a narrow grass verge that ran alongside the Manse, we
were hailed by a figure that straightened up from a rose bed
and came over to the low wall. It was Shuna Balfour-Kinnear,
the lady of the Manse.

"Quite nice today," she said of the brilliant summer morning.
We were already learning that in Scotland understatement is
an ethnic characteristic; "quite nice," "no' bad," and "bonny"
are used when we would employ superlatives.

"We're being very fortunate with the weather," I agreed,
making a mental note that next time I should avoid "very" so
that my language should not be clothed in colors too bright
to blend in with the local muted tones. I introduced her to
Harl.

She pointed to a meadow that sloped away up the hill.
"We've just bought the glebe." The glebe is a field attached
to a manse where the minister could graze his sheep and cow.
"The Church of Scotland refused to sell it to us when we
bought the Manse—God knows why. Then we got wind that
some London architect was negotiating to buy it to put up
one of those ghastly contemporary houses: all wood and glass

and soaring lines. So Husband went to see them, and told them they didn't want that sort of thing being built beside an ancient landmark, and they agreed to let us have it instead, though they made us pay through the nose, canny old clerics. Impossible to best them. Quite a relief all the same. We're having the fences fixed so we can put our Charolais herd out to graze there, and our horses will have the home park to themselves. Come in and have some coffee and a biscuit. Frightfully busy, so I can't offer you anything grand."

We accepted the invitation that seemed to have blown over her shoulder as if she weren't responsible for it, and went back along the lane to wait at the locked gate of an enclosed courtyard, while she rounded up half a dozen yapping terriers and shut them in what appeared to be a row of stables, from which the clamor of their protest continued noisily while she let us in. The garden paths were covered in raked gravel and not a weed showed its head. As we approached the front door, a tall figure in white moved away from a side window, withdrawing with an effect so wraithlike that I thought it was more likely a light curtain billowing in a gust of wind.

Inside it was chillier than out of doors. She left us beside the feeble glow of a two-barred electric heater set in the hearth of a baronial fireplace in a great, stone-floored entrance hall. Another interior familiar from the English novel: threadbare Oriental rugs, faded Sanderson chintzes on sofas and easy chairs, dun watercolors of loch and mountain, framed sepia photographs of stern Victorian men and women and starched, frocked children, piles of tattered horse-and-hound magazines on the hearth. Harl examined the contents of a couple of glass cases filled with shards of pottery and pale clay jars that seemed to be of great antiquity.

She came striding in with a tray. "It's only instant coffee, I'm afraid," she said briskly; "no time to brew the real stuff. One of the new pups is ailing and I'm waiting for the vet to get here, and the girl who comes in to clean hasn't turned up this morning—which happens more often than not." The coffee was weak and watery and scaldingly hot, and there was a plate of digestive biscuits.

Harl asked about the pottery in the cases.

"It's pretty ancient stuff, actually. Husband fancies it—one of his hobbies. We've lived abroad a good deal, and he was always picking up bits and pieces when we were out in Africa and the Middle East. He's a quantity surveyor, worked a lot for oil companies, so there was always lots of digging going on and he would snoop about and pick up the odd pot. He's always preferred living out there; he can't stand the Scottish climate. But it's not my cup of tea; I hate the heat. Always loathed living out there, actually. All those wives. Nothing to do but sit around the British Club idle, drinking their gin slings or playing tennis. Not for me, thanks, that kind of existence. And no decent schools for the boys—had to educate them myself."

"You're a teacher?"

Her laugh was like the high whinny of a startled horse. "Me! I never even matriculated from grammar school. I had to leave school in the fifth form to take care of my mother, who was an invalid. But I certainly never let *that* hinder me! I was determined that the boys should get into Geddes Academy, here in Perthshire. It's a first-rate school; my brothers went on from there to good universities. In fact, the reason why we bought this drafty old manse is because Geddes Academy is nearby. I corresponded with the headmaster all the time we were out in Saudi. He sent me the curriculum and book-lists. I had the books sent out from Edinburgh and I jolly well taught the boys myself. Set them lessons every day, corrected their work from the teachers' manuals, wouldn't let them off anything. I was jolly strict—maintained the highest standards. Had to. It's very hard to get into Geddes, and that was where I was determined they were going. Stood no nonsense from them. We came back to Scotland five years ago, when I'd had just about all I could take of the heat and dust and dryness. Told Husband I was taking the boys home, and he could come or stay. He came. Took this job in Stirling. The boys sat the entrance exam—it's a pretty stiff exam—and all three of them were accepted." She set her cup down in its saucer with an air of conviction. "The older two are both at the university now. And Ninian (he's the youngest) is a day-boy at Geddes."

Her determination and her achievement, both so formidable, silenced us for a while. We munched at our digestive biscuits, filled with awed admiration. "Well," I offered, "you've done a remarkable job. It seems that everyone we know has problems with their children dropping out of school, trying different ways of life, searching for themselves—as they say—in some pretty strange places."

She set her shoulders back and lifted her chin. "Children are like animals," she said. "They do *exactly* what is expected of them. I've trained my dogs—when I whistle, they obey—and I've trained my boys. I *accept* nothing that falls short of the standards I *demand*. That's what I expect, and that's what I *get*."

Agog and chastened, there was no response we could make to this absolute view of child-rearing; it left me feeling vaguely disreputable and of dubious moral caliber. I rose from my seat murmuring that we would detain her no longer from her chores, wondering if she regarded our own glaring lack of pressing duties as a form of feeble self-indulgence.

She walked us past her orderly herbaceous borders to the gate; her flowers, I had no doubt, bloomed in this manner because that was what was expected of them. Could it be, I wondered, that the existential unease that plagues me prevents my backyard garden in New York from flourishing like Shuna Balfour-Kinnear's?

"You're the first non-clergy to live in the Manse?" Harl asked.

She nodded. "And we're not churchgoers either, in spite of the proximity. I've only set foot in the kirk once since we've been here: for the baptism of Mrs. MacFadyen's great-grandchild. The whole glen was there that day. Husband grumbles every Sunday morning when the service is on, because the lane gets parked up outside our gate. Apart from that, there's no disadvantage living so close to a church and graveyard."

I refrained from asking her about ghosts, as she doubtless expected immaterial manifestations to keep out of her way. I did ask, though, if she knew why the grave of Miss Jane Honeyman was outside the church wall.

"Oh, there's some local legend about it. I forget the details. Ask Jessie MacFadyen; she knows all the old stories. I must go and cook the dogs' meat now, and I still have to hose down the stable floors," she said, more to herself than us, and bade us a brusque goodbye.

The dappled sunshine of the tree-bordered lane was a delight after the chill of the Manse. "All the same," I remarked to Harl, "she'd have made an admirable wife for a Calvinist minister."

"Did you notice a face looking out of the window when we were at the front door?" he asked.

"Oh, you saw it too. I thought I had seen a ghost. . . ."

Shuna Balfour-Kinnear had said she would like to see how we had fixed up the old reservoir keeper's cottage. A week later I called to invite her to morning coffee.

At eleven o'clock sharp on the appointed day, there was a yapping and barking commotion outside, and the lady of the Manse rapping on the door and hallooing like John Peel.

"What about the dogs?" I asked, when I came down to greet her and six toylike pups all energetically investigating the garden.

"Oh, don't worry about *them*." She blew a peremptory toot on her whistle and the dogs left off their sniffing exploration and came to heel at once. "Sit!" she commanded, and they all sat down on their small haunches, eyes fixed on her, expectant for her next command. "*Where* is Bessie?" she asked sternly. "Bessie!" A blast on the whistle brought the delinquent Bessie tearing through the gate of the kitchen garden to join the others. "Bad girl, Bessie! Sit. And no nonsense."

The dogs knew, and I knew, that there would be no nonsense. We went in. I showed her round the house, and she looked curiously at everything, but, disconcertingly, offered no comment. We had coffee upstairs in the living room. "Quite a nice view of the loch," she allowed, looking out at the water, which was an almost Mediterranean blue that day, whipped up by a brisk breeze into wavelets that scattered disks of sunlight over walls and ceiling and milk jug and teaspoons. The family had gone out over the hill to buy milk at the caravan site. I hoped they would return in time to see the small platoon of Jack Russell terriers awaiting orders on our terrace; it would be hard to convince them that they remained like that for the hour and ten minutes of her visit.

She was wearing a skirt of tobacco tweed, a beige twin set, stout brogues. "What do you *do* with yourselves all day long?" she demanded.

"Well, we hike in the hills . . . and explore the countryside," I answered feebly, knowing how slothful and unproductive our existence must seem to her. "And we're getting to know all the villages around here . . . churches . . . Roman camps. . . ." I petered out.

"And at night? I see you haven't got a wireless or television."

"We read." I sounded apologetic. We were all getting through three, four, five books a week. And that summer, and every succeeding one, we would read a Dickens novel that would pass from hand to hand, the children threatening to expose plot and dénouement to each other when they teased or quarreled. We could not get our hands on enough long, engaging books, and were at the village library at least twice a week, blessing the Victorian novelists for the heft of their works; we stopped wherever there was a bookshop, and were always borrowing books from the Hunters. There was quite literally nothing to do at night if one did not read. Under Mrs. Balfour-Kinnear's hawklike eye, this now seemed to be an effete and listless way for a vigorous family to fritter a summer away. I longed to be able to tell her that we spent our evenings oiling our guns, or currying our horses.

"Well," she said, "I envy you. I hardly have time to look at a newspaper. Apart from the dogs and the beasts and the horses, there's the garden, and I have to do most of the housework because the girl that comes in to help is unreliable and incompetent. And I also have a mentally disturbed mother to take care of." She helped herself to a chocolate biscuit and munched it matter-of-factly. "Chronic melancholia."

I recalled the pale, gowned figure that had dissolved away from the window. So, there was a Mrs. Rochester at the Manse. "It must be difficult for you," I said. I took care not to say *very* difficult.

"It is never-ending." She spoke in the same clipped curt tone as when she spoke of boiling the dogs' meat or waiting for the vet; affectless, and without a trace of self-pity. "It was another reason why I decided to come back from Saudi. There was no one to take care of Mother; her companion had died, and my brothers wanted to put her in a home, but I didn't think it was the right thing to do."

"Does she need a lot of care?"

"She wanders," she said. "She is under the illusion that she has lost something that she must get back. She gets out, and doesn't know where she is or what she's looking for—so she wanders. Then everyone in the glen has to go searching for her. Last winter she got out in a snowstorm. She was missing for ten hours. Luckily she couldn't get too far because of the deep snow. Donny MacIver found her sheltering in one of those ruined cottages up at Braeburn, to everyone's relief. I can never leave her alone for long; keep her locked in her room when I go out. If I have to get away to a dog-show—it's essential, you see, for a breeder to show at competitions—I have to employ someone to stay with Mother. Costs the earth, but I breed show dogs. I take a lot of prizes." She spoke then, at some length, about the dogs, manifesting for the first time some warmth and feeling.

She glanced at a man's watch strapped to her bony wrist. "Ten past twelve. Get carried away rather when I start talking about the dogs. Must be getting back now. Don't like to keep Mother locked up for too long, and I have to change the dressing on one of the Arab mares; she has an ulcer on her hoof. The horses are Husband's little hobby, but he's never there when something needs done." As we went down the stairs, she remarked, "Husband said we ought to invite you for dinner. But I told him I was sure the reason you'd bought this cottage was specially to get away from dinner parties and all that sort of thing you must have so much of in New York." She emitted her high-bred whinny; I made some non-committal murmuring sound that fortunately was lost in the din of the dogs' enthusiasm as their mistress emerged onto the terrace.

I let them out through the picket gate at the bottom of the garden. She organized the dogs into a marching squad and strode off along the bank of the loch. While I was washing up the coffee things, there floated down from the forestry road the high-pitched yapping of the puppies, silenced suddenly by the shrill note of the silver whistle: a dottily heroic sound from an intrepid lady engaged in imposing order on the small chaos of her own existence—as if, by blowing with the right note of authority on her whistle, she could bring all of life to heel.

A day came at last when we were commanded to present ourselves at Glencorrie House. At about eight-thirty on a Monday morning the phone disturbed us at breakfast.

"Mrs. Gordon? This is Jessie MacFadyen."

"Oh, good morning, Mrs. MacFadyen. How are you?"

"Fit as a flea, m'dear, fit as a flea. Now, I want you and the doctor to come and visit me on Wednesday night."

"Thank you. We'd love to." I felt I should bob and curtsey as I spoke.

"Right. Be here at half-past eight, then. We'll drink a bottle of wine and have a little chat. Goodbye for now. . . ."

We walked there over the hills in the quiet of the early evening, the light from the westering sun slanting across the sheep-dotted slopes. The sheep never seemed to leave off cropping as long as they were awake; even when they were not visible on a black, moonless night, we would hear the tearing sound of their teeth pulling up tufts of grass.

There was a smell of wood smoke as we climbed the hill behind Jenny's cottage. Their gray cat was curled up, asleep, on the doorstep, and the window of their living room glowed with the eerie cold light of the television set. The sweet-smelling smoke rose up in a thread on the windless air, to merge with the blue bowl of the heavens set over the glen.

In about half an hour we emerged from some woods above the church, onto the last quarter-mile of the winding driveway of Glencorrie House. The golden limestone of the small mansion seemed a solidification of the evening light.

We presented ourselves in hiking boots and jeans, hoping, as we tugged the brass bell-pull, that we had not been expected

in cocktail outfits. The indefatigable Mrs. Darroch, in the role
of butler, let us in and ushered us through to the drawing
room, where a bright fire burned in the grate. "Doctor and
Mrs. Gordon is here," she announced.

Mrs. MacFadyen strode forward to shake our hands. "I
didn't hear the sound of your car on the drive. . . . Oh, walked
over the hill, did you? Well done! I'd do it myself if I were
still your age. Come and sit by the fire now. Don't really need
the warmth tonight, but I always say a fire's company. My
dear Mrs. Darroch lights it for me whether I ask for it or not.
'You don't want to be chopping sticks when there's so much
to be done,' I said to her this evening. But no, she's set in her
ways and likes things *just so*. I don't know where she finds
the time. She mowed the whole front lawn this afternoon
between tea and dinner, though of course we *have* got an
electric mowing machine. They're quite dangerous, though.
She had an accident with the lawn mower last summer; took
off two of her toes. And now that it's the tourist season, things
tend to get rather hectic at the Lockup—that's my son Gavin's
bar and disco, you know—and they phone for help, and I have
to run Mrs. Darroch over to the Castle so that she can wash up
the glasses. Have you been there yet? You should go; they've
done up the dungeons quite nicely. It got a writeup in the
Courier last spring. Gavin's having an excellent season this
year: the caravan site is full, and the Lockup is crowded every
night. Now, Doctor, if you wouldn't mind drawing the cork
from this bottle, we can all take a glass of wine."

On a small table in front of the fire, glasses and a few bottles
of Chablis were set out. As our glasses were being filled, Mrs.
Darroch appeared with a silver dish of tiny sandwiches garnished with mustard cress, set them in front of us, and hoisted
a small tree-trunk into the fire. "Oh, well done, Mrs. Darroch.
She's an absolute jewel of a woman," she confided when Mrs.
Darroch had quit the room after replacing a full ashtray with
a clean one.

The wine was light, crisp, and perfectly chilled, and by the
evening's end both bottles had been polished off. "Either of
you smoke? . . . No? . . . Well, I jolly well do." She fitted a
cigarette into a long jet holder, and lit up languorously from

the flame Harl struck for her from a box of kitchen matches on the hearth. Her style seemed to me very much of the thirties; I could see her consorting with Lady Metroland and Mrs. Beaver. We had dined about an hour ago off lambchops with crisp local cabbage and floury, nutty Ayrshire potatoes, followed by rhubarb with thick cream; we now found ourselves munching cucumber sandwiches, potted salmon sandwiches, and smoked trout sandwiches that we dared not decline.

Mrs. MacFadyen's skirt was short, and her legs were good; she crossed them and leaned back in her baronial chair, puffing and nibbling and sipping, waving the long cigarette holder about, stabbing the air for emphasis. "I came to this house as a bride over fifty years ago. We were married in Glencorrie Kirk, and as we walked out, over the wee wooden bridge, back to the house for the wedding breakfast, there were bairns from all around the district strewing rosebuds along the path before us. My husband's family had owned a very large and famous biscuit factory—we exported all over the British Empire. You would find MacFadyen's shortbread and oatcakes on the shelves of any high-class grocer at home and abroad: Durban, Sidney, Calcutta, Rhodesia, Kenya, Malaya. My husband's father bought this house and Glencorrie Castle; it was all part of the huge estate owned by the Honeyman family. Unfortunately, my husband had . . . you know"—she raised her elbow and flicked the wrist—"a weakness for the bottle, and he let everything go to pot; we had to give up the factory, his health gave in, and he died and left me to carry on."

A log shifted in the grate and sparks flew up the chimney; the lawns beyond the windows were still bathed in light, though a clock on the mantelpiece chimed ten times. Jessie MacFadyen ground out a cigarette end, fitted another into the holder, and refilled the wine glasses. "When I came to live here after I was wed, there were . . . I cannot remember how many servants: maids, cook, housekeeper, chauffeur, gardeners. That garden was a bonny sight to see; people would come from all over the county when the rhododendrons along the driveway were in flower. Mrs. Darroch takes care of the garden now—she does her best—but the rhodies don't have the show they used to have. And we had shepherds and a farm manager and agricultural laborers; it was like a feudal village we were responsible for. And now, it's just Mrs. Darroch and me to run the whole show. Let me show you the house."

She conducted us round with pride and obvious pleasure in the grace of its architecture. Ten rooms radiated off the large center hall, which was lit by three domed skylights—clerestory lights, she told us, a prized architectural feature. The handsome marble fireplaces were of Adam design; the original rich ornamental plaster cornices and rosettes in the reception rooms were still intact; the shelves of the library were filled with old leather-bound volumes. "These books were here when my husband's father bought the place lock, stock, and barrel from the Honeymans. One of the Honeymans' sons is wanting to buy the library back now, but I will not part with a single volume. 'Feel at liberty to consult the books whenever you wish,' I informed him. 'All I ask you to do is to telephone beforehand and make sure it will not inconvenience my housekeeper.' "

I would have liked to examine the collection, but we were whisked off to the dining room. On the massive Victorian sideboard was an array of polished silver serving pieces and tea and coffee services. "Mrs. Darroch likes to keep a good shine on the silverware. Alas, this is all that's left of it; we've had to dispose of quite a lot of it to tide us over hard times." The oval Hepplewhite dining table was elaborately laid with one place for dinner: embossed antique silver flatware set for many courses—soup, fish, meat, dessert, savoury. "Mrs. Darroch prefers to reset the table after I have had my dinner each evening; I take my breakfast and luncheon in the small sun parlor near the kitchen, so that she doesn't have to lug heavy trays such a long way *three* times day. In summer, of course, afternoon tea is served in the garden under the oak tree on the lawn."

The furnishings appeared to be an accumulation of the styles and fortunes of two hundred years of continuous occupation: ponderous Edwardian and Victorian stuff mixed with the elegant simplicity of Hepplewhite and Sheraton. Upholstery and draperies were of rich fabrics now worn and faded; the carpets were tatty; the bedrooms, surprisingly furnished in a Hollywood style of art deco that once more brought Lady

Metroland to mind, must once have had a certain splendor, now overtaken by shabbiness. In all the rooms she had us admire the wallpaper—flocked, sprigged, Regency-striped— which had been hung with professional precision by the versatile Mrs. Darroch.

She swept us along back to the fireside.

"I'm afraid you'll not see our ghost," she said. "She only likes to appear late at night when all is still. She visits me sometimes as I sit at my desk in the library."

"Who is she?"

"She's known as Gray Jane. She's the ghost of poor wee Miss Jane Honeyman, who was the granddaughter of the man who built this house."

"And she haunts the place?"

"She appears to me once in a while," Mrs. MacFadyen answered with complacency. "I feel an overpowering sense of her presence, and I know she is reading over my shoulder. As I look up, she fades away—a misty form dissolves and disappears. The other evening I was studying her accounting book. She was a very careful housekeeper and kept a detailed record of every penny she spent: thirteen shillings for a ton of coal, sixpence for having it put in the cellar, and so on. As I turned the pages, I was strangely aware that she was beside me. She is a benign presence and means no harm—and she is certainly welcome here. After all, this is her home where she was born and lived almost a hundred years."

"We were looking at her grave the other day, and we wondered why she'd been buried outside the church wall," Harl said.

"Ah . . . thereby hangs a tale. You see, she was determined to be buried in Ayrshire, where the Honeyman family originally came from, and where they have all been buried in a wee village kirkyard since the seventeenth century. Well, she had the misfortune to depart this world in January of a terrible winter of snowstorm and blizzard. It was impossible to convey her to Ayrshire; the roads were all under snow and the horses could never have got through—this was 1894, remember. So they waited a while, and waited, but there was no sign the weather would break. When everyone began to ask, Well, in the circumstances, why not bury her in Glencorrie Kirkyard, which is, after all, a bonny place to lie? it was revealed that she had written in her will that if her last wish was set aside and she was buried here at Glencorrie Kirk, she would return and haunt the glen for all the days to come. At last, when the family and the minister could no longer decently delay the burial, it was decided that the only way they could carry out the letter of the will would be to bury her outside the kirkyard. So a small exit was cut into the kirk wall to allow access to her plot, and there she lies, not in the kirkyard, but alas, not in Ayrshire either. This ruse did not pacify her, and she is still seen wandering through the kirkyard and in the fields by the riverbank, and on occasions she pays a visit here, to her old home."

Hiking home through the gloaming after having drunk many glasses of wine was a strange experience. Like the late departed Miss Jane Honeyman, we seemed to float just slightly above the grassy hillside as we made our way back. I half hoped, half feared that we would encounter her misty form along the riverbank, but she manifested no interest in the new people up at the loch. It was past eleven, and light enough still to make out the track that took us through the woods where it joined up with the forestry road. Jenny's cottage was in darkness, and so was the Camerons' farmhouse down in the valley. Country folk go early to bed, and it was only New Yorkers, keeping late hours, who would be abroad in the glen near midnight. Headlights of a car rounding the curve of the hill road raked a white swathe across the night, and the sound of a motor roared into the Camerons' barnyard; one of the wild grandsons was returning from a night's carousing. The sheep dogs set up a ferocious barking as the slam of the car door echoed through the glen; a rough voice swore evilly at them, and they fell silent.

We reached the heather embankment that sloped down to the loch. Below us, the black surface of the water gleamed, sending out orange streamers from the glow of light from the windows of our house. It had a mythic quality, warm light shining from a solitary dwelling in a dark landscape, a meta-

phor from a folk tale: shelter, warmth, domestic order, revealing itself in a solitary light reflected in dark water in the isolation of the hills. We scrambled down the slope, went along
the bank of the dreaming loch, and let ourselves into the garden, through our small white picket gate under the rowan tree
arch that kept witches away.

"Did you enjoy your visit at Glencorrie House?" Jenny
asked the next day, when we stopped at her cottage to return
a scythe.

We told her about it.

"Och, she's a character, she is," Jenny said. "You have to
hand it to her, though, the way she battles on, trying to keep
up appearances to what they were in the grand old days, when
even royalty used to eat MacFadyen's biscuits; she'll always
tell how it said 'by appointment to His Majesty King George'
on every packet of oatcakes. Robbie had to go up and see her
last week about a fence she claims the Forestry Commission
had promised to mend. It was after tea, though she doesn't
have *tea*—she has *dinner*. Mrs. Darroch took him through to
the drawing room, and there was Mrs. MacFadyen, lying on
the sofa dressed in a long pink evening gown, wearing earrings
and a necklace, he said, and smoking away with that long black
cigarette-holder of hers. She was drinking coffee from a cup
about as big as a thimble, while Mrs. Darroch was clearing
away the dinner dishes in the dining room. When he finished
talking to her about fixing the fence—she didn't even ask him
to sit down; kept him standing the whole time—he took a cup
of tea in the kitchen with Mrs. Darroch. And Mrs. Darroch
is right proud of her mistress; she told Robbie how she usually
dresses for dinner in a long gown and her good jewelry, even
though she might just be having a bit of herring and a potato
and some rice pudding for her meal, and she uses all the good
family silver and china and crystal, though she is eating all on
her own. You have to admire her for trying to keep up the
old standards, even though everything is changed for the
worse for her."

We agreed that indeed one had to admire her.

CHAPTER
7

Still Waters

Living in the hills, the sound of the bleating of lambs became as familiar to our ears as the wail of sirens and the blare of transistor radios on the streets of New York. While we worked in the garden or tramped through the hills or sat reading on the sunny terrace in front of the house, there was the accompaniment of the piteous cry of a lamb looking up from its grass-cropping and for a moment unable to locate its mother; there followed the hoarse, fostering response of a ewe, several octaves lower, the lamb then skipping over to suckle anxiously on the pendulous udder. In early summer the lambs were about three months old, with curly white coats—touching and extremely engaging to watch as they gamboled and pranced stiff-legged on the green. Words like *meek* and *mild* occurred in the mind of the beholder; and one began to understand why, in the language of poetry—the Bible, the psalms—the lamb is a metaphor for innocence, helplessness, and purity, and the shepherd is the benign protector:

> "The Lord is my shepherd.
> I shall not want.
> He maketh me to lie down in green pastures.
> He leadeth me beside still waters."

The words of Psalm 23, learned in grade school, floated to the surface of the mind. And "Little Lamb, who made thee?" we would go about asking, until at last our daughter, who commits her favorite poems to memory, wrote out Blake's *The Lamb* on the back of an invoice from Angus McWhirter, "Fishmonger and Poulterer," and taped it on the door of the little china cupboard in the kitchen. There it remained year after year, so that when one went to take out a plate or a cup, one paused and read the lines:

> "Little Lamb, who made thee?
> Dost thou know who made thee;
> Gave thee life and bid thee feed
> By the stream and o'er the mead;
> Gave thee clothing of delight,
> Softest clothing, woolly, bright;
> Gave thee such a tender voice
> Making all the vales rejoice?
> Little Lamb, who made thee?
> Dost thou know who made thee?"

It would take a few days at the beginning of each summer for the spirit to readjust to this Old Testament setting, and gradually we would begin to experience a quality of peacefulness that, until then, we had known only briefly, or in passing; as if day by day the heart slowed down to a more even pace, the blood moving more leisurely in and out of its chambers. Even the children lost their restlessness and were subdued by the more tranquil rhythm—the long slow hours of hill-walking, reading, the deeply restful sleep—that Glenauchen imposed on us.

To the farmers, the flocks were a means of livelihood, a source of constant labor and anxiety: dipping and clipping, maintenance of fences, vet's bills, market prices to be watched. To us, they were a metaphor for some ancient, tranquil, pastoral time: a time that existed, perhaps, only in myth, legend, poetry; an idea of something lost that the heart eternally longs to regain—the sense of which we were privileged, each summer, to experience. And we accepted our exile from it at the end of every summer, recognizing that to be immersed in it year-round would be an experience far removed from the shepherd's pipes playing the unforgotten melodies out of that lost time in the life of the world.

"How long is a sheep dog's working life?" Harl asked Dougal over a pint of beer when we found him at the bar of the hotel pub one evening.

"I had a dog—twenty years old—had to put a bullet through its head. I'd like to do the same to that old collie that does nothing but snooze at the back door of the farm, but my granny's too soft. 'Let it live out its last days in peace,' she says, but I say it's nowt but a waste to feed an animal that doesna' work for its living." Swarthy, unshaven, handsome in a dissolute way, he drank down a chaser of beer after a shot of whiskey. "You never can tell what you're getting with a sheep dog. I had another one—gave three hundred pounds for it—just refused to work; had to put a bullet through its head. This new one my granny's just bought—it eats chickens. Hope we don't have to destroy the bugger. They're canny beasts, though. Old Mr. Campbell that used to be head shepherd on Lord Dougdale's estate—he'll tell you about a dog he bought once that herded the gardener and his whole family into a corner of their cottage; kept them there for I don't know how long, until someone brought his trainer in to call him off. Sometimes they're worked so hard that their hearts just give in."

"How many sheep do you have on the farm?"

"Between two thousand and three thousand head, we usually have. But it all depends on a number of factors. The weather: if there's a bitter cold spring with snow falling after the lambing, we lose a lot. And it all depends on the market: sometimes we get good trade for our lambs, some years we just cover what they cost us. . . . It's my turn now; what will you be drinkin'—same again?"

Patterns were laid down that first summer that gave shape to all the summers we spent in those hills. Once a week we would drive to the Hunters' farm, and over one of Helen's excellent dinners we would recount our doings, our forays into the countryside, the charms and eccentricities of the neighbors and village people we were getting to know. On the weekend they would come out to Glenauchen to dine with us. They took great pleasure in this enterprise they had initiated, and approved of the way they found us more cozily installed each time they visited. Bob relished any stories we told of the glen Mafia. Any of their children who were home from school (or the mandatory middle-class adolescent rites of passage, such as going overland to India, or working as an attendant in an insane asylum, or being self-supporting by having a "dung route" in a rural area of Devon) would come along too.

We would take a walk in the hills after dinner, the fresh mountainous air a good antidote, according to Bob, to the inclination to fall into a pre–middle age, postprandial torpor before the fire. The children—who took to each other as their parents had done twenty years before—would remain behind to do the washing up. Too replete, usually, to contend with any slopes, we would keep to the forestry road.

From the house windows, the red earth that had been turned up could be seen as it wound through the green for a distance of some five miles. Deep vertical furrows had been ploughed up and down hillsides, the tiny conifers being planted in rows on the ridged humps thrown up by the plough blade. That first summer the young saplings, pine and larch and fir, were about shoulder-high; each summer when we returned to the glen, like our adolescent children they had sprung up and were inches taller, their limbs thickening, branches spreading, the pale young green of their needles darkening and obscuring the overturned earth of the hill. Wild flowers and grass started to recarpet the ground, and with each summer, the purple-pink willow herb, heather, bluebells, lady's bedstraw, and ragged robin grew like healthy tissue over the cut, so that, at last, only someone familiar with the view could discern that the mauve shadow girdling the hill concealed a road.

Until one year, the four of us stood at the far end of the forestry road, from which our loch looked like a small mirror dropped in the valley, the clump of trees surrounding our house a smudge of darker green brushed with the tip of a paintbrush on the bright green of the pasture, and Bob observed, "See what's happened—the trees are taller than any of us. It's grown into a pine forest." And indeed, in the way our children grow day by day without our noticing, a dark green forest now covered the slopes, and reflected deep green in the waters of the loch.

Bob, trained as a botanist, was an excellent companion on a hill walk, able to identify for us, by family, genus, and species, the flora of the hillside. "This tiny flower? It's *Viola*, family Violacae, *viola tricolor*, but it's known as wild pansy. See, it's yellow and purple like a miniature pansy. This is thyme growing along the banks of the loch; here—crush the leaves and you can smell it; *you have a bank where the wild thyme blows*. Rosebay willow herb—it spreads like a weed, though a handsome rosy mauve weed it is. It's also known as fireweed. Those are foxgloves—digitalis—very useful if we should have a heart attack from all this climbing after too much food and wine."

We would gather bluebells to keep in a small stoneware jug on the kitchen mantelshelf. "These bluebells are really harebells," said Bob. *Campanula rotundifolia*. It's the true bluebell of Scotland; what they call bluebells down in England are really wild hyacinths that only flower in April and May. Ours bloom from July to September."

While we picked the delicate blue flowers that grew thickly on the slopes, we talked of how odd it is that Western man has such a deep-seated need to classify, categorize, sort, codify, and systematize, from the broadest category through the most minute variation. We name things to give them reality. Without our consciousness of the world—without the Word—the world would not exist. "Our Linnaean heritage," Bob said. "We impose systems upon the chaos and disorder all about us, and this way we can delude ourselves that we are in control." He pointed out some low bushy plants with dark blue berries in among the heather. "Blaeberries—the wild version of your American blueberries. They're still soor—" he grimaced and spit one out—"but you can eat them with oatmeal and cream in a few weeks' time, or make them into jam."

At the far end of the forestry road the pine belt ended abruptly at a dry-stone wall, and the sheep of a neighboring farmer grazed the smooth slopes. As we walked back, the loch held the radiance of the twilight in its depths, while the solidity of the hills was starting to dissolve in shadow all around us. Bob spoke of the primeval woodlands of Britain, telling us how much clearing had taken place for soil cultivation by the end of the Middle Ages, and how in Tudor times the oak forests had been cut down for sailing ships and for timbered houses, so that a land that had been covered by forests began to find itself short of timber. The fuel shortage became so serious that coal, which the Romans had used during their almost four centuries of occupation, started to be mined again to warm the hearth.

He told us about the subterranean upheaval thirty million years ago that folded the earth's crust into ridges that formed the Himalayas and the Alps; the spreading shock of these disturbances caused volcanic eruptions through the hard rock of southern Scotland, throwing up the hilly rock formations that the glaciers of the ensuing Ice Age then smoothed and eroded into their present contours around us. Edinburgh Castle sits upon a glacial ramp above the core of a Miocene volcano, and the lochs of Scotland are glacial lakes formed by the action of ice plates carving away at the bases of mountains. The thaw began some twenty thousand years ago, and at first the primitive evergreen forests covered the land. Then came the oaks, the elms, and the beech—the trees that Constable loved to paint—replacing the pine as the climate grew warmer.

In the hush that had fallen over the basin formed by the ring of darkening hills, was immanent the ongoing, timeless flow that had formed this ancient landscape. Below us, a single yellow light was reflected on the water: our house, a small, man-made shelter, constructed of the granitic rock hewn out of the stony slopes of these majestic old hills.

When the children had finished washing up while we were out walking, those who had achieved the legal drinking age would take off for the Lockup Pub in the dungeons of Glencorrie Castle, to drink beer and observe the goings-on between the locals and the vacationers from the caravan site. If ever there was brawling or fisticuffs to report on their return, at least one of the wild grandsons was sure to be involved.

We tried to discourage any of the younger generation from

coming into the living room as we sat before the fire murmuring and sipping and watching midnight gather over the loch. "No one under the age of forty allowed in the living room after dinner," Bob said. "This room is resairved for the grownups. The young are taking over the world; we must unite to maintain a last bastion against them, here at Glenauchen at least." Sometimes the young people would infiltrate, or we would relent, but generally they were content to gather round the downstairs kitchen fireplace, and bursts of hilarity and argument would float up through the floorboards.

Upstairs, the grown-ups murmur, the fire glows, the Glenmorangie suffuses benignness. Helen is always as amused and engaged by Bob's conversation as we are. His bedside table, she tells us, is piled with books on the treatment of diseases of dairy cows, jumbled together with his well-thumbed and underlined volumes of Proust. Once, at the Perth cattle market, while waiting for some of his beasts to be auctioned, thinking of how Proust had written about the death of his beloved grandmother, Bob found himself overcome with grief; so that no one in the crowd of farmers, cattle dealers, gillies, and shepherds should see the tears that filled his eyes, he had had to take himself off to a nearby pub to restore his composure with a couple of whiskies.

"Tell them what happened this morning, Bob."

"Airly this morning," Bob murmurs from the depths of the armchair, "she rouses me up to tell me that a rabbit who has been chewing up the vegetable garden is sitting in the middle of the lawn. So I rise from my bed and fetch the gun, and take aim from the bedroom window, in my pajamas and still half-asleep. A pairfect shot. The rabbit keels over. I turn around, and there's Helen with the tears running down her cheeks. 'What are you greetin' for?' I ask. 'That poor little bunny rabbit,' she says."

We all laugh, including Helen. "It looked such a pathetic thing, lying there, dead on the lawn, that I felt bad that I'd asked Bob to kill it."

She encourages Bob to tell all his stories. "I read in the paper, Helen, that a woman shot her husband because his memory was going and he kept telling the same stories over and over."

"Och, that's all right," she answers with equanimity. "My memory's going as well, so I don't remember that I've haird them all before."

Around midnight, Helen would remind us that there was a real world beyond our hills—"You have to be out of your bed early to feed the beasts, Bob Hunter"—and we would rise reluctantly from the fireside and walk them to their car. In high summer, the pink and dark red honeysuckle bloomed in profusion over the front wall of the house, perfuming the night air with its sweet heavy scent. We would stand at the white-painted gate and watch till their car lights disappeared in the valley below, on moonless nights the darkness so black it was almost palpable; then, succumbing to the effect of the "guid hill air," we would turn in and sleep as though drugged.

With each succeeding summer we would come to know the stones and paths, the sheep-trails, the rocky outcrops, pools, and lochs, the music made by the water of Glenauchen Burn as it cascaded down the hills, every turn and bend of the river as we walked along its banks. Halfway up Ben Shawe, near a rock shaped like a throne for an ancient king, we found the source of our spring, and we would climb up there just for the pleasure of listening to its sound at the very spot where it gurgled up out of the recesses of the earth and gushed into clay pipes that had carried it down, its flow uninterrupted for over a hundred years, to our kitchen sink and our bath-room.

The more familiar we became with the area, the more curious we became about its history and the nature of the life that had gone on here for centuries. In the tiny branch library in our village, and in the first-rate county library at Perth, I browsed through old volumes, turning the pages back to the past to try and grasp a sense of how it had been. A helpful librarian at Perth led me to *The Statistical Account of Scotland—drawn up from the Communications of the Ministers of the Different Parishes*. This account had been accumulated by "circulating among the Clergy of Scotland a variety of Queries for the Purpose of elucidating the Natural History and Political State of the Country" starting in 1791. It made fascinating reading

on days that were too hot for hill walking or when it sometimes rained. The accounts varied according to the temperament and literary skill of the contributing parsons, some giving
only bald facts, others indulging in flowery language, many of
them writing in lucid prose that was a pleasure to read; most of
them, it seemed as I read, painting perhaps a rosier picture of
contentment than the statistical facts of the poverty of the
larger part of their flock seemed able to substantiate. Their
descriptions tallied, in large part, with the idealized pastoral
perfection we all like to believe existed once in a time before
our own.

On their rambles, our children had come upon an abandoned
village that we had read about in the *Statistical Accounts of
1884* as a thriving wool-milling community. On a day when
they were all three away at the farm helping Bob with the
haying, Harl and I set out to take a look at this place they had
found.

We struck off the forestry road just behind Jenny's cottage,
keeping to a high sheep-trail toward the whitewashed church
we could glimpse in a clearing among some woods about three
or four miles distant. In the valley below us, the clear-winding
river ran sparkling over its rocky bed, sheep grazed, an infre-
quent car, toy-sized, passed along the glen road. The occasional
farmhouse or cottage that dotted the landscape was in a proportion just sufficient to domesticate the scene without diminishing its natural, unspoiled quality. The sheep-trail led over a
stone bridge; down below, the burn boiled noisily and dark
pools swirled.

Across the bridge we came upon the remains of the abandoned hamlet, stone cottages with only the side walls and
pointed gables still standing, their floors overgrown with grass
and weeds. These were "but and ben" cottages—in Scottish
dialect *but* means "back" and *ben* means "front"—the dwellings
consisting of two adjoining rooms, the standard crofter's
cottage all over Scotland. Before the thick-coated breed of
sheep was developed to withstand the rigor of winter out on
the hills, the sheep would have crowded with the family into
the but and ben.

We peered into the gaping spaces where doors and windows

had been, and saw smoke-blackened stone skeletons of great hearths that had warmed vanished households. Massive chestnut trees, their burred light green pods suspended like small lanterns among the dark glossy leaves, flourished in and about the ruins, dipping their branches into deserted homesteads.

Beside the bridge one house stood intact and appeared to be occupied; as if the whole forsaken village was their backyard, chickens scratched and clucked outside the gate; children's toys were strewn about: an overturned tricycle, some plastic cars and engines, a red and green rubber ball. Picked out in stone on the wall of the house, we read "Braeburn."

In the *Statistical Account* I had read: "There has been for some time past, at [Braeburn] in this parrish, a mill, on a small scale, for spinning wool." This must have been the mill, we concluded.

A small dog hurled itself through the gate snarling and yapping, followed by a young woman with a child at her knee and another on her hip. We struck up a conversation; she turned out to be a friend of the Kirkbrides and knew who we were—Mr. McWhirter, the fishmonger, had pointed us out in his shop. Her husband was a shepherd working for the curmudgeon Geordie McCaskie; the derelict hamlet, she told us, lay on McCaskie's property. She had been a hairdresser in Glasgow before her marriage. Did she not find it lonely living in the only occupied house here? Oh, she was far too busy to feel lonely. She pointed to the flowers and vegetables abundant within the walled garden of the old mill, told us that the bairns kept her on the go, and besides, she had a back room set up as a hairdressing salon, and several of the glen women came each week for a wash and set. The children, both boys, stared, round-eyed and silent, while we spoke with their mother.

She was incurious about the history of the ruins among which she lived, and could tell us little. Later, we asked around and learned that the hamlet had centered on the woolen mill, and that there had been a blacksmith's forge. Some of the older glen folk recalled a sweetie shop there, owned by an old widow, that had served as the postoffice; Mrs. MacFadyen told us that for a penny the schoolchildren could buy a pokeful of boiled sweeties—"bullseyes" and "soor-plooms"—enough to keep sucking on for hours. Bullseyes we remembered from our own childhood as pillow-shaped lumps of peppermint candy striped black and white; curious, however, about what soor-plooms might be, we asked once at the sweetie shop on the High Street for a half-pound of "sour plums," our request eliciting blank incomprehension, until Harl suggested I try asking for *soor-plooms*. "Oh, soor-plooms—sairtainly we have *those*," and the old lady measured out, from a labeled glass jar, a scoopful of varicolored hard sweet-sour candies.

We had been told that the sheep trail we had taken to Brae-burn had once been the main road through the glen, a thorough-fare that had evolved from the old drove road that had been used since earliest times to drive sheep and cattle to be sold at cattle fairs that were held in the district. But in the 1830s a new turnpike road had been built skirting the foothills—our present glen road—and life had moved away down the valley, the hamlet of Braeburn was abandoned, and nature moved back in and relentlessly took over. Wild flowers bloomed on the cottage floors with weeds and thistles, creeping plants climbed out of windows, ewes brought in their lambs to crop beside remains of hearths, and the air was filled with the unceasing babble of the millstream, which made its way through the romantic desolation as busily as it had when its energy had been harnessed to the mill-wheel of the industrious little community that had once labored on its banks.

All over the Highlands one comes across these abandoned but and ben cottages: a sad legacy of the infamous "Clearances" of the first half of the nineteenth century that sent masses of impoverished Scots abroad from the native land that could no longer maintain them. The events that led to the Clearances can be traced back to the early history of the Scottish people, who, until the middle of the eighteenth century, had lived under a feudal monarchy that had developed out of the earlier tribal systems of the four groups that make up Scotland: Celts, Picts, Scots, and Britons. The spread of Christianity in the sixth century gradually brought cohesion to the different groups; between the eighth and eleventh centuries, the tribes were further united by the necessity for defense against repeated Scandinavian attacks by Danes and Norsemen with such formidable-sounding names as Ketil Flatnose, Maelbrigte Tooth, Harold Fair Hair, and Magnus Bareleg.

By the middle of the eleventh century the kingdom of Scotland was ruled by Malcolm III—the same Malcolm who slew Macbeth, and whose history Shakespeare drew upon. From the thirteenth century onward, the unification of the Scottish people was strengthened by their wars of independence against England's attempts, in the next four centuries, to absorb her northern neighbor. It was in 1314, at the famous battle of Bannockburn, which took place on the outskirts of nearby Stirling, that a small force of Scots, under their self-proclaimed king, Robert the Bruce, defeated the cavalry of the English king, Edward II, whose forces far outnumbered them. Defying the orders of the Pope to submit to the English king or be excommunicated, Bruce's nobles replied with a declaration that echoes down through Scottish history: "For as long as one hundred of us shall remain alive we shall never in any wise consent to submit to the rule of the English, for it is not for glory we fight, for riches, or for honours, but for freedom alone, which no good man loses but with his life."

By the fourteenth century, the clan system prevailed in the Highlands—a grouping half tribal, half feudal, in which kinsmen and retainers adhered to a definite chief whose power over them was arbitrary and absolute. They caused great disorder in the land, defying all authority including that of the crown, feuding with each other, fighting, plundering, killing, raiding for cattle or for women, with a strong belief in magic carried over from pagan times. The lands of the chieftains were worked, in tiny small-holdings, by tenants who owed them absolute allegiance and could be called upon to fight whenever their chieftain needed them. Their small-holdings were called "crofts," and the crofters all kept some sheep—small creatures with meager coats; inbred for centuries, these sheep were thought to be unable to survive the winters outdoors, and the practice of housing them indoors with the family throughout the cold season was not conducive to the growth of thick coats. But in the middle of the eighteenth century, it was discovered that they not only survived but flourished out on the hills in the winter. New breeds were introduced: the Linton black-faced variety that browsed around our loch, and later the Cheviot breed with its fine wool.

So sheep farming began to be engaged in on an ever-increasing scale, encouraged by the markets that had opened up as England expanded its colonial empire, and augmented by the introduction of the turnip as fodder. But as for the poor crofters, their own numbers were increased by the introduction of the potato and by the generally improved conditions that arose out of the more orderly and prosperous state of the country around the turn of the eighteenth century; overpopulation became the problem.

The capacity of the crofts dwindled as their inhabitants multiplied. Their chiefs neglected their ancestral responsibilities to their tenants, who, as their lives became more wretched, became liabilities to landowners who needed more and more space for grazing the sheep that were now becoming such a profitable business; so profitable that it was found to be more viable economically to have sheep, rather than men, occupying their estates. So they set about dispossessing their tenants in favor of the sheep. Small landowners were offered three times the rent to let out the land for grazing; all over the Highlands impoverished crofters were evicted, their hovels burned. Whole families were put onto ships and sent away to Canada; some, unwilling to submit to being forced from land occupied for generations by their ancestors, tried to hide out in the hills but were sought out and hunted down like game.

The Clearances are a tragic and shameful episode in Scottish history; Scottish song and poetry are filled with the keening sound of a people mourning the loss of their wild and beautiful ancestral land that could not support them and forced them into exile. Names of Scottish towns, villages, and hamlets are place-names all around the world in countries where the exiles settled. Thousands of sheep were put out to graze where small crofts had been amalgamated into large holdings—nibbling the grass and thistles that flourished among the stony ruins of humble cottages.

In the postwar years it became fashionable for middle-class

people to buy and restore these picturesque crofters' cottages to use as second homes.

There are more Scots living abroad than in their native land.

We went on up the hill out of Braeburn. Reaching a crest, we looked back. The young woman lingered still at the gate, watching us, her baby on her hip; the older child and the dog shared a game with the ball on what must once have been the village High Street. Smoke rose from the chimney pot of the only occupied house, floating away above the fallen and gaping walls and hearths, over the tops of the noble chestnut trees, and dissolving in the clear blue of the sky.

CHAPTER
8

The Village

Auchterbraehead, our nearest village, eight miles out of the hills, stands in relation to Glencorrie as Athens to the ancient Greeks, London to the inhabitants of Elizabethan England. It was our center of civilization; the source of our staples: bread, meat, and wine; the location of the library, bank, and post-office—it was our connection with the life of the mind, commerce, communication. The narrow glen road twists its way through the Blairrossie range, emerging to overlook the splendid sight of the valley of Strathmuir, turning to run down the valley into the High Street of the village.

Like most Scottish villages of that size, Auchterbraehead consists of a High Street, about half a mile in length, lined by quaint old houses with shops and banks and pubs occupying the ground floors. Our first stop, at the top of the High Street where countryside and village abutted, was a small dairy farm, where we would pick up rich milk and thick cream produced by cows which grazed in the meadows beyond the stone barn. A very small old woman, her face and clothes wrinkled and rumpled, giggled when she answered our ring at her doorbell, giggled while she fetched what we asked for from the refrigerated room beside the barn, giggled while we paid her and as she waved when we drove off; we never knew if we were the cause of her uncontrollable risibility or if she were privy to some ghastly cosmic joke.

On our return each summer we would be welcomed with warmth by all the tradesmen—"twirling the ends of their mustachios at the thought of all those nice fat dollars you'll be handing over the counter," Bob observed with a villainous look. Angus McWhirter, HIGH-CLASS GROCER, FISHMONGER, AND POULTERER, as his sign proclaimed—a jolly red-faced man dressed in a bright blue nylon jumpsuit rather like an astronaut, was helped in the shop by his white-haired mother, whose dignity was so imposing that she looked far more the grand lady of the glen than did Mrs. Jessie MacFadyen of Glencorrie House.

A manifestation of the British character, orderly queues, formed themselves naturally outside shops; customers awaited their turn patiently, and pushing or shoving were unheard of. Standing on line while those ahead of us carefully inspected three tomatoes, or selected a pair of kippers as though they were making a major commitment for which no redress would be available, or gravely offered opinions on brands of marmalade, or pondered over the choice of streaky versus Ayrshire bacon, we would have to train ourselves anew each year to shift down into a slower pace, reminding ourselves that we had no pressing engagements, no schedules to justify the speedy release of adrenaline through our systems. As the queue inched forward, we would survey the day's offerings ranged in the shop window: small punnets of mustard cress, vivid green; strawberries; raspberries; tight-skinned, yellow-green gooseberries; red currants for jelly and black currants for jam; fresh herrings curled silver-gray on beds of parsley; fillets of white fish; kippers which had been smoked to a burnished gold over chips of oak wood; smoked haddock, which we would make into kedgeree with rice and hard-boiled eggs in a lightly curried cream sauce; mackerel, both smoked and fresh; honeycomb from the hives of the gardener at Gleneagles; round pats of hand-churned butter from the farm of Mrs. Cameron's older daughter, who still milked her cow by hand twice each day; cauliflower; cabbage; green beans; English cucumbers two feet long; grapes, oranges, and bananas, expensive, imported from hot, exotic lands, arranged with the respect due their high prices; small Scottish tomatoes, sweet and full of flavor, raised only in hothouses in this cool climate. Over the threshold and in the shop were the staples: onions, carrots, potatoes, a limited selection for New Yorkers accustomed to the trans-seasonal and transcontinental availability of farm produce.

In the early years I would have to bring from New York a summer's supply of garlic, but somehow the news of Mediterranean cuisine seeped eventually into those hills, and small wizened heads of garlic began to appear in McWhirter's grocery. Occasionally there would be giant green marrows; planning one day to do a stuffed marrow when the Hunters were coming to dinner, I was disappointed to find them sold out. "Were ye specially needing it, then?" Mrs. McWhirter asked, full of sympathy for my culinary predicament. "Dinna fash, dear—we'll find you one." The small, plump woman who had worked there for most of her sixty odd years was dispatched, in her smock, to the neighbor on the High Street who raised marrows in his back garden; by the time I had come to the end of my shopping list she was back, panting and smiling, the large dark green marrow, still warm from where it had been plucked out of the sunny bed, clasped to her bosom.

In the month of July, when all the soft fruits ripen, country women fall into a frenzy of jam making, considering it sinful to leave a single berry to waste on a bush when it could be frugally put by for the dark, fruitless winter months. Helen, driven by demons, would be up at dawn, her jam kettle bubbling, the farmhouse warm with the fragrance of boiling fruit; whoever came by in the afternoons and evenings would be dispatched to the kitchen garden with bowls to fill with berries. One summer there was an unaccountable sugar shortage during the jam-making season, and housewives traveled out to distant towns where, they had heard, the precious substance was available. Each time I shopped at McWhirter's that sugar-lean season, Mrs. McWhirter, unasked, would surreptitiously slip a couple of two-pound bags of sugar into my order, broad winks and hints and nudges signaling the nefarious nature of the transaction, as though we were dealing in cocaine. As a summer visitor I did not go in for the jam-making frenzy, but it would have seemed ungracious, I felt, to hand back to her the newspaper-wrapped sugar bags so generously smuggled over the counter. I supplied Helen and Jenny Kirkbride and Tottie MacIver with my unwanted stock of contraband. "It pays to know influential Yanks, even in the boondocks," Bob commented.

Mr. McKenzie, the butcher, smelled always of whiskey, no matter how early in the day one came into his shop. Burly, his complexion ruddy, he wore a long blue-and-white-striped apron, and would slice off what I asked for directly from the carcasses that hung from hooks on the walls. He would not sell meat that was not properly aged. "I canna let you have any of it today, I'm afraid, it hasna' hung long enough. What aboot some tasty lamb-kidneys instead?"

Scottish lamb, the ribs and prancing legs of the wooly creatures that gamboled on our hillside, has a gamier flavor and a finer texture than American lamb, and is sweet and strong-flavored when cooked rare—though the British prefer their meat well-done to a point that dries it out. "We don't like actually to see the blood running from it," Helen would aver with a shudder, while Bob, more primitive perhaps, liked the way we broiled our chops and steaks rare and pink. Scottish beef, raised and fattened in the rich green hills, is prized, though not always available; much beef is imported into Britain from New Zealand and Argentina.

"I have a nice piece of Scottish beef this morning," Mr. McKenzie would tell us, confidentially, across the counter; the next time we were in his shop he would listen with the satisfaction of an artist who hears his work praised as we described the superiority of the local beef over American factory-raised beef. He enjoyed knifing off large, thick steaks for his carnivorous American customers. Britain is a poor country, and we noticed that meat was bought in sizable cuts mainly at the weekend—the traditional "Sunday joint." If we ever wanted a roast of beef or lamb on Tuesday or Wednesday, there would be none in the shop; he could let us have it, he would tell us, on Friday or Saturday. Over the years, we became more herbivorous, and I grew aware of his disappointment as we spoiled the image he had of us as steak-happy, red-blooded, money-loose Americans.

On Wednesdays he always baked steak and kidney pies, crisp, light puff paste topping chunks of meat baked tender in a rich gravy; with pickled beets and Scottish tomatoes this became a standard Wednesday lunch dish at Glenauchen Cottage. While he sliced and trimmed and wrapped our purchases, Mr. McKenzie liked to engage us in discussion of American politics; he was well informed and curious, his opinions veering well to the right and heavily enveloped in whiskey fumes.

Two tiny old ladies owned the drapery shop that sold yarn and fabric and needles and thread and men's socks and baby clothes. They liked to tell us how they had been enthusiastic hikers in their youth, and they recommended expeditions to us—climbs, views we should not miss, shortcuts, and ancient monuments to visit; they were always keen to hear where we had been, and how it looked these days. "I mind how one summer my cousin and I hiked all the way from Wigford to Strathmorlie," one told us. "It was just after the Great War, and he was back safe from the trenches. And I mind how it was a hot day, and we stopped to ask a drink of water at Back Hills Farm, about five miles above Strathmorlie—you must have been past it when you walked to Kilbride Loch. And the wee wifie at the farm, she had seven children, and she helped her man with the milking and the beasts as well. And she told us that she used to walk over the hills to Strathmorlie to buy what was wanting—bags of coal it sometimes was—and she carried it home on her back. She worked three hundred and sixty-four days of the year, she told us (not complaining, just telling what she tholed) but New Year's Day she always took a holiday from her labors. 'And do ye no' weary?' we asked her. 'Och, I ha' nae the time to weary,' she told us."

*   *   *

There were two antique shops on the High Street—"for all the rich folk who come to the glen for the golfing," Meg Cameron told us when we stopped by to visit at the boutique where she worked in the mornings, "and the American cattle breeders who come here to buy Aberdeen-Angus beef cattle." She sold Scottish souvenirs, bits of mohair knitting and weaving, and knick-knacks to the same clientele. There was also a HIGH-CLASS TAILOR AND PURVEYOR OF FINEST SCOTTISH TWEEDS AND WOOLENS, two doors down from the teashop. James Drummond Begg, grandson of the original tailor, ran the family business.

Harl, like Thoreau, distrusts all enterprises that require new clothes, and it is only with difficulty, and when his clothes are undeniably shabby and worn, that he can be prevailed upon to enter a clothing store. (He is also color-blind.) But one day a golden opportunity presented itself. On a sunny August morning, as he sat, relaxed, on a low wall outside the pub, reading the morning paper while he waited for me to join him for morning coffee at the Copper Kettle, I nabbed him. Convincing him that it would be almost painless to have a sports-coat made for him by James Drummond Begg, rather than drag around the New York outfitters, I persuaded him to accompany me up the stairs to the tailor's rooms. Once up there, though, in the portly presence of the solemnly dignified Mr. Drummond Begg, among the bolts of tweed stacked on the shelves, he withdrew from the enterprise, refusing to offer an opinion or preference, leaving it all to the tailor and me. As though in an advanced catatonic state, he allowed his arms to be lifted and his chest, shoulders, and waist to be measured; then he retired behind his newspaper while Mr. Drummond Begg showed me bolts of cloth and I selected the fabric. Mr. Drummond Begg remained inscrutable, apparently unsurprised by the behavior of his client. He knew, from the glen Mafia, that we were the folk from up at Glenauchen Loch.

The jacket would cost fifty pounds, he informed me, and would be ready in October. But we would be back in New York by then. "No matter," he said. "We will post it on to you. We make a lot of suits and sportscoats for American gentlemen. We have many clients from Texas and your midwestern states who come over to buy pedigreed cattle here,

and many who come for the golf. Only this morning we posted
two suits to a gentleman in Hollywood—a film star I believe
he said he was—and another to a gentleman in Connecticut.
We are quite accustomed to dealing with customers this way.
You can rest assured that you will find it quite to your satisfaction, madam." I wrote out the check and gave him our New
York address. Harl folded up his newspaper, the tailor accompanied us courteously to the door and wished us a good day,
and down the steps we went to have coffee at the Copper
Kettle.

Bob was highly amused at what he called the incident of the
bespoke overcoat. "Och, how they love to *rip off* the Yanks,"
he crowed, until we convinced him that a hundred dollars for
a custom-tailored Scottish tweed jacket would not, back home,
be tallied a rip-off, not to mention the difficulty of getting
Harl into a clothing shop in New York. Bob relished my description of the unfazed politeness with which Mr. Drummond
Begg had accommodated Harl's catatonia. "Och, the British
are very accepting when it comes to dealing with odd folk
and eccentrics—never bat an eyelid in the face of the most
bizarre dottiness. Anyway," he added, "he probably got the
impression that Harl is some dotty millionaire."

In October, the bespoke overcoat arrived in New York,
folded in tissue in a stout box; a beautifully tailored, well-
fitting garment of indestructible tweed, which still looks good,
and ages without ever losing its aristocratic quality.

Mr. Baillie, the bank manager, welcomed us back each summer as though our custom really made a difference to the
bank's revenues. "You spice up his life," Bob said. "It makes
a change from farmers asking for overdrafts, and ironmongers
and drapers wanting a wee loan. How many branch managers
d'you think have customers from New York?"

"Mind you," he remarked one rainy day when he had waited
in the car while I went in to cash my first check of the
summer, "to treat you with favor is one thing—to bow you
out of the bank and then fling his jacket over a puddle for
you to step on—I thought that was carrying things a bit far."

Mr. Baillie was always intrigued by our relationship with the Hunters, who signed our checks, paid our bills, made purchases, and arranged various repair jobs over the winter for Glenauchen Cottage. "I presume you are related to the Hunters?" he inquired once, discreet.

"Only by friendship," we told him.

"Ah . . . the best kind of relationship," came his smooth reply, though the fact that there was no blood tie between us seemed to obfuscate the matter further in his view, and he continued to look perplexed.

Before leaving for Scotland every summer, we would transfer a sum of money from our New York bank to Mr. Baillie's bank, and I would phone or visit him to announce my return. One year I called him from the public phone booth outside the library in Auchterbraehead.

"Hullo, Mr. Baillie. Here I am—back again."

"Welcome back to Scotland, my dear."

"Has the money I transferred from New York arrived yet?"

"No, it has not. But don't let that trouble you. You just carry on exactly as though it's here."

What a change, I thought, as I replaced the phone and stepped out into the bustle of the sunny High Street, from the treatment we accepted from our bank in New York. There everything is controlled by a giant computer central to the system like a spider squatting in the middle of a web—a computer that stores even my grandparents' names in its prodigious electronic memory; a system that seems to ensure that whenever one becomes friendly enough with a teller so that one's existence, identity, and solvency need not be confirmed on a small television screen by the spider each time a check is cashed, one finds that the teller has been transferred to another branch, and the impersonality of commerce has been sustained with mandatory facelessness.

In his discreet way, Mr. Baillie was curious about this place in the hills that lured us from such a distance each year. "Would you like to see Glenauchen Cottage?" we asked him one day. It appeared that he had longed to see it ever since he had first advanced the money for its purchase. So we invited him and his wife and two children to tea one Sunday afternoon. It was a gray day, cool, with lowering clouds. We did the right thing as far as tea went: scones with raspberry jam, mustard-cress sandwiches, fruitcake. After tea, Mrs. Baillie and I remained by the fire while the fathers and children took a walk round the loch.

Soon the gray clouds turned into a soaking drizzle, and from the living room windows we could see the small group at the far end of the loch. There was no rescuing them from the rain. They returned chill and damp. The children lit a fire in the kitchen and hung up socks and sweaters to steam out. Upstairs, though, Mr. Baillie sat by the fire, declining an offer of dry clothes, looking thoroughly damp and depressed. The wind swept gray veils of drizzle across the dark surface of the loch and against the windowpanes. "What does one do with a damp bank manager on a rainy Sunday afternoon?" I muttered to Harl in the hall. "Try offering him a drink," he suggested.

"Oh, Mr. Baillie, how would you like a glass of whiskey to take away the chill?" I asked.

His face lit up and he beamed at me, beatific. "Oh, God bless you, my dear," he answered earnestly. A couple of glasses of Glenmorangie, drunk neat, and soon the damp and gloom accumulated at the lochside were dispelled; so efficacious is its power, in fact, that after a while the sun broke out and the loch turned as blue as the sky.

The village library occupies a large room at the back of the Village Hall, and is open two afternoons a week and on Saturday mornings. At the beginning of each summer I would walk into the library after an absence of almost a year, and the librarian would look up from her desk, greet me as though I had been in the previous week, and hand me, from a small wooden filing box, the library cards for the whole family. In spite of its size, this little country library proved a rich source of reading matter. The pickings, so far as fiction went, were slim: all the popular American best-sellers loaded the shelves with their bulk, and there was a sprinkling of the later American classics: Faulkner, Scott Fitzgerald, and Hemingway, but no Hawthorne or Mark Twain, and of Henry James only *Portrait of a Lady*. Of the better-known contemporary novelists ubiquitous on both sides of the Atlantic, there were plenty, in among an undue proportion of Gothic novels and light romantic fiction. We found, though, many of the English novelists we had read in our youth—like Arnold Bennett and H. G. Wells, who could be reread with pleasure; the children were also much taken by the chronicles of the *Five Towns* and *Mr. Polly*. For staple fare, there was sufficient Trollope, Mrs. Gaskell, and Evelyn Waugh; it seemed that one or another of us took out *A Handful of Dust* and *Scoop* every year, for there always seemed to be someone lying on the sofa laughing fiendishly at Waugh's black humor, and insisting on reading the more outrageous bits out loud to whoever wandered into the sitting room. And there was Dickens, who kept us awake on those long summer evenings when we read so late that ours was the only light that shone in the slumbering glen. The poetry and philosophy sections were excellently stocked; and an extensive selection of Scottish history, literature, and country writings enabled us to learn more about the history and nature of our area of Perthshire, which we came to know better and feel closer to each succeeding summer.

Our Glenauchen summers were characterized by a great sense of space: the skies were spacious, and the hills where we walked rarely encountering another living soul; and the evenings were spaces used for reading. One of us was always waiting with impatience for someone else to finish a particular book; one year, various members of the family were constantly to be found sniffling over *Dombey and Son*, and those who had read it threatened to tell those who had not if little Paul Dombey would live, or if Walter had really drowned at sea or would return to the arms of poor Floy. Philippa once threw a book at Neil and a noisy altercation ensued because he divulged to her, in the middle of her absorption in *Bleak House*, that Esther Summerson was the illegitimate daughter of Lady Dedlock. And there would be enthusiasms, each summer, for books which we would urge each other to read, like Edmund Gosse's autobiography, *Father and Son*, and Shiva Naipul's *Fireflies*.

Perhaps the experience of reading was more vivid at Glenauchen because of our isolation: so much silence, so much space, so little of the common interchange of daily life to dilute the full strength of what we read. We took our books neat as we took our malt whiskey neat—ideal circumstances for reading. We always brought home from the library, constantly renewing them when they fell due, weighty anthologies of poetry, to pick up and leaf through in a moment of idleness or boredom, or between books; each poem that one dipped into had an intensity that would send the mind reeling like the sudden sight of a golden hawk drifting on the blue air in the valley below.

At the border of the village, where the roads petered out into farmland spread in rectilinear fields like green tablecloths laid down in the sun at the foot of the hills, a weaving mill, built beside a racing millstream, functioned still as it had done for a century and a half in the hands of the same family. The water that rushed down out of the Blairrossie Hills once supplied the power that worked the shuttles. With the coming of the industrial revolution, the mill had switched to steam, and the original steam engine still functioned, the furnace stoked with coal by a man so old that he might have been the Original Stoker himself.

The engine was displayed with great pride by the present owner, who enjoyed showing the plant to visitors; it was a handsome piece of machinery, built with the same Victorian sense of fine craftsmanship that distinguished Glenauchen Cottage—an object sculptured in black iron, with polished brass rods and pistons and even-toothed whirring ratchets and gears, its parts all smoothly oiled and sending power to the dozen or so looms handled by local women.

For generations, the young owner told us, fine-quality cotton fabrics had been woven into men's shirtings; a fair amount of the product was exported to a well-known shirt manufacturer in New York. The owner had taken a university degree in political history, we learned, and then returned to the village to take over the business when his father died, feeling committed to carry on an enterprise that had been in his family for so many generations. He took us about among the clatter and din of the great noisy looms to watch the operators weaving the pin-striped and small-checked shirtings in restrained patterns and quiet colors that would be made up into very British-looking shirts. He had a great affection for the efficiency of the steam engine, one of the few still being worked in Scotland, and was pleased to be able to provide employment for the village people; some local families had worked at the looms for several generations. Each year we would stop by, fascinated, to watch the women, each one silent and in control of her great clumsy-looking clattering machine, the heavy shuttles banging with deafening noise, back and forth, throwing the woof across the tight-strung warp threads to produce, out of all the din, a fine web of cloth; we would buy lengths of the fine-woven cottons to take back to New York, charmed each time by the young mill-owner's pride in the skills of his weavers and the high quality of his fabrics, and by his dedication to a long tradition of accumulated experience.

In nearby villages along the foothills, we got to know several small family-owned mills that produced tweeds and woolen fabrics, and knitting mills that turned out the sweaters for which Scotland is famous; they all stood where originally they had been built beside millstreams, but the noisy shuttles, which must have damaged the eardrums of the loom-hands and made conversation between them impossible, were now powered by electricity.

There is an ancient tradition of wool weaving in Scotland. The earliest Britons kept flocks; fragments of woolen cloth have been found in Neolithic burial mounds; and the ancient Celts excelled at dyeing, even in Roman times weaving many-colored checkered plaids that are still characteristic of Scottish woolen fabrics. In the Middle Ages, and until the eighteenth century, the Scots wore these woven plaids belted, the upper part forming the shawl and the lower half the kilt.

As far back as the fourteenth century, records show that the plaid cloth was woven on hand-looms in the peaty smokiness of peasants' cottages. By the seventeenth century home weaving had grown to a cottage industry, since the peasants needed to increase the bare living they eked out of farming, and during the eighteenth century weaving came to play a significant part in the economic development of Scotland.

The invention of the fly-shuttle and the spinning jenny brought the industry out of the cottages into small mills that were powered by water until the Glaswegian James Watt's development of the steam engine; cotton mills then sprang up all over northeast Scotland, able to draw labor from the impoverished Highlands. Out of this ancient tradition of spinning and weaving, Scotland's textile industry, using cotton imported from America and wool from her own native sheep, became one of the country's major trades and exports.

The Victorian authenticity and charm of Gleneagles Station was maintained for the benefit of the guests and personnel of Gleneagles Hotel by British Railways, who owned the hotel with its three golf courses that were the Mecca of all serious golfers. The little station had the appearance of a toy structure in a child's miniature railway set. It nestled beside the green hills, with meticulously maintained flowerbeds; pots of geraniums bloomed in the station lobby, which was trim and always fresh-painted, its Victorian brass embellishments bright with polishing. There were two platforms, immaculately swept, four sets of railway tracks, and an old-fashioned waiting room with an ornate fireplace. A fire burned most days in the small hearth in the office where the clerk dispensed tickets from behind ornate iron grillwork. The stationmaster, with his whistle and flag, wore a red-and-black-striped waistcoat and peaked cap exactly like the toy stationmasters our children used to have in their railway sets. In our early years in the glen, there were still gas lanterns hanging along the platforms that were individually lit when dusk fell, but these were later replaced by electric lights, which detracted from the charm of the place. There was no public phone, no taxi; if the arriving traveler was not met by someone with a car, or by the limousine from the hotel, there was nothing but the prospect of a lonely walk along the country roads.

We had afternoon tea at Gleneagles just once, and a splendid affair it was. The hotel, a great granitic building that looked like a historic, rather ostentatious mansion, was in fact built as a hotel in the nineteen-twenties. It was set in acres of formal gardens with sweeping driveways, and there were usually a number of Rolls-Royces and Daimlers parked here and there. It was constructed in the grand hotel style of the great European establishments, with a flourish of vast halls, lounges, salons and dining rooms, deep carpeting providing an air of hushed awe—that deference encountered in the great cathedrals and wherever enormous wealth is catered to. There was much wood paneling, carved mahogany, brocade, and discreet formality; expressions remained inscrutable when sheiks, golf champions, or movie-stars passed through the lobby.

The waiters were solemn and dressed like footmen. Afternoon tea was ceremonially served at low, round tables in a large lounge where French windows overlooked the gardens. One did not order—there was a set ritual. After one had been ushered in and seated at a table already set with fine bone china, a footman brought a silver teapot, milk-jug, and hot water pitcher. A choreographed succession of dishes then appeared in an order as set and instituted as the Japanese tea ceremony. A plate of crustless, triangular savory sandwiches was followed by scones and girdle-scones (the latter, a type of small pancake) served with butter and a pot of jam. Later, a three-tiered dish of assorted tea cakes, buns, and sliced fruitcake was placed in the center of the table; just as one prepared to sink back, replete, the footman appeared to refill the hot water—for by now the tea in the pot had steeped to a dark, strong brew—and to offer generous wedges of *gâteau*, garnished with coffee or chocolate butter-icings, layered with raspberry or apricot preserves, lavished with whipped cream.

A tea of this sort, like high tea at Tottie MacIver's, displaced one's regular cultural habits of food intake, so that dinner or supper the same evening was out of the question, and by midnight one was in the grip of earnest pangs of hunger. So we did not take to dropping in at Gleneagles for this midafternoon repast, though we would send our guests there for the experience.

CHAPTER

9

The Tenants

The summers at Glenauchen, just as Mr. Greenleaf had predicted, were warm and mostly dry. But our first summer was unusually warm. No END TO HEAT WAVE IN SIGHT, proclaimed banner headlines in *The Scotsman* after three or four days of temperatures in the low eighties. Down at the caravan site they lay about beside the burn, stripped to the skin, their pallid, almost unhealthily white flesh given up in sacrifice to the sun god; old gentlemen removed ties and shirts and sat reading the paper in undershirts, and stout, bare-armed wives served tea at folding tables set up on the grassy verge at the side of the main road.

"It's like the French Riviera along the glen road," Bob reported one Saturday afternoon when the Hunters were visiting us. "All the gairls in their wee bit bikinis; if the weather continues like this, the glen will turn into a veritable St. Tropez. Mediterranean skies—look at that wine-dark loch—your celestial messenger on the train certainly *wasn't kidding* about the good weather." But the Hunters would feel quite uncomfortable when the mercury rose above seventy. "Our northern systems are not adjusted to deal with such extreme heat," Helen murmured, wilting, her fine fair skin flushed, fanning herself with a wide-brimmed straw hat.

We had a houseful that weekend. A nephew had hitchhiked up from his university in England and a couple of the Hunter children were spending a few days with us, so sleeping bags were spread on floors in the downstairs bedrooms. The loch burned indigo under the unclouded sky; the sheep in their thick coats, too hot to nibble the dry grass, gathered and lay down wherever there was a scrap of shade surrounding our property, huddling where the belt of trees cast shadows that shrank as the sun rose higher overhead. Like the sheep, we all lolled about, inert on the sloping lawn, on the terrace, constantly replenishing our tiny refrigerator's meager supply of ice.

On Sunday afternoon, an ennui that had settled over all of us was inexplicably and suddenly displaced by a form of midsummer madness. No one was ever sure how it came about. We all knew that the loch was a reservoir, and we had never given it any thought as a place where one might swim—Scottish lochs, after all, do not conjure up visions of aquatics. "Why don't we all go in for a swim?" one of the boys said idly, rhetorically probably, and in the next moment the lawn and terrace were empty; minutes later, it seemed, they were in swimming suits, running down over the greensward of the bank of the loch, and shattering the blue surface of the water into sparkling cascades as they all plunged into its chilly depths.

The folly was contagious; soon Harl had joined them, and a party of Glaswegians—two men and a girl who had been fishing farther along the bank—caught by the delirium that quivered in the still, heated air, stripped to their underclothes and flung themselves in.

I stood watching the scene from the terrace, wondering if I should join in. There was no movement, no sign of life anywhere in the landscape; even the birds had fallen quiet in the heat of the afternoon. The ancient hills ringing the loch, green sentinels separating us from the world outside; the sheep huddled in the shade; the glad cries of the plunging, splashing creatures delighting in the pleasure of the water—the moment was caught, sylvan, mythic. But instead of Pan's pipes I heard the ring of the telephone. In the coolness of the stone hall I picked it up to hear Tottie MacIver's agitated voice. "We've just received word that there's a party of people from the caravan site *swimming* in the loch!" she announced, in tones

her ancestors must have employed to warn the approach of a
wild Highland clan with murderous intent. The glen Mafia. . . .
We had forgotten that it operates without any visible means of
connection.

The criminality of our behavior slowly dawned on me. Here
we were, respectable landowners in the glen and party to this
unlawful, unseemly activity. "We haird that some of them are
swimming in their *underwear*," Tottie went on, her shock at
this further evidence of depravity raising her voice to a pitch
of high indignation.

"*Really!*" I exclaimed, my feigned horror making me, in
that moment, accessory to the crime. "I'll go right down to the
loch and chase them off."

"I just phoned to let you know that big Angus Taggart is
on his way over from Kilbride Loch with his dog. He'll stand
no nonsense from anybody; he's a right terror when he gets
going. And Donny's on his way as well."

I hung up the phone and sped down to the loch. "Out—out—
hurry!" Like a sheep dog I herded the whole dripping party
back into the house, covering their traces as we retreated,
picking up towels off the grass and off the line, hosing down
the terrace to remove the implicating wet footprints.

The three Glaswegians, however, paid no heed to my warning. Obviously they were types who would never have survived
the slaughter of the warring clans; it was too delightful in the
cold water of the loch, and they continued splashing happily
about. It was not long before big Angus came striding from
his car with his lean, muscular Alsatian padding beside him. I
met him at the gate and headed him through the kitchen
garden to prevent him from picking up any hint of our com-
plicity in the afternoon's crime. "They've all left," I said
vaguely, "but those three wouldn't come out."

Guilt-ridden and uneasy, I stood by the picket gate as he
tramped to the lochside and with one great bellow had them
all out of the water. I never knew what he said to those three
Glaswegians, dragged out and dripping on the bank in their
sagging wet underclothes. Whatever they told him, it seemed
to me that it was foregone that their role was to be a sacrificial one. If Tottie hadn't presented me with the *fait accompli*

that authority was already on its way over, I might have had
the chance to explain that we were the culprits; but her assump-
tion of our innocence—her presumption that it was *us* against
them—made my situation inadmissible. Along with my reason-
ing went the suspicion that her phone call was a friendly
warning, and that her role in the episode was to provide us
with a cover-up. By admitting our guilt I would blow the
whole carefully contrived plan.

Soon Donny's blue van came toiling up the hill, and out he
stepped, officious and dapper in his Sunday clothes, and even
more rigidly righteous than on weekdays. He delivered a sermon to them; the two young men each in a single wet garment,
the girl in her two scanty bits of underwear, having to listen,
in the overheated air, to words scorched with hellfire and
brimstone and sin. Like a citizen of Minos's Crete I stood there,
witnessing the sacrifice of someone else's sons and daughters—
regretful, but knowing it must be as it was.

Donny thoroughly enjoyed himself; probably the heat had
been too much for him, too, and here was the perfect vent for
his rage, which simmered chronically against the decline of the
West in general, and the depravity of contemporary youth in
particular. "Yobs!" he said to me with much satisfaction when
he joined me in the garden after having sent them away with
raised arm and quivering forefinger. "Tinks! And on the Sabbath too. And not even a bit towel to cover their nakedness!
I sairtainly gave it to them—riff-raff that Gavin MacFadyen's
caravan site attracts to the glen. Cheeky they wair, too, until
I told them, 'Yer lucky I'm not takin' you in charge—tres-
passin' upon Water Board property, as well as disturbin' the
peace and privacy of Dr. and Mrs. Gordon.' "

Donny and I looked each other straight in the eye. Did I
receive, in that look, a certain acknowledgment that a farce
was being enacted, a face-saving farce, with each of us knowing the lines to be said, the roles to be played? Was I getting
a message from him that our guilt must remain unacknowl-
edged, that presumably a lifetime of summers lay ahead, and
we, as members of the establishment, separate from the yobs,
were under the obligation to maintain a certain facade that was
more important, in the circumstances, than candor?

Is this what he was obliquely letting me know? And had Tottie phoned really to warn us? Or did they truly believe that the respectable burghers they took us to be would never go a little crazy during a prolonged Scottish heat wave and jump collectively into a loch that supplied the county's drinking water?

Bob was highly amused when he heard our story. "Och, the glen Mafia; I told you there's nothing gets past them. Maybe a few of the sheep are bugged for sound. Did you notice if any helicopters were hovering about? Or hikers with walkie-talkies?"

There had been no one, I assured him; it was too hot.

"Too hot for anything except a dip in the loch. What a sleister about nowt! Donny runs the purification plant; he knows a wee dip in the loch couldn't affect the quality of the water. What do they think they're doing coming over with ferocious dogs!"

Bob, however, remained convinced that they had known we were swimming, and had phoned to warn us. Helen subscribed to the view that it was the yobs from the caravan site they were after, in their wrath against Gavin MacFadyen's commercial activities in the glen.

"It was an elaborate glen-Mafia pseudo-subterfuge, enacted for your protection," Bob summed up.

We would never know. I took the precaution of hanging the wet swimming suits up to dry in the kitchen, for one thing we did know now was that invisible eyes watched everything that went on; in our isolated spot of countryside, we could be seen.

In the many hot summers that followed, we discovered places where we could swim. Way back in a cleft of the hills, where Glenauchen Burn flowed before pouring itself into the loch, were a couple of rock pools, more suited to a dryad, but deep and clear enough to cool and refresh us. All around, the bracken and gorse were thick enough to conceal us from view, and the only creatures we ever disturbed were the grouse we startled up out of the heather and an occasional renegade family of sheep who had run away to evade the clipping or the dipping or the sheep-sales. And for swimming in earnest, we would drive an hour to the East Neuk of Fife, where along the coast were strung out half a dozen ancient fishing villages with stone harbors and sandy beaches; here, after one had bathed, one could visit a thirteenth-century church; or buy freshly smoked kippers or mackerel, or visit a small working pottery and come away with hand-thrown stoneware porringers and mugs.

So it turned out to be no hardship, really, that we could not bathe in the loch on our doorstep.

On an afternoon during that first summer, I was dreamily preparing a gooseberry fool; the family were out, making their first assault on Dalrioch, the hill about two thousand feet high that rose from the east bank of the loch. From time to time I checked their progress through the binoculars from the living room window, their figures antlike as they clambered up through the bracken, and then returned to the kitchen to press the slightly sweetened, stewed gooseberries through the sieve with a wooden spoon until there was a dishful of thick puree. Gooseberry fool is a traditional dessert, affording as much pleasure in the making as in the eating. I stirred an egg custard into the fruit, mixing until the green and yellow amalgamated into a shade of bronze one sees in medieval tapestries; poured it into a glass dish; and set it to chill until it was due to be served for dinner accompanied by whipped cream.

Washing up was also a pleasure. The low sink was set under the window that overlooked the front garden and the loch, so the dishes in the warm, soapy water seemed only incidental to contemplation of the shadow of a cloud moving across the water, or a pair of birds scrapping over a morsel of something on the terrace, or some bees dipping into the bowls of the large orange poppies growing under the window.

There were footsteps along the flagstones, and Donny came round the corner of the house and waved through the window; the front door stood wide open to the sunshine, and I called to him to step right in. Tottie had sent us a few heads of lettuce from her garden. Donny accepted my offer of a cup of tea, apologizing that he couldn't stay for more than a few minutes as he was very busy.

He stayed for an hour and a half, and was still sitting there at the kitchen table when the others came down off the hill. He comes from the Isle of Lewis, and Bob says there's nothing a Lewis man likes better than talking; he was in a state of indignation that day, having just read in the local paper that Auchendoon, a famous historic mansion in a nearby county, had been bought by an Arab oil millionaire who was going to use it as a hunting lodge. "It's been in the same family for I don't know how many centuries—they got it from the English king for their help in putting down one of the Jacobite risings, I've haird. And now—would you believe it!—this sheik is going to be moving in there with his harem of wives and concubines. And, to make matters *worse*, they've got themselves an architect who is going to redo the whole interior of the mansion in Moorish style. It's a national disgrace; what is this country coming to! So there they'll be on the glorious Twelfth, out on the moors in their long white nighties, shooting at the grouse—it wouldn't surprise me—with rounds of machine-gun fire. The Lord only knows what will become of our Scottish ways if this sort of thing is allowed to go on."

I refilled his teacup, and ventured that perhaps the laird was as much to blame as the Arab sheik. "After all, he knew who he was selling it to, and he knew they weren't going to change their desert robes for kilts and sporrans."

"Well," Donny allowed grudgingly, "perhaps that's so, but you really canna' blame the poor mannie; the taxes are killing, and they canna' afford the cost of keeping up these grand old places. Did you know that some of them have the roof removed from their castles and mansions? If there's no roof on a building they don't have to pay any taxes. Tottie tells me the old Marquis of Knockinlaw had the roof taken off Knockinlaw Hall and has moved into the lodge keeper's cottage. It's only these robbers from the oil-producing countries can afford the upkeep of castles nowadays."

"But Scotland's an oil-producing country now," I reminded him.

"A fat lot of good it's doing us," he grumbled. "It's difficult and dear to lift it up from under the North Sea. Half the time the weather's so fierce there, it's a wonder they can work there at all. And *we* canna' get away with paying *our* labor a few pennies a day like they do in those places in the desert; you'd have the unions on your neck in no time."

Donny would not appreciate, I conjectured, the historic irony in the change of circumstances: For a few centuries the British upper classes had enriched themselves fabulously by paying the natives of the colonial empire a few pennies a day for their labor; now, it seemed, the oil sheiks were having their day. It struck me that the reverence of the average Briton for the titled aristocracy is so ingrained that it can be regarded as a national characteristic; Donny and Tottie were no different in this respect from Virginia Woolf, who, with all her worldliness and sense of irony, confessed to a thrilling response when she received letters written on the crested note-paper of some ancient, noble family.

Donny declined a third cup of tea, and turned his wrath upon one of the wild grandsons, with whose tractor he had narrowly escaped collision on the hairpin bend of our hill road. "Covered in sticking-plaster his face was; brawling in the pub as usual. Tottie haird that he had to have I don't know how many stitches taken on his forehead—but that hasn't wiped the cheeky grin off his face. . . . And have you haird what's happened to Commander Napier's cottage?" It appeared that a weekend cottage, as isolated as ours, belonging to a retired naval commander, had been stripped during the owner's midweek absence of all its copper piping and lead guttering: items, according to Donny, that fetched high prices on the appropriate market. "Even the countryside isn't safe any more from yobs. And what happens when they're taken before the magistrate? They're let off with a warning; their parents are told to exercise better control over them! They should be soundly whipped instead of molly-coddled. They've all gone soft and good-for-nothing. I tell you, there's no respect anymore, for property or persons or institutions. This country is in great danger—I can see nothing but trouble in the years ahead."

Donny was our prophet of doom who could sense change in small signs. We became accustomed to his railing invective against the trade unions; against wealthy Arabs, Germans, and Japanese taking up the privileges once reserved for the British aristocracy; against the falling-off of attendance at the kirk and the "nekkidness" of the sunbathers at the caravan site. He was the messenger who brought the news that all was not as well with the world as our idyllic existence in the hills led us to suppose.

His monologue was interrupted by the family coming in full of enthusiasm for the splendid views from the hilltop, after a climb that had taken amost an hour up but only twenty minutes for the down-hill slither. "We had a good view of your loch and your house," David told Donny.

"But you couldna' see the mother and father swan and their seven wee cygnets that live on our loch," he said. "You must come over and visit them. When the father swan is away getting food, we sometimes see the mother taking all the bairns for a ride on her back—it's a bonny sight. The same couple has been coming every spring to our loch for the last five years. Tottie feeds them every day."

Over a fresh-brewed pot of tea, Donny came at last to the point of his visit. "Now, what were you thinking of doing with this place over the winter when you're all back in America?"

We had thought of leaving a key with Robbie Kirkbride and asking him to be our winter caretaker.

Donny shook his head gravely. "That wouldna' be a wise thing. You would be taking a risk to leave the place unoccupied. Such an isolated situation it is—it would an invitation to vandals. Tottie and I were thinking that it would be best for you to try and find a tenant to rent it while you are not here."

We consulted Bob. "Perhaps he's right. An unoccupied house might draw intruders. Problems in paradise. . . . The best thing would be to put an advertisement in *The Scotsman* toward the end of August: 'Stone house beside loch in the Blairrossie Hills.' That'll get them. It got you."

*   *   *

Tucked away in our hills, some ten miles off, was a large Edwardian manor house belonging to a Scottish gentleman of means with a well-developed sense of social responsibility. Feeling that the Edinburgh Festival catered only to the urban middle and upper-middle classes, and to droves of foreigners, he decided to turn his mansion into a summer theater that would make available the riches of music and drama to the culturally deprived inhabitants of rural Scotland. All summer there were ongoing programs of plays, chamber music, and solo recitals. The Hunters insisted that we go at least once, and on a fine summer evening we arranged to meet there for a performance of a play by a young British playwright.

The place was organized along the same lines as Glyndebourne—a poor Scot's Glyndebourne, Bob said—and patrons were expected to dress formally, the women in long gowns; cocktails were served before the performance, and a buffet dinner during the intermission.

Harl and Bob compromised their distaste for formal attire only to the extent of jacket and tie; Helen and I put on long dresses, and we all entered the handsome library at cocktail time in great style. Everyone appeared very genteel and earnest, their demeanor implying that they were here for improvement as much as entertainment. Bob said that the local kulaks—at whom all this good taste was aimed—were not only indifferent to the fancy carryings-on, but couldn't afford the high price of the tickets, and that most of the audience were university lecturers and the middle class of Edinburgh, for whom it had become quite the fashionable way of spending a summer's Friday or Saturday evening.

While the drinks were being fetched, I wandered around to inspect the titles of the books, which were not very clearly visible because of screens of fine-meshed metal covering the glass doors of the bookcases. "What's the chicken wire for?" I asked Helen when she joined me with our drinks.

"Book pinchers," she explained. "Since he opened up this place as a theater, so many of his precious volumes began to disappear off the shelves that he's had to secure them behind wire."

I gazed around at the patrons: well-dressed women with fine

complexions and rather elaborate hairstyles; the men, quiet-spoken, courteous, some in formal evening dress, a few decked out in the kilt; the rest in lounge suits or good tweeds. An unlikely-looking bunch of kleptomaniacs or book lifters. Helen and I looked at each other and drank up, as if saluting our perplexity.

The great hall of the house had a minstrels' gallery surrounding it on three sides, and had been turned into a charming little arena theater. The play was well performed by competent professionals, and during the intermission there was an excellent buffet supper of cold meats, salads, strawberries and cream, and wine. When we had reassembled in our seats for the last act, a man appeared on stage in a kilt that hung awry above his knees, from which wrinkled woolen stockings drooped. Was he going to do a vaudeville act, I wondered, a comic turn about a drunken Scottish nationalist from Glasgow? But he appeared to be a member of the household who was offering raffle tickets at five pence each for a prize of a bottle of champagne; proceeds from the raffle were to go toward the continuing operation of this rural theater, which, he announced, in spite of its great success and grants from various arts councils, was being run at a loss. At the equivalent of ten cents each, the sale of tickets went well, each of us buying a fistful from the kilted man, who hopped about with much energy, up and down the tiered rows of seats, counting out the pink slips of paper and giving change from a worn leather sporran suspended in the center of his swinging skirt. A cheer went up when the winning ticket was drawn and claimed by a stately, silver-haired matron in wine-colored crepe de chine and silver sandals, and the play went on.

As we walked through the formal gardens back to the parking lot, I commented on the dishevelment and earnestness of the man in the kilts who had conducted the raffle. "That man," Helen said, "is the lord and master of this whole estate, and the backer of this whole enterprise."

The black currants ripened on the bushes that had provided jam for the wives of successive reservoir keepers; though the crop was not large, I decided to make a few pots of jam to take back to New York. A taste of the tart preserve at home in New York would evoke our hillside garden and the surrounding glen in a mouthful.

Currant picking is a tedious business, a lot of labor being expended to gather just a bowlful of the small, jewel-like fruits. As I picked, a stranger hailed me from the stableyard gate, talking in broad Glaswegian; he and his family were wanting to picnic on the banks of the loch—would that be alright? Who was I to deny a workingman's family from a cold, sooty city a day in the sun? If they were planning to do any fishing they would need to get a permit from the farm down the hill, I called out. How much was the permit? Fifty pence. No . . . they were not intending to fish. I turned back to my currant bushes. Would I mind—his voice came over the hedge—if they took a shortcut through our garden? His auld mither was disabled and it wasna' easy for her to walk far. Certainly, I agreed.

The small gate in the hedge of the kitchen garden swung open, and a procession trailed past me along the path: the man, followed by a tiny old lady moving with sprightly skill on crutches, two stout middle-aged women, another man with fishing gear, two young couples, and an assortment of children. There were fourteen of them in all; they filed by, laden with cushions, deck chairs, picnic baskets, thermos flasks, rugs, and a large red and green umbrella. A few of them nodded at me in a distant, wary way, but most of them merely ignored me as I stood there holding my bowl of berries, somewhat taken aback at this Glaswegian invasion of the garden. They filtered out through the small white gate that led onto the banks of the loch, and soon their gay umbrella was impaled in the thick turf and their numbers and their picnic paraphernalia were disposed all about it. The children went rolling down the grassy slopes, shouting with delight, a transistor radio providing background din that sent the rabbits scuttling for shelter in the bracken; great quantities of fruit, beer, and sandwiches were set out on the rug, while the two young men settled down on the shore, fly-casting.

A signboard at the turnoff of our private road proclaimed: No Parking. No Camping. No Picnicking. If Donny spotted them there would be trouble. He would banish them, even the disabled old granny, from the precincts of the Water Board. But not I. With my non-Scottish accent, and what Bob called my wishy-washy liberal guilt feelings about our privileged access to this glorious landscape, I was in no position to keep trespassing natives at bay. Let Donny deal with them if he must. I would get on with my jam making.

The bubbling fruit gave up its ruby juice, and bright pink foam frothed on the surface as it boiled; the small house filled with fruity fragrance, and the four pots of jam that resulted from my labors were sealed and ranged on the shelf to be carried back to New York at summer's end, to wreak their magic on our breakfast toast for the first few months of the fall.

In the late afternoon we all watched through the living room window as the Glaswegian cohort wended its way back through the garden, across the stableyard to where their cars were parked at the side of the hill road. A small child slept against its father's shoulder; the hampers were empty; Granny swung contentedly along between her crutches; and one of the young men carried at least five fine brown trout hooked together in a flagrantly unconcealed bunch. Their day of illicit pleasure had been undiscovered and unimpeded by the hand of authority.

At the end of our first August in the glen, we placed an advertisement in *The Scotsman* for tenants to occupy the house as caretakers, for a nominal rent, from mid-September until mid-June. We stirred up an odd lot of strange folk leading shadowy lives at the edge of what is considered normal society, the sense of isolation and privacy evoked by our advertisement drawing them out of murky areas where they contrived to survive.

Our first applicant was a slender blonde woman with an educated English accent, in her mid-thirties, her clothes showing taste and money; after a most cursory look around the house, she said it would suit her very well—she would take it. Would she live here all alone? we inquired, mentioning the isolation of the place. No, she would have her nine-year-old son with her. Her husband, she said, was . . . um . . . away . . .

away for a while—would be back in about fourteen months; she hadn't been well, needed some peace and quiet. "*I must have some rest,*" she said, more to herself than us, fists tight on her Liberty Cotton lap.

Had she thought about the problem of school for the boy? Oh, there was sure to be a decent private school in the neighborhood. The neighbors tell us they are often snowbound in the glen in winter, we told her. She stood up, looked out of the window at the loch, turned to face us; there were dark shadows under her eyes. "It will be *alright*—really it will— I *must* have this place. I'll pay any rent you like; money's no problem."

Some extremity of her situation gave a sense of the furtive, of something dark and desperate for a place to hide away. We felt we were being heartless when we said that we were really looking for someone to take care of the place, maintain the grounds, keep up repairs. Something seemed to cave in within her, and she looked suddenly haggard, years older. She left, her snakeskin shoes and bag, and the sleekness of her maroon Jaguar, somehow diminishing her person.

We felt awful as we closed the gate and walked back across the stableyard, as if we had driven a waif out into a snowstorm. "Do you think perhaps her husband is doing fourteen months in jail?" I asked Harl.

"That's *just* what I was thinking," he said.

Our next prospective tenant was an intense young American from San Diego in blue jeans and western boots, curly-haired and attractive. He was studying to be a wood carver, he said, and had discovered that the finest wood carver in the world, Alexander Shillinglaw, lived right here in our own village of Auchterbraehead. He had read about him in a book on wood carving, and had immediately determined to make his way to Scotland and learn the craft from him. With his wife he had arrived in the village a month ago; they were staying in a bed-and-breakfast place until they could find a permanent place to rent.

Had he already started to work with the wood carver? we asked. Well . . . there was a slight problem. . . . The thing was that he had come to Scotland without making prior arrangements; that is, he hadn't thought to write first to old Shillinglaw to ask if he would take him on as an apprentice. Intensity flashed in his dark eyes as he tried to convey to us his sense of his own dedication. "You see, once I made the decision that I would train under *him* and no one else, there was no stopping me; I had to get moving right away. My wife and I threw up our jobs, sold our car and furniture, bought our plane tickets, and came right over."

His story was conveying to us more of a sense of romantic imbecility than a serious pursuit of his craft. "We arrived at Gleneagles train station, hitched a ride into the village—they don't even have taxis here—this really is the boondocks—no kidding. I asked at the postoffice which was Mr. Shillinglaw's place (he lives right on the High Street), and I went and knocked on his front door, and told him I was here to learn the craft from the finest wood carver in the world!

"Trouble is," he continued, "this book I'd read was quite old, and it turns out that Mr. Shillinglaw's seventy-five years old, and he has some illness and he doesn't take students. Matter of fact, his wife didn't even want to let me into the house to just visit with him. I had to do some pretty fast talking; told her I'd come all this way from the U.S. expressly to see him—finally talked her round. Then, when I got to him at last, he said *no way*; he was too ill to take me on. But I wore his resistance down," the young man told us complacently. "Went to see him every day. Told him how I'd sold everything just for the opportunity to work under him; told him he owed it to posterity to hand on what he'd learned. At last he's agreed to let me come in and work with him two mornings a week."

How long did he plan to stay in Scotland? we inquired. Oh, well, they'd only granted him a three-month visa when he got into Heathrow Airport, but he'd get around that; we needn't worry on that score. But if they refused to renew it, wouldn't he have to leave the country? And then our house would stand empty. His confidence knew no bounds. He assured us he would fix things up with Immigration. Did he know he would need to have a work permit in order to stay? No kidding! Well, he'd fix it up. . . .

He had bulldozed the ill old wood carver into taking him on, but we had good health and comparative youthfulness to withstand his onslaught.

"He's like the youngest son in the fairy tale," I remarked after we had persuaded him to leave, "the one who takes the most direct path to the cave where the magic key is hidden, fearless of dragons and wizards and reluctant landlords who stand in his way."

"Except," Harl said, "in the fairy tale the youngest son generally isn't half-witted."

The third applicant turned up at about nine-thirty one night, six hours late for the appointment we had set up on the telephone. He wore a slouch hat and long, dark raincoat that he never removed, though it was a mild evening. His shoulders were hunched, he kept his hands in his pockets, and his glance slid about, taking in everything; he examined the landscape from every window. "The neighbors," he wanted to know, "are they nosey? Dropping in like—you know—to borrow a screwdriver or have a cup of tea?" His accent sounded Geordie to us—Northumberland.

There were no nearby neighbors, we told him, though the waterman came up twice each day to inspect the loch and pumphouse. He was tense, with sudden movements and questions, his demeanor shifty and evasive. Yes, the place would suit him fine. He would take it, sign the lease on the spot if we liked. He could let us have the year's rent in advance, in cash if we wanted.

I wondered if he would whip a revolver out of his raincoat pocket and fell us on the spot if we turned down his offer. Would he be planning to live here on his own? I asked. Well . . . he wouldn't actually be *staying* here . . . like . . . he wanted it for his wife and her sister. He would have to be out of the country for a while—abroad, he added vaguely, though naturally he would be visiting them from time to time when he could manage it.

We shepherded him to the front door, said we would let him know; there were several other people still wanting to view the house. He was belligerent: Couldn't we just let them know . . . like . . . that it was rented? Well, we really wanted someone who would look after the place: a caretaker. His face darkened; he reached into his coat pocket and drew out a wad of money secured with a rubber band, gesturing threateningly with it as though it were a weapon. "Look, you can have the cash right now. Just say how much you want." He licked his finger and made ready to start counting off the notes. "I'll take it for ten months and clear out in June—how much now?" If he would just leave his phone number, we murmured and demurred, we would get in touch. He wasn't sure where he'd be, he would phone us. He was in a fury; he pulled his coat collar up, muttered a surly goodnight, and the dusk swallowed him up.

We heard the stableyard gate slam and a car engine recede, and we closed the front door, Harl amused at the way I locked and bolted and latched. A character from one of those grainy old black and white movies of the nineteen-thirties, *films noirs*, come stumbling into our *pastorale*, on the run from who knew what form of vengeance. He called from a public phone a few days later, and when we told him the place had been let, he hung up without a word.

We turned down several more dubious applicants, but when three red-cheeked buxom Scottish girls turned up in a mini-Minor to view the house, looking ordinary and sturdy, we felt we could safely entrust the place to them over the winter. They were farm accountants, employed by an organization that sends qualified accountants to outlying farms to do the bookkeeping.

"Farming has become a complicated business these days," Bob explained later, "with incomprehensible tax laws and subsidies and allowable and nonallowable deductions, with new regulations thought up by ill-disposed civil servants arriving every morning in the post to disturb the bucolic torpor in which farmers prefer to wallow. It's got way beyond the simple arithmetic we kulaks needed to master to know if our profit was more than our losses, or vice versa. If you have a farm of a decent acreage, it's like running a small corporation.

"These girls," he told us, "generally come from farming families and are quite at home with the tallying of loads of hay, gallons of milk, acres of barley, and head of cattle. *And* there's an ulterior motive in their choice of profession. Say, for example, they come every so often to do the books of Farmer Jones. They look about them and they see that his beasts are sleek and well-tended; his fields are bursting with barley, potatoes, turnips, and kale; his steading is in good repair, and the farmhouse well furnished. They tot up the wee red columns and the wee black columns in his books, and they see that the profits are high and the farm is prospering. *Then*, they look about to see if Farmer Jones has an eligible son who will inherit the farm. And before too long, the Agency is advertising for another lass, because Farmer Jones has acquired a new daughter-in-law. The attrition rate is high in this field. But you can count on them being reliable girls and good housekeepers, from sound Scottish yeoman stock."

And so they turned out to be. It was evening the first time that they came to view the house, and as we left each room I noticed that one of them would automatically turn off the light. Scottish frugality has always been the butt of humor—both literary and vaudeville—but over the years we began to comprehend how the habit of frugality, ingrained in a society, has its own right-mindedness: a probity that has to do with reverence for what is given by nature for our use and our survival, and an acknowledgment of the finiteness of things. In the cold northern Scottish awareness, there is no vision of cornucopias of unending plenty; everything is prudently husbanded, valued, eked out. There is virtue in thrift, wickedness in waste—a lesson we are only just now learning as we are warned of scarcities to come, but one that every Scottish child takes in with the first spoonful of oatmeal porridge.

In his *History of Scotland*, J. D. Mackie, writing about the prosperity and economic growth of eighteenth-century Scotland, observes: "It has been said that, in a reaction against the religious furies of the seventeenth century, Scotland developed a secular spirit, turned to money-making, and according to some, magnified the virtues of thrift, abstinence, and hard work into a kind of piety expressed in the fact that copies of *The Shorter Catechism* issued to children bore the multiplication tables on the back." He goes on, though, to defend his countrymen: "To state the matter so is to exaggerate. Capitalism existed before Calvinism. . . . What is true is that the regard for truth and honesty inculcated by the discipline of the Kirk was a good foundation for success in business, and that Scottish people [were] trained to the 'economic' virtues in a long struggle against a hard environment."

And indeed they use everything up, make meals out of leftovers. Overflowing garbage cans are not a sight one comes across in Scottish towns; things are scraped bare and clean before they are disposed of. We learned, when we went marketing, to remember to bring along shopping bags, for there was no prodigal donation of the stout brown paper bags Americans take for granted; the department stores charged the equivalent of a nickel for a shopping bag. As the summers went by, though, we could not help noticing how the ubiquity of American packaging, with its extravagant superfluity, was the beginning of a rash of litter over town and countryside: an unknown phenomenon in the early years.

The girls' turning off the lights of our house as we left each room was a good indication of the sort of tenants they would make. And in fact, when we returned to Glenauchen the following summer, we found the place as clean and well maintained as we had left it, just as Bob had predicted. And, as he had warned us, the very quality that made them such excellent tenants deprived us of their tenancy, for they all left: two of them to marry farmers' sons, and one to achieve fame as "Miss Scots Lamb" in a rural beauty contest that led to a modeling job.

After the departure of the three lasses, we advertised for tenants at a university in a county town about twenty miles distant from the glen, for, as Harl maintains, academics are the truly privileged class of our times—being accorded the leisure and authority once reserved solely for the aristocracy; only the financial rewards do not measure up to the exemption from the hurly-burly of life that the luxury of their free time grants them. We hoped to find some tweedy don with a light teaching load who would prefer to contemplate eternal truths in a remote, low-rental, bucolic setting.

We ended up with a couple of graduate students. The young woman, plump, intelligent, was doing her Ph.D. in history, and appeared competent and housewifely. To our delight, she was called Miss Waterman. "This house was originally known as the Waterman's House," we told her, and we all felt it had been ordained that she should become its tenant. The young man who was her consort was a withdrawn fellow with a sickly pallor, his shoulder-length hair and wispy mandarin beard contributing to a general fuzziness of outline that contrasted oddly with the healthy concreteness of Miss Waterman. His field was sociology.

Bob disapproves of sociologists. "I even wonder if it's proper to harbor one of them under the roof of Glenauchen Cottage," he said, but he was so taken with the wholesomeness of the girl, who was the moving force of the couple, that he felt it outweighed the dubiousness of the young man's calling. "Come now, Bob," Helen chided him, "there's far worse things he could be doing—like writing pornography or plotting more effective weapons of nuclear destruction."

We were a little worried that the glen folk might be shocked or offended by our renting the place to an unmarried couple. "What if Donny finds out they're living in sin?" I said to the Hunters.

"Och, don't vex yourselves," Bob told us. "There's no need to say anything; let them just assume that they're wed. There's more depraved goings-on in a glen like this than a couple of staid academics sharing their bed and breakfast without a parson's blessing."

It was true; as the years went by and we became recognized and accepted inhabitants of the glen, stories sifted down to us through gossip and innuendo, tales of rage and passion enacted in these remote hills: adulterous relationships and threats of murder and revenge; lust and intrigue; brides left waiting in the church and babes born out of wedlock; malicious codicils to wills like laughter cackling from graves; lowered voices of respectability retailing scandals and the blots and stains of unbridled appetites. But this all took place behind an observance of respect for the received conventions; the very secrecy, the darkness, the fact that these stories were told in whispers, hints, asides, were all an acknowledgment of the moral order that ruled behavior. Those who misconducted themselves were aware that they violated its formidable authority.

So our young tenants, by living openly in sin, without shame

or secrecy, would be making a mockery of a code fundamental to the social order, and the glen folk would, with justi-
fication, be horrified; if they at least pretended to be married,
there would be no offense or insult. Hypocrisy has its place in
the ordering of a small, tight, hill-bound community—it is an
exaction of tribute to the deep-held beliefs of the others; in
cities it is possible to get by without it. We always referred
to our tenants as the Watermans, and hoped for the best.

If the Celestial Messenger had selected them for us, there
could not have been more suitable tenants. They paid the rent
each month to the Hunters, their check from a joint bank
account indicating they were wed at least in the eye of Mam-
mon. Their first October there, Mrs. Cameron telephoned Bob
from Wester Glenauchen Farm, ostensibly to ask if he could
sell her some hay. "But the truth was," Bob wrote to us, "that
it wasn't really hay she was after. Very subtle—very canny—
she turned the conversation to the tenants up at the loch. A
nice wee couple, she said they were, very quiet; they looked
to be taking good care of Glenauchen Cottage 'Mr. and Mrs.
what-was-their-name-now?' she asked in the most oblique manner, trying without actually asking to find out if they are
married. I, as adept as she at that mode of cunning circumven-
tion, said that their names were Gladys and Walter, and suc-
ceeded in talking of, about, and around the young lovers up at
the loch, without either lying *or* affirming in any way her suspicion that they are not married."

The Watermans loved Glenauchen Cottage as much as we
did; they tended it as if it were their own and planted an excellent kitchen garden, urging us to eat whatever ripened
during the summer, which they would spend with her family in
the Midlands. Every year when I returned, they would have
departed a couple of hours before my arrival; we rarely managed to meet. There were always vases filled with wild flowers,
a tea tray set out on the kitchen table with a plate of something
home-baked, and jars of homemade jam left for us in the cupboard. The jam, wild raspberry and bramble, told of rambles
through the waning days of autumn to strip the hedgerows and
copses of their jewel-like fruits, and jam kettles bubbling in the
coziness of Glenauchen's kitchen while early dusk thickened

over the loch. We tasted the autumn jam, and wondered if we would ever know the season in the glen.

All our tenants' dealings over the winter would be with the Hunters, who would drive out to the glen occasionally on weekends to check how things were getting along, and, when necessary, to engage a plumber or stonemason or carpenter for repairs. It was on one of these visits that they discovered what Bob called an illegal tenant: "a lapdog no bigger than a rat, of a Mexican hairless variety and malevolent disposition," he wrote, "that yaps hysterically and snaps viciously at one's ankles. For some reason known only to themselves, they have concealed the presence of this wee repulsive beast, chloroforming it, perhaps, or hiding it in the stable loft when they knew we would visit. But, arriving unannounced on Sunday, we found it curled up like a sleeping rodent on Mr. Waterman's lap, from where it sprang to the floor and attempted to bury its fangs in the fleshy part of my leg."

"Miss Waterman," Helen wrote, "is dressed always, when we visit, in long caftans or voluminous ankle-length dirndles. We wonder if this is so that he can hide behind her skirts. She serves a nice tea, which we have all huddled around one-eighth of the table, because seven-eighths of the table is permanently covered with a football game. Bob thinks that Mr. Waterman must be doing a Ph.D. in soccer. The sexual arrangements of the two of them, which so intrigue the glen folk, seem to us to be the least interesting aspect of their general eccentricity."

"Perhaps a place like Glenauchen Cottage naturally attracts queer folk," I replied. "For all we know, people might find us odd. And in all likelihood it took eccentrics to find such an un-likely place for us to buy."

CHAPTER

10

Cottages, Castles, and Old Drove Roads

On a warm afternoon of our second summer in the glen, the children were off somewhere, and Harl and I somnolent in the living room after a ten-mile hike ending in a pub lunch that had included several foaming tankards of ale. We were aroused by banging on the front door. Harl went down, spoke a few minutes with the caller, footsteps resounded on the flagstones and receded, and he returned looking bemused.

"Who was that?"

"Well, it was a nice-looking man, in his sixties, I'd say. Asked if we'd mind if he and his wife picnicked on the bank of the loch. Then, before I could answer, he said, 'You see, this is a sentimental journey; I was born in this house. My grandfather was the original waterman.'"

"Did you ask them in?"

"Sure. They want to have a picnic tea while the sun's out; I asked them to come in and have a drink with us later in the afternoon."

"What's their name?"

"Monroe."

"Monroe's Park. Mrs. Cameron always refers to the meadow at the back of the house as Monroe's Park."

Through the window I watched them walking along the bank: a tall, well-built man with white hair, dressed in tweeds, carrying a picnic basket; his wife beside him small and trim in a flowered print dress and cardigan, her hair set in tight waves and curls. It was an afternoon of sunshine and wind, with white clouds racing across the blue to mound up over the crest of Dalrioch.

Round about five-thirty they knocked on our door. We led them upstairs to the living room, feeling like interlopers in their house. Mrs. Monroe was English; she said she would take a small sherry. He took whiskey, and seemed as willing to satisfy our desire to know about the past as we were eager to ask questions. He was an engineer, lived in England, and took his summer holiday in Scotland, where his sister still lived. His grandfather, George Monroe, had been the first waterman to occupy the house when it was built in 1870. His father had been born and raised in Glenauchen Cottage, and became the second waterman after the old man's retirement. By the time he and his sister were born, the grandfather had died, but the grandmother still lived on with them.

"There were no motorcars in those days," he said, "but there were two horses in the stable out there, and a trap in the carriage house, where you keep your car. And my mother, and my grandmother before her, always kept a cow in the byre; the cow was always called Bessie. Mother would do the milking twice a day; she churned her own butter and made her own cream. I'm always telling the wife about Bessie's cream—thick and yellow it was.

"We kept a boat, a heavy wooden rowboat. You see, my father would cut the hay that grew in a field at the far end of the loch—it's all nettles and bracken now, I notice; by hand he'd cut it, using a scythe. When I was a lad I liked to watch him—so powerful he looked as he swung the scythe easily before him, and the tall grass falling and lying about his feet as he went forward. When it was dry enough he would tie it into bales, and I would go out with him, rowing across the loch, and we'd pile the boat high with the hay and row it back to the house, and stow it up in the wee hayloft over the stable for winter feed. Sticks for the fire, too, we'd gather and load up into the boat.

"Over there"—he pointed out of the window—"on the far right bank of the loch there used to be a small bonny wood where we'd get our kindling. But about twenty or twenty-five years ago (Ella Cameron would know the exact date) there was a terrible storm, and a hurricane tore through the glen wreaking destruction. The wee minister down at Glenauchen Kirk declared it was brought on by the sinful ways of the congregation"—his eyes twinkled as he said this—"and the woods out there were flattened like ninepins. The Camerons also lost most of their woods in that storm, and so did Jessie MacFadyen over at Glencorrie House. You can still see some of the tree stumps on the slopes. That field is part of the Cameron's farm now, but in those days we were entitled to use it to graze Bessie and the horses."

"Is that Monroe's Park?"

"Aye, that's what it was called."

"We wondered how it had got its name. . . . And did you go to school at the little schoolhouse?" I asked.

"I sairtainly did." His years of living among the English had not touched the burr and lilt of his Scottish accent. "I started there at the age of four and was reading fluently by the time I was five. *The Pilgrim's Progress* was one of the first books I ever read, just because it was the book generally to be found in the homes of literate yet uneducated folk . . . that and the Bible, of course. I remember, when I first went there, I was such a wee fellow that my legs would not carry me all the way to the school, and my father would have to take me over the hill on his shoulders and set me down to walk the last few yards on my own feet, so that my school-fellows should not know I had been carried. And later on, my sister Florrie came along too, and I had to be in charge of her because I am four years older.

"Ella Cameron and Miss Kirstie Aird and Jessie MacFadyen and Alistair Kirkland, who farms up at Rumbling Bridge—we were all at the school at the same time, though Alistair was much younger than I, and the girls much older. There was only one teacher, and he taught us all, from the smallest bairns to muckle great boys already in their teens, with braw muscles from working on their fathers' farms. Our teacher was the dominie who taught there so long, it was believed he was a fixture, like the school bell or the blackboard. That dominie, he was a right terror; I often tell the wife about him. He beat the three R's into us with a relentless strap. We children were always so feared of bruised or bleeding knuckes that we learned our lessons well and never shirked our homework. He would use the tawse on us—a leather strap—if we were stupid or bored; he must have featured in the nightmares of many a bairn who grew up in the glen. He had seven children of his own, and showed them no more pity than the rest of us.

"One of his daughters, a spirited lass—Bertha, her name was—just could not thole his brutality and his cruelty. Well, one day she defied him, and he ordered her up to his desk to be chastised. And Bertha refused point-blank to move from her seat. She sat there, as steady as a rock, and as grim in her defiance. And all we children were frozen with terror to see someone go against the will of this formidable dominie. He turned white, and fell into a terrible wrath and went after her, and she slipped out of her seat and darted beyond his reach. Round and round the schoolroom he chased her, brandishing the tawse, till finally he cornered her and caught hold of her. She was like a wild, spitting cat, and in her rage and her helplessness she snarled at him, "I wish you would fa' dead." And in that very moment he was stricken with a heart attack, and fell to the floor. A day later he was dead. We children never forgot being witness to that terrible scene."

In his *History of Scotland*, Professor J. D. Mackie, discussing education in Victorian Scotland, writes: ". . . The *Dominie* was a commanding figure to whom Scotland owes much. It is true that he gave most of his attention, sometimes in unpaid coaching, to the 'lad o' pairts' who went to the University at a very early age, not only well-grounded in the essentials of character, and of learning, but also aware that success came from industry and application." It was evident that our Mr. Monroe, the son of the reservoir keeper at Glenauchen Loch, must have been considered a "lad o' pairts" by the dominie at the one-room schoolhouse beside the burn.

"After the dominie died," Mr. Monroe went on, "they in-

stalled Mrs. Abernethy as the schoolmistress; she was just a
young gairl of seventeen or eighteen fresh out of teacher's
training college. Very bonny she was, and couthie, and we
children all liked her and heeded what we were told just as well
as we had done under the dominie's reign of terror. She was
schoolmistress here in the glen for over forty years; she and
Mr. Abernethy never had any children of their own. When
she retired—it was just a few years ago—they shut the little
schoolhouse down; it was featured on the television, I remember. And now the glen children are picked up in a bus
and driven to the school in the village, and a family lives in
the schoolhouse, just as a family lives in the Manse. Things
change. . . . There's more efficiency, I'll agree, but there's
loss, loss. . . ."

His wife sat quietly by, listening to stories she had likely
heard many times, indulging him, pleased that he had an audience eager for his recollections. Like a peddler who had wandered into an isolated community, he laid out his wares for us,
and as each brooch or ribbon came out of his tray we gratified
him with our expressions of wonder and delight, his companion prompting him from time to time—reminding him to
display the watered silk, the painted fan, the silver buckle.
"Tell them about Miss Jane Honeyman, Sandy, how she haunts
the glen; tell them about Miss Kirstie Aird on her white
horse; about that winter when you were snowed in for two
weeks."

Mr. Monroe was pleased to have found a repository for the
reminiscences that connected him so powerfully to his own
history. For us, it was as though having been uprooted generations ago, we had a need to graft ourselves onto roots that had
long gripped the earth. Living in old houses, learning their
history, and keeping it alive is a way of doing this; we had
done it in New York and were doing it here in the glen.
"What's wrong with new houses is that they haven't got a
soul—no ghosts," Bob says. So we kept open house, as it were,
for the old ghosts who disappear only when they are no longer
remembered.

*　*　*

The Monroes fell into the custom of visiting us at Glen-auchen every summer, filling in the past for us so that we need not feel we occupied an unknown landscape. As we had no history there, he made us a gift of his own; we became trustees of a past that his own son, a gifted musician dedicated to his career, had no interest in.

Mr. Monroe had gone on from the glen schoolhouse to win a scholarship to the distinguished Geddes Academy, and from there to the university. "Och, Sandy Monroe," Mrs. Cameron told us, "I mind, when he was a wee lad, and all the years he was growing up, he would go walking past here, up the hill road and past the steading, not seeing what was before him nor what was under his foot, for he had his nose buried always between the pages of a book."

The Monroes usually stopped for a visit at Wester Glen-auchen Farm on the way up to us at the loch. "Aye," Miss Kirstie Aird would agree, "Sandy was always one for the books. I prefaired horses myself—that's why *he* always took all the prizes. A clever lad, and very studious. And his sister, Florrie, as well; there was another clever one."

We came to know Florrie Monroe also. She, too, had gone to the university, and she had become a mathematics teacher, but had been stricken by poliomyelitis as a young woman and left severely handicapped, immobilized almost, needing constant care, which was provided by a woman companion who had been with her for many years. Sometimes the Monroes would bring Florrie with them for tea, which we would have downstairs, in the kitchen, as she moved with difficulty on crutches. Her body had become thick and heavy through immobility, but her face and eyes, though marked by suffering, were lively with interest and humor and intelligence. She hadn't been back in the house for a quarter of a century, and she took in with avidity all the details so dense with rich association for her.

"Over there, in that wee pantry where you've got the cooker, that was mother's buttery—d'you recall, Sandy? Mother kept all the pans of milk there, and the churn. D'you mind how that butter tasted, Sandy, on slices of new, warm bread? Sandy and I, when we were bairns, would climb that slope where the heather grows on the near bank of the loch, and in amongst the heather the blaeberries grew thick. Do they still grow up there? I wonder. We would gather a little pailful and our mother would serve them with oatmeal porridge and cream. . . ." Her reminiscing seemed to release, from the helpless body of the elderly woman, a girl who moved lightly along the green verge of the loch. "And in July, we always knew where to search for the earliest bluebells; they grew in masses on the slopes of Dalrioch."

"Those dressing rooms," we asked the Monroes, "why would a reservoir keeper's cottage have something so grand as dressing rooms?"

Mr. Monroe and his sister both laughed. "They were nae dressing rooms, my dear," Florrie said. "They were bedrooms for humble folk. My old granny and I *shared* the downstairs one, while Sandy slept in the one upstairs next door to our parents' bedroom. We shared one large bed, Granny and I did, for there was not room for more than one. The downstairs room that you use now for a bedroom was our sitting room, our front parlor. We only used it when we had company. Most of our living went on right here, in the kitchen; this was the one room that was always warm. We had a muckle black coal stove right here where the chimney is."

"But what about the big sitting room upstairs?" we asked.

"That," said Mr. Monroe, "was the *Board Room*, where the gentleman of the Water Board held their monthly meeting. We were not allowed to use that room *ever*. Mother used to go in there to dust, and once a month the fire would be lit there to warm the respectable persons of the Board members.

We were shocked.

"That's how it was in those days. They were very imposing, those gentlemen, with their beards and paunches and gold watch-chains. The room was furnished with a Turkey rug and a long table of shiny mahogany, and leather chairs with brass studs; and on the walls there were photographs of the members of the Water Board, all looking very self-important."

"But Sandy and I used to sneak up there when the weather wasn't too cold," Florrie said, "and we would do our homework at the table, taking care not to scratch it or overturn the ink bottle, for there was so much family life going on in the kitchen that it was not easy to concentrate on our lessons."

"With Granny always settled in front of the fire in a great creaking basket-chair—eh, Florrie?—knitting jerseys or reading the Bible. . . . The boardroom was ell-shaped in those days; it was only after the Second World War, I believe, that the narrow part of the room was divided off to make a bathroom for Mr. Davison, who was the waterman here after my father died. We never had the advantages of indoor plumbing in our day."

"How did you manage with no bathroom?"

"Well, there was the outside toilet, that's still there, I notice, at the side of the house. And we had basins and jugs of hot water in our rooms. And when we needed to have a bath, Mother would get a fire roaring in the stove, boil up kettles of water, and we would bathe, right here, in a tin bathtub in front of the fire."

We talked with the Monroes about the deep and abiding respect that the Scots have for education. Children of the poor who achieve higher education in Scotland are held in much esteem by all classes of society, and Bob holds that this reverence accorded to learning cuts across social and economic distinctions, and is one of the reasons why the class system has less of a grip on the Scots than it does on the English; he maintains that the Scottish working-class person is tougher, has more independence of spirit, and kowtows far less to the master than does the Sassenach across the border (Sassenach being the old Gaelic, somewhat slighting term for the English, or Saxon, neighbors).

"There is a wee, whitewashed cottage," Mr. Monroe told us, "standing near the glen road, beside the burn just past Miss Kirstie Aird's farm, with a fine garden full of vegetables— you know which one I'm refairing to? Well, an old retired shepherd lives there with his wife; for many years he was head shepherd on one of the great estates up in the northern part of the county. Now, their son (who was a fellow-student of mine at Geddes Academy) is vice-chancellor at a very famous

Scottish university. So you see, Scotland is a bit like America, because with an education you can go as far as your ability will take you."

After a visit one summer, we were standing in the hall with the Monroes, helping them on with raincoats, taking leave of one another; the door to the downstairs bedroom used by the children stood open, revealing sleeping bags on the floor among a confusion of boots, books, sweaters, and general evidence of adolescent disorder. From the hall where he stood buttoning his raincoat, Mr. Monroe looked into the room, seeing something other than the marks of youthful life carelessly abounding.

"The Room," he said. "This was always called 'The Room.'" He invested the words with solemnity as if he were saying "The Throne Room" or "The Sacristy."

"*The Room*—we children seldom ventured in there. It was filled with shiny furniture and cut-glass vases and china ornaments, everything polished and dusted and immaculate. A china cabinet stood over there in the corner with our mother's best cups and saucers in it. It was used only on very special occasions, like when the minister came to tea. And I recall some very distinguished company here, one afternoon a long, long time ago. Sitting in there, there was . . . let me see now. . . . There was Lord Haldane, and J. B. S. Haldane, and Sir Edmund Gosse."

"Here, in that room! What were they doing at Glenauchen?" we asked.

He was gratified that we were impressed. "Well, you see, my grandmother and old Lady Haldane, Lord Haldane's mother, both celebrated their hundredth birthday on the same day. So they made a visit, coming over from the big house on their estate outside the village, to congratulate our granny on having lived a full century. Sir Edmund Gosse, who happened to be a guest staying with them that weekend, accompanied them on the outing. And there they all sat in The Room, with Florrie and me hanging back shyly; my mother served tea out of her best tea set, and they were charming and gracious, and questioned me when they learned I was a student at Geddes, asking me what I intended to be when I grew up. My grandmother died the following year, and so, I think, did Lady Haldane."

"Did it never occur to you," we asked him one year, "to buy Glenauchen Cottage for yourself when the Water Board put it on the market?"

"Aye, it did. The thought occupied my mind for a time. . . . I talked it over with the wife, and we concluded that since our son's interest is all in his musical career (he spends more time in Europe than in Britain) there would be no point in having this place if he never could come here. So we thought better of it."

"Well, if we ever decide to sell Glenauchen, we'll offer it to you first, just in case," Harl told him.

"Though I can't imagine that anything could induce us to give it up," I added.

"I like to think of it belonging to you," Mr. Monroe said. "I told the wife that you folk appreciate the spirit of the place, and that gives me a good deal of satisfaction."

One of our favorite hikes, over the years, was to Castle Gloom and the village of Douleur; it became a custom, ritualized by the high tea Tottie always set up for us on our return.

When I was a child in southern Africa, our family would take our summer vacation in the same place every year: a rented cottage on a sparsely inhabited cove on the coast of the Indian Ocean. The pleasure most vividly recalled—over and above the isolation of the white sandy beach, the rocky, jagged coastline, the banana palms, the fields of sugarcane and pineapple, and the avocado groves flourishing above the sand dunes—was the delight of the return each season to a loved and familiar landscape: the unyielding permanence of a particular flat rock where one loved to lie and read, the recognition of the briny scent of the frond-filled rock pools, the remembered sound of the slough and sigh of the waves just beyond the garden's paw-paw trees and hibiscus hedge when one lay in bed at night. There is comfort and reassurance in rediscovery, in finding things fixed in reality as they are in memory; it gives a sense—or illusion—of continuity.

Our return to Glenauchen each year held the same fixed-rooted pleasure. "When are we going to do the Douleur hike?" we would ask each other. "When shall we arrange the walk to Auchterbraehead—to Ballycoultry?" As we discussed them, we savored the pleasures these hikes offered.

For the hike to Douleur, we would arrange to leave our car at the MacIvers' in order to make the round trip a manageable distance by cutting off the four miles each way from our loch to theirs; from their place, through the hills to the village of Douleur and back, gave us a ten-mile walk with time to dally and explore. To reach the trail, which was the remains of an old drove road, we would have to skirt the MacIvers' loch, lingering to admire the pair of swans that year after year made their summer home there, raising a small fleet of cygnets and sending them out into the world, but themselves returning each spring to lay their eggs. They occupied the loch like haughty aristocrats; aware of their white-plumed grace and beauty, they deigned to eat the food Tottie brought up to the loch for them every day. For years they had lived on Glenauchen Loch, she told us, when old Mr. Davison, who was the last waterman, lived there; but after he died and the house stood empty, they moved the royal quarters to her loch. The female maintained her imperious air even when she carried her squeaking, fluffy, golden-brown brood on her back, crossing the water like a stately galleon under a full load.

Beyond the loch we would pick up the trail that wound through the hills, where, apart from the rare hiker, we would encounter no one but the sheep. The quiet was stirred only by the sound of lambs, bird-song, and the water that broke out of the ground and tumbled in slender cataracts downhill to join the burn that flowed through the glen, disappearing underground in some places and leaving the ground boggy and oozy for our boots to squelch through. Wild flowers abounded, bees were industrious among them, and in hot weather small columns of clegs (black flies) would escort us, buzzing above our heads, impervious to the switches we made of bracken to shoo them off. Stone walls marked farm boundaries we would cross by climbing over wooden stiles; Scotland, unlike England, has no law of trespass, and one may walk where one chooses so long as gates are closed behind one and no damage is done to land or livestock.

The trail started to climb the last few miles, growing steadily steeper, so that we toiled up in silence till we reached the summit; there, spread out before us, lay the beautiful vale of Douleur: a small stone village clustered in the shallow saucer of the foothills; a church spire pointing heavenward; a surrounding patchwork of cultivated farmland in rectangles of variegated green in early summer, turning the color of brass and copper as the season ripened, then straw-colored in the thinning autumn light after the harvest was taken in, with random patches of purple-brown and earthen-red when the soil was turned over in regular ridged rows by the blade of the plough. The pastures stayed green even through the depths of winter, we learned from Bob, nurtured by the soft-falling rain that kept the country moist and lush. Beyond the farmland, low green hills went rolling away, diffusing into the misty plain where the River Forth gleamed, winding its way to the sea.

Clinging to the steep hillside below us, overhanging a precipitous forested gorge, was the ruin of Castle Gloom: a fifteenth-century stronghold of one of the fiercer clans, its history one of murder, pillage, and conflagration; the waters that flowed past the ruin into the chasm below were known as the Burn of Douleur and the Burn of Grief. The view that we gained over the sweep of the valley had afforded the medieval clan a measure of defense and preparedness against their enemies.

We would sink down on the grassy hilltop, struck by the view, and when we had regained a second wind we would descend the rocky incline that led to the cobbled paths and smooth-mown lawns around the castle, which is maintained by the National Trust of Scotland. Through the great portico was the courtyard where the medieval horsemen had come clattering in, their horses' hooves striking out sparks on the cobbles, dismounting and throwing the bridles to the ostlers, who would take the foaming, sweating beasts to be watered at the carved stone drinking troughs still standing around the walls. Worn stone stairs led down to the dungeons, where no sunlight penetrated the dank dimness of cells like stone closets; there prisoners had been held, tortured, and killed, the iron rings for their chains still fixed to the walls, the place holding a lurid fascination, particularly for the children.

Inside the castle we would wander about stone chambers with massive fireplaces, around whose blaze the communal life had been conducted: the heave and commotion of cooking and feasting, plotting and loving and dying; the welter of masters, servants, animals, and children; the smell and smoke and grease as the carcasses of whole sheep and oxen were seared, rotated in the flames by hot-cheeked, fatigued turn-spits. Only rush matting and animal skins came between the castle's inhabitants and the chill of stone paving and walls; perpendicular openings in the thick stone of the walls let the light in and the reek out; arrow slits in the turrets protected the sentry yet allowed him to let fly at the intruder. So chilly were those vast chambers on a hot summer day that the cold there in winter was unimaginable to us.

On each level, a tiny room let off from the main chamber, and here was the privy: a stone seat built into the wall, with a hole in the middle that dropped down all the way to the dungeons where the hapless prisoners lay chained; the children were fascinated by this primitive form of household plumbing, their sympathies wholeheartedly with the poor wretches whose tribulations must have been intolerably compounded by the effluence dropping down on them from their tormentors above. Medieval hygiene was so rudimentary that periodically the residents would have to vacate their castles for a season, the clan chief and his kin and cohorts moving to another castle until time and the sweep of seasons rendered their own habit-able again.

The upper floors of the castle were in ruins, and there was exhilaration in emerging from the stairs into one of the great, time-wrecked chambers to find sky and clouds for a ceiling, the sunshine throwing the fractured stone remains of walls, ramparts, and turrets in black shadows across the light-flooded floors, casting a tessellated pattern where the sun spilled over what was left of the crow-step gables around the tower. The tower leading to the ramparts was gained by mounting a narrow stone turnpike stairway; its granite treads had been spooned into shallow cavities by five centuries of footsteps ascending, spiraling dizzily round and round to emerge at last on the ramparts, which opened to the view of the valley spread out in front and the broad range of our hills at the back. From the height of the ramparts the village looked toy-sized, set in its checkerboard of cultivated fields, smoke wisping from cottage chimneys, the bright red of a toy tractor snail-trailing along a lane, and a miniature steamship on the river in the far distance smudging the sky with a plume of smoke—anachronisms in the tranquillity of this medieval landscape.

It required only the slightest flick of perception to picture the feudal villagers in their leather jerkins carting supplies up the cruel incline to the castle, beating the animals as they toiled pulling the loaded wagons, skidding as rocks and stones slithered downhill; or to hear the ring of the horses' hooves in the courtyard way below, the sentries patrolling the ramparts armed with bow and arrow, while in the green, flower-bordered quilt of the garden laid out on the terrace—where we could now see the caretaker's wife's laundry blowing dry on a line stretched out beside beds of cabbages and roses—high-breasted ladies in wimpled headdresses must have strolled among the herbs and flowers or sat lost in a dream with the quiet splendor of this view in their eyes, their needlework forgotten on their laps, servants scurrying about cursing, swabbing, skinning, peeling, slaughtering, grinding, roasting, boiling, scrubbing, for their masters.

Depending on the weather or our mood, we would make the descent to the village either by the road the medieval villagers had used or else by the paths and railed footbridges overhanging the gorge, which the National Trust maintained for the more venturesome or foolhardy to descend through the chasm that dropped from the castle terrace to the village below. Here, in a green, damp shade created by leafage of gigantic trees and thick undergrowth, the path led past a series of cataracts, waterfalls, and swirling pools, as the river hurled itself over the gorge, and the sunlight penetrated only in thin arrow shafts to dapple the leaves and water. Sliding and slithering (for the sunless paths were always muddy and slippery), clutching onto handrails, vertiginous, the din of the falling water roaring in our ears, we would gain the bottom at last; the water's boisterousness tamed into a picturesque burn forded by arching stone bridges, it ran under the High Street, and went on its way to join the headwaters of the Forth.

There was a small golf course at the foot of the gorge where the houses of the village started, and a tea shop called the Red Rooster, run by a buxom young woman who served excellent homemade soups, sandwiches, and cakes. Here we would stop for lunch, receiving always a warm welcome from her. "Well, how are things in New York?" she would ask as we came stomping into her clean place in our muddy boots after we had stopped to admire the latest rosy-cheeked baby parked in its carriage outside the kitchen door. It seemed as if there were a different baby sitting there in a state of healthy contentment each summer when we emerged from the gorge, and the little troop of toddlers and small-fry who entertained themselves on the lawn seemed to add an ambulatory recruit to their ranks every year, while the mother serenely baked and served her scones and tarts and cakes in the tea shop, which occupied an annex built on to the family's cottage.

The village of Douleur, which housed the famous Geddes Academy, was rather more sophisticated than our own, catering to the school faculty who lived there, and also to the families of well-to-do executives who moved there in order to be eligible to place their children in the school, from which entrance to a good university was a certainty. There were two "gourmet" shops that sold imported delicacies, including such exotic fare as Uncle Ben's Rice, Hellmann's Mayonnaise, and Ronzoni Lasagna among the French cheeses and tins of pâté and caviar and chestnut purée; the wine shop had a good selection of French and Italian wines, and there was a book shop, a few boutiques, and a Danish coffee shop.

In the *Statistical Account of Scotland*, Douleur was described by the minister of the parish around 1798:

The water of [the river] which runs from E. to W. nearly divides the parish. [The river] is not navigable, being a small but beautiful stream of pure limpid water . . . it gently glides over a bed of pebbles, where, finding itself at ease (as it were) after having been dashed and broken in its narrow and rugged channel, through the parishes of [Glenauchen and Muirhead], it seems to sport itself in many beautiful meanders; winding from side to side in the valley, as if loth to leave the delightful haughs of [Douleur]. . . . The air in this place is remarkably pure and healthy. . . . As a remarkable instance of this, the minister, in the whole course of his parochial visitations from house to house, did not find one single sick person in the parish; and scarcely any complaining of ailments such as coughs, shortness of breath etc.

The minister was as much taken with odd characters as we are, and described a "Literary Shepherd":

There is living at present in this parish, in a very advanced age, a man who was bred up, and lived merely as a shepherd, and who received only a common education, and yet possesses a valuable library of books, containing upward of 370 volumes, consisting of folios, quartos, octavos, duodecimos & decimoquartos. They are upon many different subjects, as divinity, history, travels, voyages, etc., besides magazines of various kinds . . . including a complete set of the Spectator, Guardian, Tatler, Rambler, etc. They are all of them his own choosing and purchasing. . . . The books are all clean and in excellent order. He was born in 1712, and lives in the same house as his brother and sister . . . all three remain unmarried.

We would do a little shopping in the village for Penguin paperbacks, stationery, stamps, olive oil, fresh-ground coffee, or wine vinegar, which were not available in our own village. Packing our purchases into a small backpack and then starting the largely uphill hike back to Glenauchen, we would arrive at the MacIvers' loch in the early evening, muscles aching, but with that curious sense of exhilaration and achievement that a long, steady hike gives rise to; we would flop down into the coziness of Tottie's parlor and prepare ourselves for the onslaught of one of her high teas.

Over the hills rather than along the glen road, the distance from Glenauchen to our village of Auchterbraehead was about ten miles; this walk we always arranged to coincide with a day that Meg Cameron worked at her part-time job at the village boutique, so that we could ride in with her and walk back; or else we would take the hill walk there, to meet her in the late afternoon for a lift home.

The trail we took, an old drove road, was well known in the district. Miss Kirstie Aird used to ride it as a girl: "A bonny canter it was, all the way over to my uncle's farm, Glenrazie; it lies on the side of the hill overlooking the village. You'd not encounter a living soul all the way there and back. Och, I've never really felt at home in my wee car the way I did on the back of a horse."

Old Mrs. Cameron recalled how, when she was a girl of nine or ten, her sister Kirstie caught the measles and she was sent away to stay at Glenrazie with her auntie. "I mind that day very well," she told us. "Kirstie was that ill, and my mother was in a swither how to send me there, and she asked me if I feared to walk there alone, over the hills. But I felt very brave, and I set off with a wee basket on my arm with my clothes in it, and some buttered baps to eat on the way. Och, but it turned out to be longer than I'd bargained for, and my wee legs began to ache, and halfway there I wearied and could not go on. I sat down on a rock and I was near to tears, for there was nothing all about but sheep and a few wild beasties. My uncle's farm was still a long way off, but I had come too far to turn back. So I ate my baps, and drank some water from the burn, and pushed myself on, and when at last I got there, my auntie just took my basket from me and asked me to go out and pick a dishful of black currants for a tart, as if it was just a wee bit stroll I'd taken."

In the sitting room at the Camerons' farm was a framed photograph of two little Victorian girls: Mrs. Cameron and her sister, Kirstie, aged seven and ten, in high-necked, tight-sleeved, full-skirted long frocks, hair tied back with big bows, their faces smooth and untouched as fresh fruit. Yet the way they would be sixty years later was already discernible. In Ella Cameron's plain-cut features, her good sense, dependability, and a certain purposefulness and stoicism of expression and demeanor were evident, so that any mother would trust her on a long, lonely walk through the hills. Miss Kirstie Aird, the younger, pretty, vivacious, fair curls escaping from the constraint of a hair-ribbon, chafing at the immobility demanded by the photographer under his black cloth—they must have had their hands full coping with this high-spirited lass. One gazed into the old photograph, reaching to sound the fathoms of the lives of the two women who grew out of those girls riveted by the camera. The pretty one never marrying. . . . Was there some disappointment? A change of heart? An inability to break the knot that tied her to her father? Or had she not wanted domesticity? Everyone still recalled vividly what a figure she struck astride her horse, fleet and light over the hills, until the years reduced her to using the small puttering car she could never get the hang of. . . . The older sister, the plain one, marrying the neighboring farmer, needing to draw deep on the source of that stoicism to deal with the husband's early dying, the raising singlehanded of children and flocks, bringing up the wild grandsons after their father went off with another woman and their mother moved away to a big city; in that purposeful stride of the old woman over her land, crook in hand, the strength, though battered, still showed.

Along the drove road there are no telegraph poles or overhead wires to distract the eye; the world and its business fall away out of mind. There is something mesmerizing in walking for hours through the grassy silence of hills that roll on like waves of the sea; each new vista gained at the summit of each climb is a further unfolding of undulating green. When we had just started out on a hike, we would chat, point out things

to one another, argue, caught still in the frayed edges of daily
life; but as we continued, gradually we would drop into a
silence imposed by the solitude, the steady rhythm as heart
and lungs and muscle pumped in cooperation with each other,
the oxygen we inhaled out of the bright air filling the lung-
sacs, invading the blood, invigorating the long muscles that
pulled us uphill. One falls, after a few miles, into a trancelike
state, calm, at a remove from ordinary existence, yet with a
clarity of awareness, so that the particular hue of the over-
arching sky, the form of each wild flower, the texture of gorse,
heather, bracken, the gush of water springing from the cool
dark of underground sources and sparkling over stones, the
suck of oozy mud on one's boots, the white scut of a rabbit
startled from its lair—each thing perceived is augmented with
its own keen significance.

A steep ascent to a stone cairn on a distant eminence becomes a valid *raison d'être*; the summit one is heading for
seems eternally unattainable—one's wind and muscle will
never bear one to the top—but one plods on, dealing with the
task by lifting one foot, then the other; then one reaches a
crest only to gain the perspective of a further peak, still higher
up, still not attainable, the stone cairn outlined against a yet
far-distant horizon.

Toiling up such an incline, there is no reason in the world
why one should go on, persist, in this self-imposed, heart-
bursting, lung-forcing irrationality; one is, after all, a free
agent, and the choice of that particular hilltop is arbitrary, a
whim—no one is forcing one to continue. But something drives
one on; here is a struggle, self-enjoined, its purpose in no way
connected with the life one lives down on the plain; and yet—
in some indefinable way—it does have to do with the self that
one has to confront down there on the plain. The climb has imposed an imperative that must be addressed; there is no question but that the task undertaken must be accomplished. Its
exact nature no longer has any significance beyond its demand
to be completed although the heart is thundering, pulses boom
in the ears, and legs move on powered only by will, for their
own endurance is gone. There is brief respite in stopping to

drink icy water scooped from a stream in cupped hands, but no lingering, because, now, the imagination suddenly can encompass the peak as a reality and there is an urgency to scale the final incline.

Harl always reached the top ahead of me, and would wave encouragement, shout down about the splendor of the view that awaited. Once I was at the top, my accumulated exhaustion vanished in the instant of the accomplishment, and the grandeur of the view from such heights conceded an absurd feeling of triumph. When one has rested, and taken in the view, the path downhill is a reward, bestowed for endurance.

One afternoon, a few miles out of the glen into the hills, we were granted a most remarkable sight on the opposite flank of the deep gorge our path skirted. Two shepherds with three working sheep dogs were gathering a flock that was browsing over hundreds of acres. The silence was fragmented suddenly with the sharp, peremptory yap of the dogs, the shepherds' directions ringing out to form a sort of invisible net that surrounded the scattered flock. Gradually, the unconnected white dots began to converge—randomly dispersed cells responding to the electric impulse of the authority discharged by the men and dogs. The sheep's protest swelled from ragged bleating to a concerted din, over which the shepherds' voices floated: "Come by!" if they wanted the dogs to converge on the left flank; "Away to me!" for the right; "Back!" or "Fore!" for backward or forward instructions—to which the dogs responded with the uncanny precision imprinted into their herding instinct over generations of breeding and training. Men, dogs, and sheep could be seen from where we sat as interacting elements of one vast, pulsating organism. Soon the separate white points on the broad hillside were clotting up into blobs, knots, clumps, snarls, balls of creamy wool, pulled off and spun out into long threads as they were teased out of the mass onto the narrow sheep-trails; and then into separated white running stitches embroidering the green path, as if a vast snarled skein of yarn were being untangled. Along the trails the sheep ran, down the hill through gates that hung open for them to pass through. The bleating, crying, protesting of sheep and lambs, the barking dogs, the shepherds' cries that had filled the air with din and energy, diminished as they dropped away out of view.

We felt privileged, as though, unexpectedly, we had been given orchestra seats for a performance of a classic play with seasoned actors; it had been an extraordinary accomplishment we had witnessed: the exercise of men's imagination and will upon natural creation—a powerful force like a great hand on the landscape gathering up and imposing order upon existing chaos, creating constellations of form out of scattered randomness. The interaction—its swiftness and efficiency built out of ancient, painstaking training and cooperation between three different natural species—was awesome to watch, against the grandeur of the huge spreading haunch of these hills, which had been gouged and smoothed into their present form by the great shifting ice-plates of the glacial epoch. Over the quiet that had flowed back into the void left by the departed flock, floated the far-off echo of the dogs' barking as they finished their work.

Tramping through the hills along the trail that had been used by cattle drovers taking their beasts to be sold at the huge eighteenth-century local cattle fairs, we would reach at last the steading of an old farm, Glenrazie, which had belonged to Mrs. Cameron's uncle, and know that we would soon be out of the Blairrossie range. We took care to avoid a field where we knew a bull was penned. He was a splendid sight, glossy black against the green; his form, his power, his short stumpy legs and massively muscled body, all merely equipment to power his reproductive system—and to defend it. The absoluteness of his bullhood as he stood, glowering in the field, encompassed him like a field of energy. We warily skirted his domain.

A pine forest, another farm with a well-tended steading, cows drinking at a small pond, children's toys lying about in the farmyard—the trail turned then into an unpaved road skirting the estate wall of a great Edwardian mansion of golden limestone, with a view of the village and the green sea of hills to the west; a steep downhill walk of about a mile would bring us to the far outskirts of the village where the weaving mill stood beside its millstream.

We would make our way past modest eighteenth-century cottages whose front doors opened directly off the narrow sidewalk, whitened doorsteps in front and small secret gardens at the back, occasionally encountering housewives with shopping baskets, and walk up the sloping street that joined up eventually to the High Street of Auchterbraehead. Here, depending on the time of day, we would stop at either the Blue Kettle Tearoom for tea and scones, or the Three Bells Hotel's pub for tankards of draught beer.

There is probably nothing that tastes quite so good after a strenuous hike as a tall mug of pale ale, at room temperature, drawn from the cask, the light effervescence sending up a foaming creamy head. Bitter and malty on the tongue, it slakes one's thirst and imparts a sense of light-headed ease. On the last few miles of a rigorous hike, it was often the image of this foaming tankard that kept one going. Harl and David would regularly take a walk of about fifteen miles, which included scaling the 2,363-foot summit of Ben Brechin, ending up in a small village in the Hillfoots—as the locals call the string of tiny villages that border the western valley of our hill range. Here I would pick them up in the car at an appointed hour, making use, while I waited for them, of one of the few laundromats in the district. Scanning the trail one day, I caught sight of them coming out of the hills at a gallop, as if pursued by bears; they scarcely stopped to greet me so great was their haste. "What's wrong?" I called out as they charged past along the High Street. "It's five minutes to closing time," they answered over their shoulders as they headed into the cool oaken dimness of the Bird and Bottle. Inside, I found them triumphantly wiping the foam from their lips, and half-quaffed pints of ale on the bar before them. It was a hot day, and it was only the thought of a couple of pints that had supplied the energy to slog it through the hills, they told me.

"The air is dry and good in summer," the minister of the parish wrote of Auchterbraehead in the eighteenth-century statistical report, "but rather moist and damp in winter . . .

when the sun has not influence sufficient to dissipate the vapours which are attracted by the hills, and the most frequent winds blowing from them must necessarily occasion a moisture in the air." According to Meg Cameron, the last few summers before our arrival had been extremely moist and damp. "You don't know how lucky you are," she told us. "Since the time you bought the house at the loch, something's come over the weather; in fact, the summers are a wee bit too warm for my preference." I, of course, held the Celestial Messenger on the 9:55 to Nottingham responsible for the balminess of the summers, but Harl had his own theory. He maintained that I kept the interior temperature of Glenauchen Cottage so high that the escaping heat gradually was altering the ecology of the glen; often he would come into the cozily warm house from the outdoors claiming that tropical flora were starting to flourish around the loch, with monkeys swinging from lianas and parakeets competing in song with the local bird life.

Our maps, guidebooks, and rambler's handbooks referred often to trails we would hike as old drove roads. Wondering what they were, we looked in the library and found a book, *The Drove Roads of Scotland* by A. R. B. Haldane, a fascinating account of the droving trade that arose, around the fourteenth century, out of the wild and lawless history of the primitive Highland tribes, for whom cattle were practically a form of currency and cattle thieving a way of life.

In the mountainous uplands of Scotland, where the land is too harsh for cultivation, as early as the twelfth century cattle were the main source of wealth, and by the middle of the sixteenth century cattle theft appears to have been a major occupation of the Scottish people. No amount of legislation, Haldane writes, could deter a custom "ingrained and deeply rooted in the character of the people." As far back as the early Iron Age kings, cattle raiding—as in Homeric Greece—had been a favorite sport.

A beginning of legal commerce in cattle seems to have come about in the late sixteenth century; old records show the regular passage of cattle between Scotland and England in toll-gate receipts of the time: two pence for each head of cattle crossing the toll bridge. In 1607, during the reign of James VI, a treaty recommending free trade between the two traditionally antagonistic countries was adopted, following on the Union of the Scottish and English crowns in 1603, when their common interest in the defense of the Reformation required them to cooperate in the face of ancient prejudices and jealousies that remained entrenched, and, to a lesser extent, exist even to this day. By the middle of the seventeenth century, cattle trade with England was an essential part of the economy of Scotland, and the revenues from taxation on cattle rose as the tolls, levied at the customs posts, increased. The wily Scots, however, familiar with every contour of their hills and glens and rocky crags, evaded the taxation by crossing, unobserved, away from the border posts. They were fined for tax evasion if they were caught; records show that in 1628, fines extracted from drovers were used to build a new castle for the king. But the droving, legal and illegal, went on for nearly four centuries, the hooves of the cattle going southward on the time-worn routes, stamping trails into the landscape that were easy for us to follow still.

Between the sixteenth and mid-nineteenth centuries the droving trade became an important activity. Scotland was described as a mere grazing ground for England. Under the land-tenure system, in which the tenants were entitled to grazing rights, the land tended to become overstocked, and, as winter approached, it became necessary to reduce stocks. Since the cattle could transport themselves to market, feeding along the roadside as they went, droving was the inevitable solution; it flourished, and a long tradition of trade, legend, song, and poetry arose out of it. Haldane points out that the literature, poetry, and history of the Scottish peoples is a continuous story of cattle raiding. A fierce adventurous people, hardy, at home with the inclement climate and the use of arms—their folk tales are filled with the brandishing of dirk, poniard, broadsword, and cudgel, with a love of plunder, cunning, and foray, with cattle always the prize or the cost. So the cattle droving of the more settled eighteenth and nineteenth centuries was a natural transition out of those violent and turbulent earlier times.

The books we read about the drovers altered the landscape for us, enriching it with the history and experiences of that vanished breed of men. Walter Scott wrote of them in a story, "The Two Drovers"; and Rob Roy, the original of his novel of that name, was an important and successful castle drover until, ruined by a fluctuation in the market and the bad faith of a trusted partner, he absconded and became an outlaw and a folk hero.

According to eighteenth-century writings, the drovers were strong, hirsute wild men, dressed in kilt and plaid shawl, smelling of leather and peat smoke, and hung about with knife and fork, dagger, pistol, broadsword, and snuffbox. They were licensed to carry arms to defend themselves against cattle thieves, raiders, and "blackmailers," early members of Bob's glen Mafia—of whom Rob Roy was one of the best known and most feared. He would sell insurance "premiums"—protection money—against the loss of the drovers' cattle, half of his men being employed selling the premiums, which guaranteed the return of stolen cattle, while the other half kept busy stealing the cattle.

The drovers were hardy men, carrying, for food on the long journey, oatmeal and a few onions, which they would replenish along the way, and, according to Walter Scott, "a ram's horn filled with whiskey . . . used regularly, but sparingly, every night." They might also carry preserved dried blood left over from the bleeding of the cattle in the spring and autumn—a practice common as well among the southern African Hereros; this, with the onions and oatmeal, would provide the makings of "black pudding," a traditional dish much favored by the Scots, though not by us; we found it to be dark, stodgy, and unpalatable, though on a long cold hazardous journey, sleeping in the open every night, it must have been a tasty and nourishing dish—so long as there was sufficient whiskey to wash it down. Collie dogs would accompany the drovers as they moved the herd slowly southward, traveling ten to twelve miles each day. If a drover remained in the South to work at the harvest after disposing of the beasts, the dogs would be turned loose to make their way back home on their own, stopping to be fed at the same farm or inn where they had stopped for refreshment on the way down; the next year, on his way south again, the drover would pay for the food that had been given to the dogs.

A drove could number up to three hundred beasts, with one drover to about sixty animals, and en route to the important cattle markets in the nineteenth century there could be thousands of beasts stretching for miles. As the wages for droving were not high—about a shilling a day in the early eighteenth century, three shillings a day by the first half of the nineteenth century—those drovers who could afford the luxury of a pony rather than slogging on foot alongside the herd would sell homemade articles along the way: hand-woven cloth and knitted garments. Haldane recounts meeting an old man who could still recall the last days of the droving trade; according to this man, the drovers frequently passed through villages knitting as they jogged along.

There were no maps available for them to plot their routes, and they had to rely on skill, experience, and information from other drovers to move great flocks and herds across the country, finding grazing en route, fording turbulent rivers, changing the course according to imperatives of wind, storm, and mists. The trails they followed were the marked tracks pounded into the earth by the hooves of herds trampling the southward route over generations; the sites of the stances (the open grazing where they would rest and water the animals overnight) are to this day greener than the surrounding countryside. At the start of a journey the herd was intractable, straying continuously, as the homing instinct, which is powerful in sheep and cattle, urged them back to known and familiar pastures; day by day, as the memory of the old grazing places grew dim, they became easier to handle.

Some of the drovers never slept under the shelter of a roof; at night they would wrap themselves up in their plaids, even then having to keep an eye out for straying animals or cattle thieves. Walter Scott, in the introduction to *Rob Roy*, tells how he was given a vivid picture of the hardiness of the drover breed by an old man who, when he was fifteen was sent with his father on an expedition to recover twelve head of his master's stolen cattle. Rob Roy had been sent for, and gravely assured them that the "mad herdsmen" could not have removed their booty too far; he promised that their beasts would be recovered, and asked the shepherd and his young son to accompany his band so that they could help drive the beasts back after they had been retrieved from the thieves. Unwilling and apprehensive among the band of wild Highlanders, the boy and his father had no choice but to go with them. They traveled a day and a night, were brought at last to a valley where a great herd of cattle grazed, and were instructed by Rob Roy to identify and take away their master's animals. Then an old woman appeared out of nowhere, crying and screaming at them in Gaelic, but when they told her "in the best Gaelic they could muster" that they were under Rob Roy's protection, she let them pass.

They rejoined the waiting bandits and started back home, traveling till nightfall, when Rob Roy called a halt for the night on a bleak moor, "across which a cold north-east wind, with frost on its wings," blew cuttingly. The Highlanders lay down on the ground to sleep, wrapped in their plaids; the boy was told to keep himself warm by walking about watching the cattle, but at last, half-frozen, he crept up and lay down beside one of the bandits, wrapping himself in a corner of his plaid, and fell asleep. Waking at dawn, he was horrified to find he had uncovered the huge man's neck and shoulders, which were now caked, by exposure, with hoarfrost; expecting to be beaten, he waited with dread for the burly man to awaken. But all that happened was that the man stood up, shook himself, wiped off the hoarfrost with his plaid, and remarked that it had been quite a "cauld neight."

Sunday droving was prohibited by law in a time when the Church had great political power, and there are records in the eighteenth century of drovers being punished for passing through a town on Sunday and not attending the church service; but they continued to ignore the Sabbath in the press of their commitment to get the cattle to market. These men, practically penniless, entrusted with thousands of pounds' worth of cattle, had a reputation for honesty and fair dealing over centuries of great historic and political change, and underwent enormous risk and hardship to deliver the cattle entrusted to them.

Crieff, a small, pleasant county town, is set in the slope of the Grampians. It has a spa, imposing Victorian hotels, and a High Street with shops catering to the tourist trade. It was a place to go when we needed to buy sweaters and woolen goods at one of the many mill-shops in the town center; we found there, too, a bakery where we could get the best loaf of white bread we had ever come upon—a loaf with a good crusty exterior and a chewy wholesome crumb (better than cake, the children said, consuming vast quantities of it with local butter and the homemade jam Helen kept us supplied with all summer). Harl would always make for the poulterer and fishmonger opposite the baker's, where pigeons—for which he has a fondness—were sold: wild wood-pigeons, plucked, dressed, and ready for the oven. I would slow-braise the tough little birds with wine and bacon and pot-herbs for his delectation alone, as the rest of the family did not care for them.

For us, Crieff meant woolens, white bread, and woodpigeons; but from Haldane we learned that until the mid-eighteenth century it had been the major center for the cattle trade in Scotland. The cattle market was known as the "tryst," and to the Crieff tryst the herds and flocks were driven in from the North, the West Coast, and the Hebrides; for a period it came to be one of the main financial centers of the country. The trysts, according to reports of writers of the day, took place in an atmosphere of great tumult and excitement. The commercial transactions, arguments, and bargaining went on in a variety of regional accents—Scots, English, and the Gaelic of the West; the livestock, farmers, dogs, drovers, gillies, buyers, and sellers surged in a multitude at the center of the grounds. Around the borders, tents, booths, and stands were set up by food vendors; bankers' clerks exchanged money; fires blazed under great cauldrons in which mutton broth seethed and steamed; and, in among the throngs, fiddlers, beg-

gars, ballad singers, gamblers, jugglers, and thieves plied their
skill and cunning and art. The market took place under the
patronage of a local nobleman, who held a court to settle dis-
putes as they arose and to maintain some sort of order at the
fairground.

After 1770, the main tryst moved south to Falkirk, where
trading was easier for English dealers who would not have
wanted to venture further north into the wild Highlands to
do their business. In order to avoid the toll of one shilling per
score of cattle and five pennies per score of sheep, many of the
drovers heading down through Crieff and Perth steered their
flocks and herds up into our hills, and led them over the grassy
paths that we learned to know on our hikes, down the slopes
and into our glen. And in the bleating of scattered sheep we
encountered, the lowing of black cattle whose grazing we
disturbed as we tramped along the old drove roads, we sensed
the unending stream of beasts over the centuries herded by the
drovers, for whom the journey, Walter Scott wrote, "exer-
cised the Celt's natural curiosity and love of motion. . . . The
Highlanders . . . [are] masters of this difficult trade of driving,
which seems to suit them as well as the habit of war." Our
walks took us through the hills, through quiet days and long
twilit evenings, and through centuries of the life lived out in an
ancient land where evidence of the past lies everywhere about,
in the same way that the huge boulders left in the wake of
the Ice Age lay alongside the paths we walked.

The increase of population, more efficient use and cultivation of the land, and its enclosure by owners of fields and
pastures behind dry-stone walls and turf dikes, as well as the
setting aside of vast estates to preserve game from hunting, and
the gradual imposition of fees for grazing on land that traditionally had been open common—all conspired against the
drover's trade. The building of a system of roads and public
highways, on which drovers could be prosecuted for obstruc-
tion and litter, encroached more and more on a way of life
that had assumed free passage across the land as a law of nature.

And when the steam engine came into use, it was found easier to move cattle by steamship, and later by rail. In the years following 1835, droving gradually declined and faded into the mists of folk tale and legend, leaving, however, a tradition of public access. Many of the old rights of way are still in use over the countryside; the public can freely walk there without fear of trespassing.

In the introduction to Haldane's book, we had read of an old road that crosses our hills. Reading his description of the trail, which "local tradition marked . . . as one which was in use in the latter part of the eighteenth and much of the nineteenth century by droves of cattle and sheep bound from the Highlands to the great market at Falkirk," we decided to locate the old path and walk its length. We arranged a ride into the village with Meg, intending to look for the track described in the book, which should, if we could pick it up and follow it, lead us back to our glen. We left the village behind us, tramped up the steep road leading into the hills, and then followed several likely-looking grass paths all ending nowhere; we returned each time to the mossy walls of a large estate behind imposing iron gates.

Determined to find the trail, we decided to inquire at the house we could see beyond the gates, set well back from the road. We crunched up the sweep of the graveled driveway in our hiking boots, and reached the front door of a large stone house that commanded a splendid view of the hills across the valley. There was a shooting-brake drawn up in front of the house, but no other sign of life; we rang the doorbell once, twice, but all remained still and silent. Then, at a side door from a jutting wing of the house, a woman in a white apron came out to drop some vegetable peelings in a dustbin. We approached her, explained that we were trying to find the start of the old drove road, and wondered if anyone in the house possibly could direct us to it. "Och," she said—a thin, friendly person with red hands and a broad local accent—"I ken just where it is; it's no' far from here," and she gave us precise directions. Soon we were hiking along the winding drove road that, over the years, we came to know so well.

Later that day, we passed Jenny's cottage as we made our way back up the forestry road. She always liked to hear where we had been hiking, and we described the big country house where we had stopped to ask the way. "That's the Haldane place," she said. "It must have been their cook you spoke to; I know her from the Rural Women's Institute. He's the Mr. Haldane who's written a book about the drove roads."

So—we had gone directly to the source.

CHAPTER
11

A Brace of Grouse

Passersby were a rare occurrence at Glenauchen Cottage: an occasional fisher, a workman from the Forestry Commission asking for his teakettle to be filled at our sink, a driver who had taken a wrong turn knocking at our door for directions out of the hills. Callers always caused a faint flurry in our seclusion—a small pebble dropped into a quiet pool radiating mild ripples.

One evening in early August, when none of the children were at Glenauchen, I was standing at the sink, scrubbing the thin skins off Ayrshire potatoes for our dinner, when footsteps rang out on the flagstones and a young man appeared on the terrace, passed by the kitchen window, and knocked on the front door. Harl was in the stable chopping wood for kindling; I dried my hands and went to see what the stranger wanted.

He wore blue jeans and an Aran-knit sweater, and in upper-class, public-school accents apologized for disturbing me and asked if he might use our telephone. "I've been up on the hill with our gamekeeper," he explained as I led him into the hall. "My father has rented the shoot on Dalrioch from the Forestry Commission. We've set out a lot of pheasant chicks on the hillside—we're trying to stock the place. There's not much game up there because of all the tree planting, and we have to go up every so often to spread grain for them to feed on. We'd just finished scattering the last bagful, and were turning round to leave, when the gamekeeper ran the shooting-brake into a ditch. We're firmly stuck up there; d'you know of any garage nearby that could send a pickup van to pull us out?"

A simple request that took the best part of the evening to fulfill. It was a Friday night, around six-thirty; everything had closed down for the weekend, except for the pubs. Harl came into the house, and between us we telephoned every garage and service station within a fifteen-mile radius—to no avail, placating the anxious young man with beer as the sun slipped down behind Ben Shawe and the shadows of the hills lengthened over the loch. We tried Wester Glenauchen Farm to see if either of the grandsons would come to the rescue with a tractor, but they were already away at the Lockup Pub. Old Mrs. Cameron suggested a couple of the neighboring farmers, whom we phoned without any luck.

The half-scrubbed potatoes lay in a pan of water in the sink, the dinner hour came and went; the young man telephoned his home in a village some twenty miles north of the glen, and instructed a housekeeper to locate his father and have him call him back at Glenauchen. He mentioned that the gamekeeper had brought his small grandson along for the drive, and he hoped the lad wasn't *girning* and wanting his mother. Assuming that under the circumstances any sensible child would be wanting his mother as well as his supper, we put a few sandwiches and apples in a rucksack with a thermos of tea and some beer, and Harl and I set off up the hill to feed the old man and the child, while the young man went on phoning everyone he knew.

About two miles along the forestry road we came upon the shooting-brake tilted into the ditch, with the old man in the front seat trying to comfort a tearful, whimpering, five-year-old boy. The sky was bright with the twilight, but a hush had fallen over the hills, even the water that ran at that spot over a rocky streambed sounding more tentative than in broad daylight. The evening landscape, given over to wild creatures for the night, must have seemed alien and hostile to a small child so far from the warmth of his own bed. He stared at us with a blank, unresponsive gaze, refusing to accept the sandwich or apple I offered, burrowing more deeply into the security of his grandfather's lap.

The old man thought the bairn would more likely take something to eat if we went away—he was a shy wee laddie. So back down the hill we made our way. By now, the young man had been in touch with his father, and help was on the way, though it would be a while yet before it got here. He would go back up the hill and wait with Willie and the bairn, he said, as it was getting dark and they might find it a bit lonely up there all on their own.

I had, meanwhile, lost all impulse to get on with the dinner I had been preparing; so we drank some beer and ate some peanuts and kept going to look out of the window—like the sister in Bluebeard's castle—to see if help was on its way up the lonely road. By the time the young man came back with the thermos, his father had called to say a pickup van was on the way. The child had eaten and fallen asleep, he told us, and old Willie was happily drinking the beer we had brought. He apologized for all the trouble he had given us, thanked us for our help, attempted to reimburse us for all the telephone calls he had made around the county, and set off into the dusk to wait for his rescuers.

We sat down to a meal of eggs and bacon at about ten, and later, when we went upstairs to drink our coffee in front of the living room fire, the darkening hillside was swept with the white beam of headlamps, and we saw the vehicles of rescued and rescuer making their way along the hill.

A week later, on a Saturday afternoon, we got back from Auchterbraehead, laden with library books and provisions, to find two dead birds, tied together at the neck, slung over the handle of the front door. "An ill omen," was my first thought. Had a witch made her way past all our rowanberry arches, or had the yobs paid a call while the house was deserted? Harl came round the corner of the house. "Didn't you have the key?" he asked, seeing me standing motionless in front of the door. I pointed at the dead birds.

"Grouse!" he said. "A brace of grouse!"

"Grouse. . . . How did they get here?"

"That young chap—it must have been that young chap we helped last weekend. He hasn't left a note anywhere, has he?" There was nothing but the two dead birds. Harl was delighted; he grew up on a farm and hunted as a boy, and esteems game-birds.

I gazed doubtfully at the two creatures slung lifeless over the door handle. On our walks we sometimes startled them up out of the bracken and heather, and they would rise up with a whirr of wings, emitting their harsh, honking cry, to take off like arrows out of our path. On our door, their yellow-beaked heads lolled, slack, their red-brown plumage sheened like taffeta with blue-green iridescence; these was no bloody sign of damage where the shot had gone in and the life had leaked out.

"We left them hanging out there and went indoors. "What are we going to *do* with them?" I said.

"*Do* with them! We'll cook them and eat them."

"I haven't the slightest idea what to do with a dead grouse," I grumbled. I was sufficiently well steeped in the English novel to know of the status accorded to grouse shooting on Scottish heath. Trollope's novels are peopled with members of parliament abandoning the affairs of the country in order to rush up to Scotland to have their bloody sport; from Jane Austen onward, the lord or squire sends along a brace of grouse to those upon whom he would confer grace or favor; people who are living in town have grouse sent to them from their country estates; parliament goes into summer recess in time for the grouse season; gamekeepers, I had learned from D. H. Lawrence, are employed to bring down the full power of the law on those who would unlawfully poach grouse; nowadays sporting Arabs, Germans, Japanese, and Americans pay exorbitantly to rent the season's use of a shoot. All this I knew, yet I found myself feeling vaguely truculent about those two dead creatures, suspended over the door-handle and demanding, by the very weight of legend and status that surrounded them, to be dealt with in a manner quite different from that required by lambchops or kippers.

On our first "Glorious Twelfth" (August 12) in Scotland, we had learned how the Scottish hunting mystique dated back to the first half of the eighteenth century, when the use and preservation of the Highlands for hunting and fishing became customary. The Earl of Malmesbury wrote in his memoirs in 1833, "This was the first year that the Highlands became the rage and that deer-forests were made and rented," he himself renting "grouse, deer-forest and fishing, all of which were first-rate . . . at £25 a year." From the Glorious Twelfth onward, the hills and moors are rife with bloodthirsty hunters stalking game, and hikers learn to watch out for their lives. The Hunter sons occasionally took summer jobs as "beaters" on one of the great estates, their employment consisting of creating enough disturbance among gorse and heather to drive the game out of hiding into the onslaught of the sportsmen's gun-shot. Bob likes to tell the story of the gillie—the servant who attends the master while hunting or fishing—who complained of the tedium of his diet, which consisted solely of salmon and grouse.

Now we had a brace of these legendary birds to cope with. Harl called the Hunters to ask for advice. Helen had cooked pheasant and wild duck, but no grouse had ever come her way. Bob, as a youth on his grandfather's country estate, had both shot and eaten his fill of them, but what happened between handing over to the servants the bag with the day's catch, and its subsequent reappearance at the dinner table, remained a mystery to him. "But I do know that you must let them hang for at least a week, with the feathers on. Not much longer than a week, though," he cautioned. "You'll want them nicely high and gamey, but not maggotty."

We hung them for a week in the little porch; the feathers lost their sheen and the birds assumed a sorry, unappetizing appearance, quite unlike the iridescent game-birds lying with broken necks and still-bright eyes and beaks in those old still-life paintings of food done by the Dutch masters. Then Harl plucked and drew and dressed them, and found them to be, in their nakedness, very small chicks. We had invited the Hunters to join the feast, but Bob had assured us that so early in the season the birds would be young and small enough to provide only a succulent mouthful each. Bob himself goes hunting in the autumn in the stubble of his own barley-fields, and brings down a few wild ducks for the pot. He says that before the harvest is ripe the birds have all been feeding on fish, which gives their flesh an unpleasant flavor; but after the harvest, when they have feasted and fattened on the gleanings of the grain-fields, the flesh is wonderfully sweet and tasty.

Helen had consulted her cookbooks for me, and had come up with Margaret Costa's method, in her excellent *Four Seasons Cookery Book*, where the recipe begins "If a brace of gift grouse should come your way . . ." and stipulates quick, simple cooking that consists of covering the breasts with fat bacon and roasting them in a very hot oven for about half an hour.

In the afternoon, Harl and I had been walking on the private road, just past the farm, and had noticed that the wild raspberries in the hedges were starting to ripen, and had collected a dishful, which reposed on the kitchen windowsill like a small fortune of rubies. While the grouse roasted, I cooked new potatoes, and the peas we had gathered from the rows planted by our student-tenants in the kitchen garden. "Give them a squeeze of lemon before sending them to the table," Margaret Costa advises, that instruction about "sending" food to the table, frequently used in English cookbooks, stirring up visions of a bustling, red-faced cook and a relay of scullions, kitchen-maids, footmen, and butlers passing along a succession of covered dishes from hand to hand until they reach the grandeur of the dining table. I sent our grouse to the table by handing the heated dish to Harl, who burned his fingers and took three hasty steps from stove to table, while I deglazed the pan juices with a drop of wine to spoon over the birds with some chopped parsley.

We sat down to the much-discussed, much-anticipated meal. All about us, the glen was in a radiance of high summer twilight, as if our stone house was suspended in some pale gold medium. I had scorched my wrist on the roasting pan, my cheeks were hot from the high oven, and I grumbled, as I served, about all the fuss and expenditure of energy over the two birds, which looked even more paltry after having been cooked. I groused about the grouse.

We each cut off a slice of breast meat, and tasted; we looked up at each other in silence as we chewed. The hush intensified as our senses registered and acknowledged what we ate. Nothing that I had taken in of the grouse mystique had prepared me for the dark, rich, velvety meat, which, as it melted on the palate, released a flowery bouquet.

"It's perfumed," Harl observed.

"It's heather. They've been feeding on the heather up on the slope beside the loch, and the meat is scented with it."

In that first mouthful the whole grouse legend was made accessible to me, and I accepted it at once, like someone who has been won over by a small revelation. No formal grace was uttered in Glenauchen's kitchen, but the grace which abounded, that evening, was acknowledged in our hushed silence, in the reverence with which we consumed the two small sacrificial birds. We sanctified the feast with claret (which is the term the British use for Bordeaux red), and for dessert there were the wild raspberries with sugar and cream.

That is the only time I have ever eaten grouse, but I became a firm convert. A few days later we were driving on a small country road when suddenly, right in front of us, a party of about five grouse crossed the road. "Run 'em over," I said to Harl. "Quick—run 'em over!" Harl gazed at me in astonishment as the birds strolled off into some woods.

We tried, unsuccessfully, through the thickets of the bureaucracy of the Forestry Commission, to contact our young benefactor—whose name we had never found out—so that we could thank him for his gift. Happily, toward the end of August, he telephoned to ask if we had ever found a brace of grouse he'd left on our door; after we had thanked him and told what a splendid meal they had made, he said he had just called to make sure that they hadn't been snaffled while we were out.

From the Twelfth of August, then, until the summer was over, we walked circumspectly in our hills, keeping away from them on the weekends when the blast of shotguns shattered the silence of the air.

Though grouse was featured on our menu only that once, like the proverbial gillie we got to eat a fair amount of salmon.

Helen and Bob invariably spent two weeks of the summer in a cabin they had rented for years in the far northwest of Scotland. This wild rocky shore, on the Minch, where the Atlantic flows in between the western coast and the Hebrides, is one of the places where the salmon swim in from the sea to make their way inland to their breeding waters. Here Bob, swathed in sweaters and waterproofs against the swirling mist and chilly drizzle, would spend the days fishing with elaborate flies made of feathers and dyed hairs from badgers and stoats—casting, reeling, waiting for the tug on the line and the contest with the hooked game. It was a temptation, he told us, to be unsporting, for just outside their cabin the burn ran, and up this burn the salmon would swim in great numbers in their haste to reach their breeding place. And here, not quite the compleat angler, one could hook with a gaff, as they passed upstream, some of the less agile fish. One year, he described with great delight how the burn was so teeming with salmon that all he had to do was fall in and clasp the great writhing silvery creatures to his bosom.

Unsporting, and probably illegal; but we would all feast on salmon when they got back from the North. Fresh Scottish salmon, pink-fleshed, poached till just done, and served with Helen's homemade mayonnaise, small sweet Scottish tomatoes, and English cucumbers, accompanied by wholemeal bread and a glass of Chablis, is a pleasant experience.

Over the Glenauchen summers, it became customary for the Hunters to break their homeward journey from the North in the glen, where I would have dinner cooked and waiting for them; we would spend the evening regaled by their stories of the peculiarities of the inhabitants of one of the loneliest, most northerly spots in Scotland, and we would bring them up to date on our summer and the activities of the glen Mafia.

Early one morning, I opened the front door to the fresh new day and stepped out to the stable to collect the newspaper left there by Donny. I was struck at once by a strange smell—rank, powerful, feral. "A bit like the smell when a tomcat has sprayed, but much stronger," I reported to the family at the breakfast table. Philippa was away spending a few days at the Hunters' farm, and only Harl and the boys were there. They all went out and sniffed about the front terrace and the stable-yard, and came back declaring they could smell nothing unusual. When I insisted that the garden was rank with it, they suggested that perhaps a stray cat had come by. "There are no stray cats—d'you think this is Brooklyn? The nearest cat is Jenny's Fluff, and she's a female." But they were all more interested in their breakfast of eggs accompanied by kippers, which they were cooking by a new technique: holding the kipper by the tail and dipping it in a jug of boiling water till it was heated through. The discussion was dropped.

The next morning the smell was there again, and the next— strong around the front door, noticeable in the yard and near the stable. "How can you *not* smell it!" I protested. The three of them looked at each other, regarded me, twiddling fingers round their temples and rolling eyes to indicate incorrigible madness on my part, and went on with their breakfast.

On the fourth day I didn't bother to mention that the smell was there again, but came in to announce that the rubbish bins were all overturned and the yard strewn with garbage.

"The sheep must have got in," Harl surmised.

"The gate's closed; they couldn't have."

"Donny might have found it open when he brought the paper and then closed it."

"That peculiar smell is still there—worse than before."

"Let's not start that again," Harl implored, and sent the boys out to clean up the mess.

After breakfast, we set out on an expedition to look for a circle of Standing Stones, marked on the Ordnance map near a village about an eight-mile drive from the glen. As we drove down the hill road toward the farm, we met the older of the wild grandsons striding purposefully uphill, carrying a gun. We pulled up to talk to him.

"Where are you going with the gun?" David asked.

His black curly hair unruly, sporting a bruise on his cheek-bone, he answered ferociously, "To put a couple of bullets through the skull of a bloody fox. Three nights now he's come slinking in amongst the chickens—murdering a few, carrying off a few, and scaring the blazes out of the rest of the brood. The auld hens are in such a sleister that they've all of them stopped laying."

"It must have been at our place too; all the bins were overturned. We thought it was the sheep."

"Aye, it's the fox alright. Bloody scavengers they are. And I won't get a moment's rest from my granny's girning till I've put a bullet through the bugger's skull."

"How will you know where to find it?" Neil asked.

"Och, one of the lads from the Forestry spied the vixen this morning; she was lying out in the sun, just halfway up Ben Shawe, with her bairns playing all around her. I'm off to get the thieving bugger right away." He stomped off, his blood aroused with the lust of vengeance.

Farther along the road we met the postman driving his little red van marked ROYAL MAIL. He handed our letters through the window. "Have you haird there's been a fox killing the Camerons' chickens?" he asked. When we stopped to fill up at the gas pump at the hotel, the attendant, a white-haired matronly woman in blue overalls, remarked that she'd heard Dougal Cameron was going up the hill to shoot a fox today.

The fox was an occasion in the glen.

It was around seven in the still-bright evening when we drove back up the road past the farm. "Wait, stop!" David cried out. "Look at what's hanging from that tree!" We all got out of the car and trooped into the barnyard. From a bough of a great chestnut tree, suspended by a rope bound round its hind legs, hung the fox; its handsome, sleek, pointed head dangling, still, lifeless, its muzzle caked with drying blood. Beside it—shocking, brutal—swung its severed tail, a glossy red plume-like brush, tied to the branch beside the mutilated body. The sight held us silent and aghast, the closeness to the wild beast depriving us of adequate response.

Soon we were joined in the yard by the whole Cameron family, including another grandson (not a wild one) with his wife and baby, all of whom occupied the laborer's cottage opposite the barn. "I told you I'd get the bugger," Dougal

boasted, his insolence more brazen than usual. "Met him slinking up the side of the hill back to the missus and the bairns
after his bloody night's mischief. Took only one bullet, right
through the skull, to kill the bugger."

"Kill the bugger, kill the bugger," the baby chanted in a
high, piping voice.

Old Mrs. Cameron looked discomfited, but the wild grandsons laughed. "That's my canny wee bairn," Dougal said. He
patted the baby's cheek, then struck the body of the fox a
blow with the back of a fist. "And when you're a muckle braw
chap big enough to handle a gun, your Uncle Dougal will
take you up the hill and teach you how to kill the thieving
murderous brutes."

The fox swung slowly to and fro in the hush of the
evening.

There was something profoundly shocking in the sight of
the lifeless animal dangling from the tree: its quickness, menace,
grace, stilled suddenly by a single bullet; the fur of its coat
rich, reddish gold, silken; blood dried around the nose, the
jawline serrated by jagged teeth lining the red mouth; the
corpse mutilated by the victor's brutish hacking off of the
brush.

Neil broke the silence. "Why have you hung it up there—
like that—with its tail cut off?"

"Because that's what we bloody do when we kill a fox,"
Dougal answered, swelling still with murderous pride.

Something had been profaned in the killing of this splendid
creature as it went coursing over the hill so splendidly adapted
to its own necessity.

All the same. . . . "We're very relieved," Mrs. Cameron
observed, practical, down to earth. "It carried off at least five
laying hens, not counting the ones it killed for sport and left
lying. It will be a while yet before the rest of the brood calms
down sufficiently to start laying. I'll have to see if Jenny
Kirkbride can spare me a few dozen, or Meg's going to find
she's short of eggs for the baking on Friday."

We were joined by the old shepherd whose son was vice-
chancellor of a university; he had walked over from his cottage
on the other side of the river to take a look at the fox. "Och

aye," he remarked, "it would have been even worse if it had got in amongst the sheep; they can carry off a wee lamb between their teeth." Slowly the fox spun on its rope in the evening breeze. Even so," the old man added, "it seems an awfu' shame to kill such a bonny beast."

Later that week, dining at the farm with the Hunters, still bemused by the experience, we talked of the fox. "Don't you think," I asked Bob, "that it must have come skulking around our front door? I'm sure that's what that rank smell was—and Harl and the boys couldn't smell a thing and all made fun of me."

"Of course it was the fox," Bob told us. "Don't you know that only women can smell the scent of a fox?"

"Now *you're* making fun of me."

"Not at all. Ask Helen. Isn't it so, Helen, that it's only women can smell a fox?"

"That's what's always been said; for some reason the scent isn't perceptible to men. It's a pity Philippa wasn't at home; she'd have smelled it and you'd have known you weren't imagining it."

When we asked around the glen if they were aware of this curious bit of folk wisdom, it turned out to be universally known and accepted.

Every year, toward the end of August, we would be awakened long before dawn by noise—great waves of panic and anguish filling all the hollows and rising up the slopes of the glen. We would know then what day this was; the clamor meant that the lambs were being separated from their mothers preparatory to being sent to market. It is a sound that has been heard here, at this season, for centuries.

When we first arrived at Glenauchen in late June, the lambs, born in March or April, were delightful wooly creatures with the soft appeal of babyhood still on them, suckling endlessly at the pendulous dugs of the ewes. When for a moment they are not feeding, they gambol about on stiff legs as if unable to contain their enjoyment of their own lambhood, but they spend most of their time and energy suckling and browsing, keeping a constant eye on the mother. A grazing lamb, lifting its head from the grass to find its mother, who had moved a few feet off, would bleat a cry of distress and hurry over to stand close beside her, needing a few reassuring sucks at the teat before returning to the grass.

As the summer came on, the lambs, growing taller, would have difficulty fitting under the maternal belly. The ewes—like any mothers of adolescents—would grow impatient with their developing, clumsy offspring, particularly when a lamb, by now as tall as the mother, would lift the mother's hind legs right off the ground in eagerness to reach the succoring teats; the mother would attempt to reject the young by moving off in irritation while still being nuzzled.

The ewes are generally mated for seven years, after which they are sold for mutton; the rams, known as *tups* in Scotland, are kept separate in well-fenced fields, except for the mating season in the autumn. Each year we returned, the older ewes would look more harried, shabby, and worn, their shaggy coats long, thick, and matted, their legs spindly. The lambs gradually would lose their soft, wooly appearance, the whiteness giving way to the black faces and legs of their breed. Sometimes, walking down the hill road with our daughter, who was assuming the legginess and awkward grace that precedes womanhood, I would look with sympathy at a ewe worn and battered from the generations she had suckled, while her beautiful lamb pranced and leaped beside her.

The lambs would be five months old in late August, when they were made ready for the sheep sales. Earlier in the summer they would have been clipped in the stone barn by the wild grandsons, who, using electric shears, swore and yelled at the protesting sheep to the accompaniment of rock-and-roll music that blared from a transistor radio suspended from an iron hook embedded in the ancient wall. In the old days, Mrs. Cameron would recall when we came down to watch, the sheep clipping had been a communal affair in the glen, with many hands needed for the laborious manual job; great meals were prepared and set out on a long table in the barn for all the neighboring farmers and shepherds, and it was a noisy, jolly gathering that broke the tediousness of rural life.

Before the sales the sheep would have been dipped in a solution that bleached their wool, so that their coats looked white and freshly laundered. The day before the bleaching, the grandsons, with the yapping assistance of their hard-driven collies, would have driven the flock down out of the hills and penned them up in the Home Park. On our walks in the hills we would often come upon small renegade bands—a ewe with one or two lambs, their coats yellowed, tangled, and unkempt— who would have evaded the dogs and shepherds at dipping or clipping time, and remained as outlaws now, too far from the steading for anyone to bother to seek them out. Wild and terrified at the sound of our footsteps, they would leap away to higher ground, the ewe calling out a warning to the scared lambs, and would stand off at a safe distance until we passed out of range before resuming their cropping.

By the time we awoke on dipping day, the glen would be rent by the baa-ing and bleating of the separated ewes and lambs; the hoarse sounds of the mothers' wretchedness filled the Home Park, while in a field at the far side of the farm, the frantic lambs formed a panic-stricken mob, their overwhelming urge to rejoin their mothers pushing them into one another, bumping and shoving. All day and all night this terrible protest quivered over everything, leaving us with a sense of disquiet, making us wish that we were vegetarian so that we need not feel morally implicated in this tearing away of the lamb from the ewe. "Och," Miss Kirstie Aird, a sheep farmer herself, reassured us with complacence, "I think the mothers are secretly relieved to be rid of their lambs; they're much too big now to fit under the teat and they push the old ones about so, still trying to suckle."

"Sheep sale tomorrow," one of the wild grandsons remarked savagely, "that'll put an end to their bloody racket."

The local sheep sales were always held on the third Saturday in August on a nearby farm in a field that abutted on the glen road. We would be up early to walk over the brow of Ben Shawe to watch. From the Home Park the dismal bleating of the deprived ewes floated up to us as we climbed the hill.

Cars and cattle trucks filled the parking area beside the field, where movable sheep pens had been set up and were already filled with the sprightly young lambs, most of whom were not going directly under the butcher's knife, but would be taken south by their purchasers to be fattened up for a season.

Around the enclosure was a gathering of farmers, shepherds, local breeders, county types—social differences being obliterated by the fact that almost everyone was dressed in tweeds and deer-stalker caps and looked ruddy-cheeked and bucolic. Owners of flocks to be auctioned were distinguished by the possession of shepherd's crooks or shoulder-high walking sticks. The auctioneer, whose father before him had conducted the local farm-auctions, stood on a raised platform in the center of the crush of sheep and humans, conducting his business in a patter so rapid and rhythmic that we were unable to recognize a word of English, though all our neighbors were privy to the mysterious tongue and the sign-language that flickered message and signal, so that sheep were "knocked down" and murmurs and laughs sent up, the whole proceeding going forward like a well-choreographed dance-drama.

The owner of the flock going under the hammer would walk proudly about inside the auctioneer's pen, crook upright, among the frightened bleating sheep, while the auctioneer described what we assumed to be the particular points and qualities of the animals, and then the bidding would start. The auctioneer must have been receptive to a raised eyebrow, a scarcely perceptible nod, or the flick of a finger, for as the bids came in we were never able to detect from whom or even from which direction he was intercepting them; it was as though there were some kind of nervous system connecting him to the crowd, along which the rapid impulses flashed to and fro. A sound of surprise or disappointment would rustle through the gathering at the price gained for each flock; then the lambs would be led out, leaping, like the sheep one is advised to count in order to induce sleep, over the low wooden barriers, and herded into a waiting truck while the next protesting group was marshaled into the auction pen.

There was an air of restrained, polite excitement at the sheep sales—a low murmur of voices, the bleating, the occasional growl and yap of the collie-dogs. The mild country folk in their subdued tweeds were in harmony with their surroundings; the auctioneer himself was out of a tradition that had begun in the days of the sheep trysts, later moved to the large county towns, and by the turn of the century had become an established way of conducting agricultural business wherever there were beasts to be sold. The auction seemed to us to be conducted in a place out of time, sustained by its own rhythms and customs, unchanged by the world outside these hills.

From the expression of rage or surly satisfaction on the swart faces of the wild grandsons, we were able to judge the prices obtained: whether or not they had got "good trade" for our wooly hill-companions. We would start our climb home over the back of the hill, and by the time we reached the brow the business was over: traffic, people, and beasts all gone, the trampled grass and some muddy tire tracks the only evidence of the morning's commerce, quietness pervading once again, the brown rabbits emerging from their burrows to scuttle swiftly through the grass, black flies hovering over the dropped mounds of sheep dung.

Back at Glenauchen, the lamentation of the old ewes diminished over the next few days, and a week after the removal of their young they were cropping peacefully in the hills, lambs forgotten, reminding us of friends whose children have gone off to college, on whom it dawns that quiet and freedom have replaced the emptiness and loss they experienced just after the children's departure.

And it took about a week, too, for us to be able to stand by in Mr. McKenzie's butcher shop, and watch him slicing the chops off a lamb carcass, without feeling disturbed by the memory of anguished protests that would rend the air and our hearts for about thirty-six hours every year in the third week of August.

CHAPTER
12

Romans in the Glen

Whenever we consulted the ordnance survey map of our district, our attention would stray from the immediate task of route planning, beguiled by place-names printed in Gothic lettering or marked with crosses, denoting ancient monuments or antiquities. From a nearby hamlet where we would go to buy fresh trout from a fish hatchery, in a line extending eastward all the way to Perth, our map showed, at regular intervals, a string of Roman signal stations and the course of a Roman road. Near a village not half an hour from our cottage was a site marked "roman military station."

We knew that the Romans had occupied Britain during the first four centuries A.D., and we were stirred by the proximity of such ancient history to our own occupation of the glen; evidence of imperial Rome lay scattered in the hills and valleys all around us. Our guidebook informed us that the remains of the Roman military station near us were considered the best-preserved example of Roman earthworks in the country. The fort, covering five acres, was enclosed within the grounds of a privately owned estate and could be visited with permission, the book informed tersely.

It wasn't until our second or third summer, on a cool, gray

Monday, that Harl and I set out to learn what the Romans had been doing in Scotland. We drove to the village around midday; there was an inn, a few houses set along the High Street, and potato and barley fields and woodland copses spreading away to the horizon. We lunched at the inn, and were served a surprisingly good meal: a hearty barley broth, followed by cold slices of yesterday's roast mutton with potatoes, cabbage, and chutney; and rhubarb tart served with a pitcher of thick cream for dessert. When we inquired at the desk how we could locate the Roman camp, the clerk pointed vaguely across the road in the direction of some woods and fields, and said if we just went along in that direction we couldn't miss it.

Our guidebook said that the site was "visible by permission" but omitted to mention from whom. At the inn they didn't know either. "The Roman camp? Aye," an old man sitting on a bench outside the pub told us, pointing across the fields. "Just keep along yon wee path by the stone dike, and ye'll not miss it."

We wandered about, trying to locate ourselves on the map; followed a leafy lane that ran between crumbling dry-stone walls; and after about ten minutes came upon a farm laborer's cottage, where we were set upon by some yapping dogs whose threatening behavior was watched amiably by three children playing in the yard. Our request, above the dogs' clamor, to see their mother or father elicited a blank incomprehension as though we addressed them in a foreign tongue. After a time a man appeared in the cottage doorway, obviously interrupted at his midday meal, and called the dogs off. The Roman camp? he said. Aye, we were in the right place. Just continue along the lane a wee way, past the steading, and we would see it; there's a wire fence goes right around it. He ducked back into the low doorway and was swallowed by the gloom of the cottage interior. The children, in their wooly sweaters, short pants, and black rubber knee-high boots, watched silently, patting the growling dogs, as we went off.

A high stone wall ran along one side of the lane. We passed a pair of iron gates beyond which a small, neglected loch lay with white mists curling from its surface. Looking between the iron spokes of the gates, we saw untended lawns, herbaceous borders rank with overgrown blooms, rich colors of unpruned roses and choking purples and pinks of lupin, delphinium, sweet william; a white-painted gazebo dilapidated and empty; a garden bench gripped to the earth by velvet moss; through gnarled beech, chestnut, and oak, a glimpse of a small stone mansion, private, mysterious, enclosed. There was an air about the estate of age and decay, like enriching loam; around the mound of earth raised by the collapse of a toppled oak, mosses flourished alongside yellow toadstools, wild flowers, and blackberry bushes—the dead oak nourishing the soil that had sustained it.

We went on, moving back deeper into the past, which imposed its own silence as we walked along ground where the Romans had walked almost two thousand years earlier—where, before the Romans and before Christ, the early predecessors of the Scottish people had hunted game, sown grain, and tended their cattle in the surrounding fields. There was a sense of the daily life that continued there, enduring through seasons, cycles, epochs, and the rise, fall, and absorption of the conquering forces.

After a quarter of a mile we came upon a fenced area. We slipped under the wire, climbed a grassy hillock, and stood overlooking a few acres of green fields pitted with series of parallel verdant ditches. We gazed all about, expectant, looking for signposts, directions, boards with precise lettering explaining, interpreting: words that would provide a context for the emptiness surrounding us.

There was nothing. Sheep grazed among the bracken and nettles beyond the grassy enclosure; some birds sang their song to whoever happened to be occupying the land at that moment. High above, an airplane passed, the monotony of its buzz muffled by the gray wooliness of the cloud cover.

"This must be the Roman camp," I suggested doubtfully.

"Must be," Harl agreed. "These ditches . . . it's some system of entrenchment."

We had both anticipated something more impressive—something for the mind and imagination to lay hold of. We gazed vaguely about. On the far side of the enclosure the figure of a man emerged suddenly from out of a ditch, stood for a moment against the sky, then went hurrying along the crest of a high embankment. There was an air of purposefulness and authority about the way he moved, and he appeared to be carrying a clipboard. "Aha—he must be the custodian." Experienced sightseers know there is always a custodian.

We hurried after him. He was engrossed in whatever it was he was doing, and scurried along like the White Rabbit in *Alice*. "Hey!" we yelled, determined not to let him slip out of our grasp, intent on having him make sense out of this very ordinary-seeming grassy area. But the wind blew the sound of our voices away, sending it streaming back over our shoulders. Harl broke into a sprint over the thick turf, caught up with him, tapped him on the shoulder. He whipped around, startled.

"Excuse me. Are you the custodian here? We'd like to know something about this place."

"Whew! I thought I was all alone here," the man said in an English accent. "Gave me a bit of a start coming at me like that."

Harl apologized. "We'd been calling but you couldn't hear us because of the wind."

"Thought it was the ghost of a Roman legionary, did you?" I remarked, joining them.

He fixed a strange, searching stare on me, remaining silent. On his clipboard I could see a map that obviously was a layout of the entrenchments surrounding us.

"Are you in charge of this place?" Harl asked.

"Heavens, no!" he replied. He looked to be in his late twenties, and everything about him was mousy: hair, coloring, clothes. His manner was awkward, and his speech stammering. "I'm up here from England for my summer holidays." He looked around the landscape in a flustered way. "As a matter of fact, I'm trying to find my way out of here. I left my mum and dad in the car back along the main road while I was looking at the Roman earthworks, and now I can't work out where the main road is."

Harl pointed out the direction we had come from, and recalled that he had seen a man snoozing in a car near the lane we had come along.

"That'll be Dad," he said, relieved. "My mum said she would be out looking at wild flowers. She likes identifying and classifying them—it's her hobby, like; and my sister's out there somewhere with the binoculars, bird-watching."

"And you've been exploring the Roman camp?" I asked.

"That's what I'm here for," he said, a little crankily, as if I should have known. "I'm spending my fortnight holiday following the route of Julius Agricola in his Scottish campaign. Look, this map here is of the Ardoch encampment; it was in use from the Agricolan to the Antonine periods."

The wind blew through his thin, light brown hair, lifting it, and seeming to ignite in his mild brown eyes the fires of an obsession. We recognized in that moment that we were in the company of an eccentric with a compelling passion.

"Julius Agricola?"

"He was the Roman general in charge of the campaign to subdue the Scottish tribes. His ambition was to be the one to bring the whole of Britain under Roman dominion. You see . . ." For the next hour he held forth on the Romans in Britain, his bird-watching sister and flower-classifying mum forgotten, his old dad snoozing in the car by the roadside pushed out of his mind by the opportunity we gave him to expound on the subject which, we learned, was the overwhelming interest of his life. We had whipped up the flame of his obsession, which burned now with a heat and light that illuminated us. On this history-soaked piece of ground, on a day in July—gray and blowy as it might have been here in the first century, the same cloud-blanket overhead, the same grass, heather, bracken, and woods concealing the brown rabbits darting suddenly out of cover, the same birdsong in the air— the place came alive for us.

As the young man described the activities that went on in a Roman fort in A.D. 80 it was as though from a corner of the field the metalsmith's hammer started to ring out as it struck the anvil, beating and forging weapons and tools; joiners and masons were at work hard by, building the barracks and the granaries to store the wheat levied from the conquered tribes, laying pipes for the water-storage tanks and bathhouses that provided hot water; engineers were hunched over their draft-

ing tables planning road-systems that to this day form many
of the main highways; clerks and medical orderlies scurried
about the day's business; artillerymen took care of the maintenance of weapons; cooks sweated over steaming pots, the smell
of fresh bread rising from the bakehouse; soldiers drilled under
the brutal discipline of their centurions, cursed, yearned for a
work-break, longed for their families, built ramparts, dug
trenches.

"We're standing right on top of one of the rows of trenches
that surrounded the rampart," the young man explained. "They
were filled with brushwood and thorn branches, and sentries
stood watch day and night; the corporal of the watch kept
the ticket with the password of the day written on it. What a
sight it must have been . . . just imagine it . . . at night: a signal
tower over here—and one there—and there—commanding
views of all the approaches, with great fires lit on them, so
that the flares would be visible for miles across country."

In the surrounding hills, the natives went truculently about
their business—wild, fierce Caledonian people, tending their
flocks, planting their wheat, paying their levies of cattle and
grain to the invaders while planning their destruction. Familiar
with the local topography, they carried out murderous raids,
stealing past the sentry-posts, determined not to let up until
they had driven the intruders from their land.

As we listened to the young man, as he expounded, eluci-
dated, answered our questions, we realized our good fortune
in running into one of that particular British species, more rare
these days than in the nineteenth century: a true eccentric, an
amateur with an ardency in a special field. His was the Roman
occupation of Britain. We never learned his name, but did
manage to elicit from him that his interest wasn't academic;
he had never been to a university, was a minor civil servant in
a town in southwest England, where the Roman influence was
longest and strongest. "When I was a lad, you could hardly
go anywhere or play anywhere without coming upon Roman
relics: remains of walls, baths, villas, bits of pottery or lead. I
wanted to study archeology at the university but my A levels

weren't good enough." Perhaps he was fortunate, I thought. Instead of becoming a dry pedantic scholar bent on publication, he sustained his passion live and fresh. "I *am* a member of our local antiquarian society, so I'm able to exchange information and ideas with other experts."

"All these ditches," I asked him, "what was their purpose?"

"I've got a sketch right here; I made a copy of it at the library when I was preparing for this trip. See, this is how archeologists have reconstructed the layout. Aerial photography shows up lines and boundaries that can't be seen just by tramping about an area. The fort here at Ardoch originally covered about sixty-three acres. That's considered a medium-sized fort; the largest would have been about a hundred and twenty acres, and the smallest, forty or less.

"The whole place would have been surrounded by high, broad earthen ramparts. The ramparts would be surrounded by a series of banks and ditches; that's what we're standing on at this moment. Here, at Ardoch, there were seven rows of trenches because the locals (the Caledonian tribes) had such fighting spirit, and hated the invaders with such fury, that the Romans needed a lot of protection against their endless forays and sorties. The ditches were filled with thornbushes or felled trees lashed together with the branches facing the enemy. Beyond that, the area would be booby-trapped with rows of deep pits, each holding a sharpened stake covered over with brushwood. You can just imagine what would happen to you if you fell into one of those."

"But what actually went on inside the fort?"

"Oh, it would have almost been like a working village in here." He showed us the ground plan. "See, there would be granaries—raised off the ground against the damp and the rats —built preferably of stone. The hutments for the troops would be built of wood, and here you can see there would be great tanks for surface water; if there was an army tilery nearby, the roofs would be tiled, because then the enemy couldn't set the roofs on fire, but otherwise they'd use thatching. The natives would have to fill the Roman granaries with their own grain, and these levies, of course, made them hate the invaders all the more. There would be barracks for the cohorts, kit-stores, headquarters, a commandant's house, even a hospital. Signal towers would be positioned to command views of all the approaches. They had bakehouses, a bathhouse with a hot water system, a construction shop for the manufacture of pottery and tiles and nails.

"To give you just an idea of the vast scale of supplies and engineering skills required to build and maintain one of these forts, it's been estimated that at Inchtuthil—a little to the north of here—the amount of seasoned wood required for the barracks alone amounted to thirteen and a half miles of timbers for the framed wattle-and-daub walling. And legionary detachments of engineers built miles and miles of roads they needed for access to the forts.

"The forts were built, at strategic points, about twelve miles apart, and they'd keep in touch with each other by signals from the towers and by armed parties. There would be frequent sorties with the natives. All winter, they'd remain here, in the wind and rain and cold, maintaining patrols. It must have been hard on the Romans, the filthy weather here, after the Mediterranean climate they were accustomed to. Then, at last, at the beginning of spring—just imagine—the guard out there on the lookout tower would yell out the news that he could see the cavalry approaching on the skyline." The young man's hand swept the breadth of the horizon. "I'm sure a great cheer went up as the word spread through the encampment that the relief party was arriving after the long, hard winter."

"How many men were there in a legion?" Harl asked.

"It went like this: Six centuries of eighty men each, under a centurion, made up a cohort. Ten cohorts made up a legion. Each legion had as its general a senator, whose tour of duty would last four years. There'd be others, too: staff officers, a standard bearer, a corporal of the watch—he'd be the chap who kept the ticket with the day's password written on it. And there were clerks, orderlies with first-aid training, a medical section, armor-smiths, joiners, masons, artillerymen to man the 'scorpions'—"

"Scorpions?"

"That's what they called the great man-killing catapults they used. And each legion had a hundred and twenty mounted men.

And they'd use non-Roman cohorts (regiments raised from among Mediterranean peoples, whom they considered expendable) to do all the dirty and dangerous work, like manning outpost forts or skirmishing ahead of the legions during campaigns."

"But what did the Romans come to Britain for? The climate was so awful and the people wild and barbaric."

"It's the old story—colonial expansion. They did to us just what we did in colonial times to America, Africa, India. The conquest of Britain had always been a dream in Roman financial and military circles. There were rumors of gold and mineral riches, though they turned out to be copper and tin and iron ore—which wasn't to be sneezed at either. The conquered British tribes were a source of cheap slave labor, and there was always the loot for the soldiers themselves."

"How did they fight?" Harl asked.

"They were masters in the art of warfare. The legionnaires fought with javelins. They would line up and first throw a light javelin for long range, then a heavier one for short range. In *thirty* seconds," he explained, eyes ablaze with the excitement of those far-off battles, "in thirty seconds, ten thousand javelins could smash into the enemy ranks. Then, in wedge formation, with short heavy swords, they would hurl themselves on the enemy while the cavalry, armed with lances, would charge on both flanks." The color rose in his pale cheeks as he described the charge. "Can you just imagine the slaughter, the carnage? It might sound bloody and brutal, but I don't know . . . in warfare of that sort, each soldier is aware of the lives he takes. Nowadays, we can just press a button and destroy a distant city and its population."

We agreed with him.

He looked at his wristwatch. "Heavens! Is that the time already! My mum and dad will be wondering what's happened to me. Which way did you say the main road is?" He scurried off, not interested in listening to our thanks. We stayed on for a while, wandering about the five-acre field that the eccentric fellow had transformed for us. A quarter of an hour later, Harl nudged me and pointed to a mound of a rampart. There, against the sky, where once a legionary soldier had stood scanning the landscape for signs of incursion by the wild hill people, stood our young friend again, gesticulating, asking in sign language which way he should go. With the exaggerated gestures of clowns, we indicated the avenue of trees that ran alongside the stone mansion beside the loch. He disappeared finally, leaving us with the ghosts of his Roman legionaries.

But he had left us, too, with our curiosity kindled to know more about Julius Agricola, this Roman general and administrator whose destiny had become so profoundly involved with that of the wild northern tribes on a cold, hostile island that kept him, for long periods of his life, away from the high civilization and lavish sun of his own Mediterranean country. We stopped off at the village library to look for books about him, and through succeeding summers and New York winters were on the lookout in libraries and bookshops for knowledge that would satisfy our curiosity. And, in the same way that our meeting with the grandson of the first reservoir keeper to have occupied our cottage had made the quality of the landscape around the cottage more accessible to the imagination, so did Julius Agricola make Scotland itself more available to us. We hiked over the same hills where his cohorts had marched, took our vacuum cleaner to be repaired in a town near where he had fought a great battle, used the laundromat in a village where one of his signal stations had stood, stopped for a beer in a pub in a hamlet on the lower slopes of the Grampians where a Roman road had run—our familiarity with the Roman past enriching the present for us, rendering it dense and many-layered, as if we wore enchanted spectacles that revealed more than was available to the naked eye.

Julius Agricola's father had been executed by the emperor Caligula for declining to do some dirty work for him. As a boy, Agricola had been more interested in philosophy than warfare, but his mother was ambitious for him to have a military career, and through the offices of Seneca (the Roman philosopher and dramatist who had been a friend of her hushand's) a military commission was secured for the nineteen-year-old youth. In A.D. 61 he was posted to the colonial war in Britain, which Caesar had first invaded in 55 B.C., and where Claudius, in A.D. 43, had landed his expeditionary forces for what was to become four hundred years of Roman dominion.

Agricola crossed over to Britain with his servants, horses, and equipment. His ability and conscientiousness soon brought him to the notice of the governor, Suetonius Paulinus, who picked him out to be his assistant, made him his messmate, and shared his tent with him on campaigns.

In the spring they set out, the legionaries carrying weapons, palisade-stakes, entrenching tools, and meal for bread and porridge; pack animals followed, bearing food, heavy equipment, and leather ridge tents called "butterflies." Every night the army would dig in, using twenty-thousand stakes they carried, planting them in the ground all around for protection. They moved forward ten or twelve miles a day.

The tribes they were subduing practiced the Druidic religion, which at this time was quite barbarous, with human sacrifice as one of its rites; the Romans felt they were destroying something evil, their self-righteousness probably as assured as that of the British missionaries in the nineteenth century who followed in the wake of military conquest, preaching Christianity in Africa and India.

Agricola's first victory, under Suetonius, was the defeat of the uprising of the Iceni of Norfolk under their queen, Boudicca; their revolt had been provoked by eighteen years of oppression, mismanagement, and despoliation of their kingdom by the Roman colonists. But the fighting so devastated the land that famine and disaster followed; Suetonius was recalled by Nero, and Agricola went back with him. There was peace in Britain for ten years.

Posted to Britain again in A.D. 70, Agricola took command of the XXth Roman legion before his thirtieth birthday. Under Cerialis, the newly appointed governor of Britain, the Romans intended to complete their conquest. Their policy was to "pacify" the whole country, then reduce the garrison and introduce municipal self-government, meanwhile enriching themselves by the exploitation of the conquered peoples and natural resources of the territory. In A.D. 72 and 73, in the course of brutal and costly fighting, they pushed northward, the landscape becoming more mountainous and wild, the natives more savage. They built stone fortifications at strategic points, and left a cohort of hardy centurions at each one to winter there and keep an eye on the locals; but the tribesmen often slaughtered the soldiers and set fire to the fortifications, and, according to Tacitus, the enemy would in this way win back in the winter what they had lost in the summer. Cerialis was called back to Rome after three years, Agricola returning as well. His daughter, at thirteen, was married to Tacitus, who was to become the historian of imperial Rome.

In the summer of 78, Agricola set out for Britain for the third time, this time as governor. After the most fearful carnage, he completed the defeat of what is now Wales, and during the winter involved himself in civil administration. According to Tacitus, he was the only Roman soldier and administrator to have returned three times to one province; by now, well familiar with the character of the peoples of Britain, he knew that force would be ineffectual if followed by injustice, so he set about correcting the racketeering, the extortion by the centurions, and all the other varieties of exploitation possible for a conquering power to inflict upon the defeated. He brought corruption under control, ran a just and able administration to which the tribes submitted, and suppressed the abuses which, in the words of Tacitus, had made the Roman peace "no less terrible than war."

His technique was to subdue the native tribes by unceasing raids and terror, then pardon their resistance and offer the beguilements of peace. He continued to move inexorably northward, overcoming the tribes of what is now southern Scotland and making raids as far as the River Tay.

An abiding concern of Agricola's was the Romanization of Britain and the assimilation of the native tribes. By now, there were no more rebellions in the South; they had all been subdued. Government was carried on by local chiefs organized in Roman-style municipalities, managing their own affairs but paying taxes to the Romans, whose courts dealt with capital charges. Between campaigns Agricola traveled about, encouraging the use of his own army's surveyors, architects, and

craftsmen for the building of towns, temples, and houses. The
natives were encouraged to speak Latin, dress in Roman togas,
build Roman baths. Romans, mostly from Gaul, went out to
the new overseas province—schoolmasters, professors, literary
men teaching Latin and law, culture and rhetoric. In his engaging book *Agricola and Roman Britain*, A. R. Burns writes
that to the Romans, the idea of a British barrister was as
comical in its day as the idea of cannibals in top hats was to
the nineteenth-century British.

The Romans drafted Britons into their army, and there was
intermarriage with British women; A. R. Burns compares the
cultural "melting-pot" of the Roman Empire with that of the
United States. The spread of Latin eliminated language barriers,
so that members of tribes who in recent generations had been
painting themselves blue intermarried with civilized, educated
Romans. The Romans took care to consider local custom carefully when they imposed their own legal and civic systems.

Once the South was subdued, Agricola had to deal with the
hostile tribes in the lowlands of Scotland—a problem that has
been likened to what the British administration in India had to
face in the nineteenth century: a hostile region, poor and wild
and not worth conquering, that nevertheless had to be subdued
for military or strategic reasons.

In the summer of 80, he built a line of forts from the River
Tweed in the East to the River Clyde in the West; he had an
excellent eye for positioning forts, whose locations he took
pride in personally selecting, and no fort placed by him was
ever taken or evacuated. In the summer of 81, entrenching
himself further north, he built a girdle of forts from the Firth
of Forth to the Clyde, then advanced as far as the Firth of Tay.
The River Earn, which flows into the Tay just north of the
hills where our cottage stands, in those times formed the northern boundary of the tribes of mid-Scotland: the Damnoni, a
mining people, whose opposition to foreign domination persisted with stubborn ferocity. So tough were these local savages
reputed to be that the Romans believed them impervious to
the damp chill that pervaded the boggy birch- and hazel-
thicketed countryside, where the wretched winters made life
a misery for the invaders. It was during this period that Ardoch

—where we had found our eccentric young informant striding the ramparts—would have been built and occupied, along with all the military stations and signal towers whose sites are marked on our local ordnance map.

But by the end of his fifth summer in Britain, Agricola had not advanced much further than the Forth–Clyde line, which says much for the spirit of resistance in the local tribes. By the end of 82, he received permission from Rome for the invasion of Caledonia.

For his final striking force, Agricola employed three legions; he had numerous auxiliary regiments, eight thousand light infantry, and five thousand cavalry. He brought his fleet up the east coast, alongside the string of fishing villages where we would go to use the beaches on very hot days. According to Tacitus, this was the first time the fleet was ever used as part of a fighting force to carry out sea-borne raids, as ships had, until then, been used only for transport service. Agricola was aware of the impenetrability of the roadless glens and mountains, bog and birch-thicket, that would have to be breached, but pushed on nevertheless. "He could not, or would not, stop," J. D. Mackie has written. Air photography shows up clearly the series of camps the Roman built at twelve-mile intervals, firm bases for patroling, attack, and defense.

A conquering army has never marched through the Highlands of Perth, our district—where we rambled, picnicked, and hiked, from year to year returning to where we remembered the bluebells grew specially thickly, or where we had spotted a doe with a fawn beside a pool in a spinney of hazel and elder. "Half-tamed, they are pretty enough for hill-walkers," A. R. Burns says of these parts; "wholly wild, they were no sort of place to take long columns of men and animals." The broad valleys to the east, though, including the foothills of our own range, have been traveled since prehistoric times, and were the route of Agricola's marching forces. His strategy was to advance along this route, blocking all the valley entrances to the Highlands by construction of forts. The forts were armed by archers, and scorpions, and were maintained without advancement over the winter.

The following spring, the penetration of Caledonia continued. The Caledonian tribes, meanwhile, joined forces under their leader, Calgacus, and organized large-scale resistance, their leaders fully capable of planning and executing a coherent military strategy. Agricola's forces, after weeks of marching, harried and harassed by the enemy's rear and flank attacks, met the Caledonians face to face, at last, for the final pitched battle, "at the very limits of the world," according to Tacitus, for defeat in that wild enemy territory in the Grampian hills, with no means of retreat, would have been disastrous. Agricola sent away his own horse, as Caesar had been wont to do, to show that there would be no way for him to escape, and took up his stand beside his men.

The Grampians, the highest mountains in Britain, derive their name from a later misspelling of the Latin *Mons Craupius*, but no one is really sure of where the battle of Mons Craupius actually took place; different historians subscribe to different theories about its exact location, working from Tacitus's account of the battle and from archeological evidence.

They must have been a formidable sight to the undermanned legions—thirty thousand Caledonians under the command of their chariot-driving chieftains, who, dressed in primitive tartans, with helmets and shields flashing, urged forward pairs of small, swift ponies; they were followed by the infantry in their thousands, half-naked, barefoot, clashing their knob-ended spears against their shields in a terrifying clamor, wild for the blood of the invaders. The Caledonians were grimly aware that this was the last point in mountainous country where native tribes could be congregated in defense of the North, and knew that they were defending, as well, the last major tract of good land in the Highlands—the rich agricultural valley whose vista opened out to us each time we gained the end of the road out of our glen to join the main highway to our village. They knew, too, that defeat would mean subjection to an imperialist power from whom they could expect only plunder, pillage, rape, conscription, levies on their cattle and corn, and slave labor underground in mines and above ground clearing forests and draining swamps. It is here that Tacitus attributes to their leader, Calgacus, his famous rallying call to battle, and tirade against the imperialists: "For robbery, massacre and rapine they abuse the name of Empire; and where they have made desolation, they call it peace." *Solitudinem faciunt, pacem appellant*—the truth of these words echoing down through wars of expansionist conquest to the present day.

Tacitus has left a detailed account of the battle, even down to the red hair of the Caledonian tribes, a particular confirmed by the inordinate number of redheaded children we would encounter in the villages of the district. *At the very limits of the world* they came face to face, the Britons fighting fiercely against the heavily armed Romans, pitching their swords and shields against the javelins, spiked shields, and bows and arrows of the Romans.

Agricola, heavily outnumbered by the enemy, was forced to marshal his troops in a line so thin that historians have reckoned it must have extended almost two miles in length— the light infantry flanked by cavalry on each wing, supported by reserves of armored men, more cavalry, and lances. The Britons, up in the hills, looked down on the enemy, and seeing how small their numbers, swept down in flanked attacks. But Agricola was a professional soldier, and well read in classic military techniques by which Alexander, Hannibal, and Caesar had won great victories; outflanking the Britons in a classic maneuver that employed the troops held in reserve for such a purpose, he broke through their line and cut them off from retreat. After terrible carnage, in the course of which some of the tribesmen "in a berserk fury hurled themselves on the Romans with their bare hands and were cut down," the Britons were routed, scattering and fleeing for cover in the woods, with the Roman infantry and cavalry in a pursuit that only darkness and exhaustion ended.

The conquerors divided the booty, while the families of the defeated tribes wandered weeping and lamenting about the bloodied battlefield, searching for survivors, dragging away the wounded, sounding a chorus of their grief and bitterness. Then "there was a great silence everywhere," Tacitus reports. "The hills were deserted; some houses in the distance still smouldered; our scouts made no contact."

"Now Britain was completely subdued," Tacitus claims, though the land-based Romans appear only to have penetrated as far north as the Moray Firth, near Inverness; but the Roman fleet did sail north up to the Orkney Islands to receive the submission of the tribes there. Leaving a northerly fort in the area near Perth, the Romans withdrew, Agricola himself leading "the land forces by slow stages," Tacitus tells us, "so that the very leisureliness of his passing might terrorize the newly conquered tribes."

It was expected that in the spring the Romans would march once again against the debilitated tribes, imposing the Roman will and way of life upon the wild hill people. But Agricola was recalled to Rome. His work was left unfinished and he was never again to return to Britain. And as the Caledonians realized that the Romans were not returning; as the harsh winter turned to spring and summer, and the crops ripened, and no invader came marching in demanding levies, they began to understand that though at Mons Craupius they had "lost a battle," they had "won the war."

Agricola's disappointment must have been bitter, but the government in Rome had its reasons. It is thought that they considered that an undue proportion of the legionary forces was being engaged in an area where there was neither rich land nor the possibility of plunder to make the commitment worthwhile, and there seemed no end in sight to the campaigning— the very horizon, as Mackie puts it, seeming to recede before Agricola as he advanced. Also, the emperor was having trouble in the Danube and needed more troops there. Tacitus, though, is bitter about the untimely recall of his illustrious father-in-law, and ascribes it to imperial jealousy of his power and victory.

Agricola returned home a hero—a famous general and governor at the age of forty-four. Domitian showered him with high honors for his triumph in Britain, but left him to live out the remaining ten years of his life in obscurity, never employing him again in government office. In his biography, which came out in the year 98, Tacitus writes in an aggrieved way about the neglect by the mighty of this great hero; but Agricola was a modest man, he comments, and lived his remaining years quietly and "drank deep of repose."

*   *   *

Our young man on the ramparts was spending two weeks charting Agricola's campaigning in Scotland. It took us many summers to trace his advance to the northernmost point that he had been able to take the Roman Empire's aspirations for conquest in Britain—the site of a fort in Strathmore that turned out to be the last outpost, rather than the base for further forward operations. The northern fortifications were gradually abandoned, and the barbaric Iron Age culture of the northern Britons was preserved into the Christian Dark Ages.

The emperor Hadrian came to Britain personally, in 122, to survey the siting of the great wall named for him, which took six years in the building and was a fortification against the trouble-making northerners. But it was too far south, and in 139–142 Lollius Urbius invaded the Firth-Clyde isthmus and built a wall where Agricola's forts had been, naming it the Antonine Wall after Emperor Antoninus Pius. It was built of turf on a stone foundation fifteen feet thick at the base and six feet across the top, ten feet high and defended by a deep ditch, with forts two miles apart along its thirty-seven miles, and Ardoch was once again occupied. This was intended as the new northerly frontier, but since the Romans were feeling a strain on their manpower, only small contingents were kept on the Antonine Wall; and it was twice overrun by the northern tribes, twice rebuilt in the next forty years, and abandoned sometime after 186. It is said that the Romans "civilized the South, but only occupied the North."

The unconquered North remained anti-Roman, while their southern neighbors made their peace with the conquerors, adopting Roman ways with enthusiasm—particularly the Celtic aristocracies. The separation of Britain into two kingdoms, Scotland and England, which persists today in Scottish nationalism's enduring desire to be independent of England, can be traced back as far as the Roman era, as can the very difference in the characters of Scot and Englishman.

But despite the continuation of the pagan, barbaric tribes in their Early Iron Age way of life, certain aspects of Roman civilization influenced the development of what would later become Scotland under the union of four peoples: Picts, Scots, Britons, and Angles. The Romans introduced smelting and the use of glass, and the roads they constructed opened up new possibilities of communication between unrelated groups. They introduced Christianity sometime around A.D. 400, as well as the concept, unknown to these primitive tribal clans, of "a power which was universal and not local," as Professor Mackie puts it; "which was organized and not personal—the sentry on the wall did his duty at the bidding of an Emperor a thousand miles away—and which, because it was so organized, was permanent and not dependent upon the life of a strong chief."

Had we gone to Ardoch the day before, or the day after—or perhaps even an hour later than we did on that gray morning in August—we would not have run into our young man from the South manning the ramparts with his maps and charts and diagrams. That five-acre field, lying on someone's farm, would most likely have remained for us a dull and incomprehensible series of turfed ditches; and the clash of the legionnaires' lances against Caledonian shields, the terrified neigh and whinny of the plunging horses, the din of chariot wheels dashing down the stony hillsides echoing through the glen, would have been drowned out by the traffic passing along the highways: the great deafening trucks bringing food and manufactured goods from Common Market countries across the English Channel. We would have heard only the buzz of mechanized farming implements plowing and harvesting the same fields that the Iron Age Caledonian tribes had been cultivating long before the Romans—or we—ever set foot in Scotland.

CHAPTER
13

Rural Rhythms

"When one lives in the country one has to have a simple soul," Mishima wrote in one of his novels. Jung, alone in his house in the country, observed, "I pump the water from the well. I chop the wood and cook the food. These simple acts make a man simple; and how difficult it is to be simple. I live in . . . modest harmony with nature."

Simple acts, a modest harmony with nature: that, I suppose, is what we are looking for each year when we lug unwieldly baggage in and out of frantic airports—swearing, in the closeness and crush and depersonalization of jet travel, and the dislocation of being in transit, that it is madness to have a country place three thousand miles from home, the effort expended far in excess of its reason.

And yet, each year, as we stepped out of the car to swing open the white gate into the stableyard, with that first rush of the hill air into the lungs and the green silence around the glinting waters of the loch came the sense of privilege that we had access to such peace and beauty.

By complicated arrangements involving time, money, and the expenditure of much energy, we gained for ourselves, for the few summer months, the opportunity to be "simple." Yet, every year, driving up the hill road, I would experience a pang as we passed a bleak farm laborer's cottage opposite the Camerons' seventeenth-century stone barn, where a young woman invariably sat on the doorstep, watching a baby and some kittens tumbling about on the path: Alison, grand-daughter-in-law to Mrs. Cameron, wife of the third grand-son—the one who was not "wild." A junior manager in a local branch of a national chain of department stores, her husband wore a suit and tie and brought his wages conscientiously home each week to the neglected cottage where his granny allowed them to live rent-free. As the summers went by, there would be new babies and kittens, last years' babies now toddling or running about or riding tricycles, the young mother on the doorstep, cigarette always alight between her lips, gazing dully into the hills, and wishing she were elsewhere—shopping at Woolworth's in the narrow, crowded streets of her native Glasgow, perhaps, or buying a newspaper-wrapped, vinegar-drenched portion of fish and chips, or eating a chocolate bar in the intimate darkness of a cinema—anywhere but this solitari-ness where nothing but green hills and browsing sheep engaged the eye.

Watching us as we appeared on the hill road each year, jet-borne from New York, waving to us as we went by, did she wonder at us coming all this way to hole up in the endless hills? There she was in fine weather, year after year, smoking, immobilized by the increasing brood of babies, the penny-pinching, the boredom; frilly undies—black and purple and crimson bikini panties—blowing incongruously on the wash-line beside the sheep-dipping pens, while a rooster strutted about crowing arrogantly in the barnyard. Our privileged time in the hills must have seemed, to her, a sentence of unflagging monotony.

Yet the stir of envy I would experience as we passed uphill through the Camerons' farmyard was for the unchanging way of life that for generations has rooted the people in these hills, imprinting them with this landscape that confers on them—the girl would acquire it or else escape back to the city—their self-sufficiency, their reserve, their inclination to understate-ment: a form of modesty that reduces the seasons and cycles

of crops and lambs and wild flowers and eternal greenness to
"quite nice" or "no' bad."

But, like all of us, they pay a price for the simple life, their
very rootedness confining them, imposing limits on their hori-
zons and narrowing the range of their possibilities. Old Mrs.
Cameron told us that she had been to Edinburgh—less than
fifty miles away—very rarely in her eighty years, and the wild
grandsons never went there: "A reeky cess-pit wi' filthy foreigners crowding you off the pavements into the bloody
traffic" was Angus's summation of that graceful city. Mrs.
Cameron did her shopping in the village ("Such a trip it was in
the old days in the horse and trap, compared with being
whizzed there by Meg in the Mini," she observed); apart from
a rare visit to Perth on farm business, and the annual seaside
holiday, her life was circumscribed by the hills. For her, the
map of the world would be charted in a form similar to Stein-
berg's New Yorker's map: comprising her farm, her sister's
farm, the village, and then, very remote, Edinburgh, England
down south, and the outer mistiness of foreign parts. She referred to New York as though it were some fabled Atlantis.

But, so long as there is a television antenna on the roof, the
world comes crowding into the most isolated hamlet, the
humblest but-and-ben cottage, the great country houses; the
pure hill air quivers with electromagnetic waves bearing American crime shows, standardized faces of politicians and news-
casters, traffic jams, rock stars, and pictures of landscapes
devastated by acts of nature or man. Windows of houses
passed in the night flicker icy blue with TV images. Mrs.
Cameron and her sister, Miss Kirstie Aird, both fine horse-
women in their day, loved watching show-jumping, but
seemed to look at shootouts under the Brooklyn Bridge and
cops chasing killers through suburban Los Angeles with equally
undifferentiated concentration. "Fiona MacFadyen (that's
Jessie MacFadyen's younger granddaughter) is going out with
one of the Bay City Rollers," Mrs. Cameron told me over
morning coffee. "Are they a soccer team?" I asked. "Och, no—
they're that famous rock group!" she explained, shocked at my
lack of sophistication.

The waters of our loch flow from some undefiled source

that springs cold and clear out of an Ice Age rocky declivity; but the loch is also a reservoir for many local communities, and the waters are filtered, purified, and chemically treated before they are led into the pipes and faucets of homes. Yet there is no way of filtering the mindlessness and dismal vulgarity fed into people's consciousness from the reservoir of possibility that television represents. We would stand on the forestry road in the evenings, looking out across the bowl formed by the hills as it filled up with blue twilight, scattered lights from isolated homesteads twinkling in the dusk, aware that the simple life this scene represented was as susceptible to corruption as if we stood overlooking a polluted city.

The square towers and battlements of Gavin MacFadyen's castle, its walls of stone whitewashed against the dark green of its forests, catch the last of the light; on a high, arrow-slit turret a television antenna is etched against the sky. Castles, fortalices, keeps, strongholds, still standing after centuries, built to withstand the bloody brutalities of warring clans, Catholic against Protestant, Scot against Englishman, are no longer impregnable; the beams from television transmitters penetrate the thickness of stone battlements and bone skulls with a power not dreamed of in the aspirations of princes, chieftains, and kings throughout history.

A repairman comes out to Glenauchen to fix the phone. He looks around the living room. "You haven't got a telly? Nor a wireless? I don't know how you stand it up here. Three days of this would send me round the bend."

Yet days and weeks could go by when there would be no shift from the simple, the tranquil, and the beautiful, and we would perceive the perfection around us as the rule. We had an arrangement with Robbie Kirkbride, who would have mown the grass and scythed the nettles just before our arrival; in the kitchen garden, beyond the clipped hedge, the tenants' vegetables and strawberries lay in neatly marshaled ranks of leafy green on the loamy soil. Every prospect was pleasing, and going from one room to the next, one would glance out of a window and fall into a trance, held there by the slopes of the hills rising greenly all around to meet the blue sky; or watching a bird swoop down where a fish had revealed its presence by a silver bubble that surfaced on the loch to send out a ripple of watery rings; or standing by while white towering clouds massed up, great sculptured cathedrals of marmoreal density forming at the far end of the loch; or gazing at a fisherman standing in hip-boots in the water reeling, casting, reeling, casting, mesmerized by his soundless, dreamlike actions.

One still, sunny afternoon, too warm for the sheep who huddled in pools of shadow cast by our trees, I was disturbed at my reading by an incessant, buzz saw–like humming, followed by a light, high-pitched sound, almost a small whine. I roused myself to investigate the source of these odd sounds and tracked them down to a corner of the large staircase window, through which light flooded in from the stableyard; here, across the corner formed by the sill and frame, a spider had built its web, where it was holding prisoner a large, frantic honeybee. The spider was tormenting its prey by making forays and retreats from the center of the web, dancing light and agile across the delicate filaments, withdrawing when the fluttering of the bee's wings agitated the air with a small, frenzied turbulence that gave rise to the desperate-sounding whining buzz which had interrupted my reading. It was a horrible spectacle: the spider's long-legged bouncing dance over the web as if to taunt its victim, followed by a withdrawal to the edge to relish the bee's terrified, futile effort to extricate itself from its delicate bonds.

I called Harl to come and help rescue the bee. "How can we take sides?" he said. "The spider's entitled to its dinner after all the trouble it's taken to build the web and trap the bee." We watched, appalled, with fascinated horror, the brutal struggle for survival in the quiet of the afternoon. But the victim claimed our pity—as victims generally do, regardless of circumstance—and Harl freed the bee from its captivity, scooping it out of the web with a spoon and depositing it outside, where, we hoped, it would recover from its shocked, stunned state, while the spider skulked off like some thwarted Dickensian villain, and curled itself up, immobile, into a malign ball. "Now it will have to build another web and look out for another meal," Harl observed. "We don't really have the right to interfere in these matters."

"It's the kind of situation where interfering is wrong and not interfering is wrong," I said. "I only hope that the spider procures its next victim without my having to witness the massacre." We settled back with our books, once more having had to purchase tranquillity by ignoring an unpleasant aspect of reality.

Donny MacIver dropped by, ostensibly to drop off a dish of raspberries, but in fact to bring us news of the swans. He and Tottie had been very concerned about one member of the swan couple who for years had made their home on their loch. The male had been missing for some weeks now, and the female and her fleet of adolescents appeared to be disconsolate. That morning, one of the forestry men, driving to work through a glen to the south of ours, the winding road swathed in early morning mist, had been forced to brake suddenly at a large mass lying across the middle of the road; he got out to find the male swan lying there, lifeless, its huge wingspread spanning the narrow road. There was no blood, no sign of injury. But telegraph poles and wires skirted the road, and he surmised that the bird had flown, in the early morning fog, right into the wires and had been electrocuted. We were all filled with regret for the destruction of the graceful, imperial bird and its long-established, monogamous marriage. In his phlegmatic way, Donny reported that Tottie was "that upset" about it; he'd found her "greeting" into her hankie at the kitchen door when the forestry man had stopped by at their place with the news. Perhaps the female would find a new mate and bring him back to the loch next spring, he'd reassured her—and himself as well, I thought, for in his own tight-bound way he was "that upset" too.

He allowed as how he had time for just a "fly" cup of tea, over which he recounted with malicious pleasure the latest outrage of his curmudgeonly neighbor, Geordie McCaskie, who had sold a ruined wreck of a but-and-ben cottage that had stood, uninhabited for decades, on a pleasant slope on his grazing lands. The buyer, a well-to-do Polish delicatessen owner from a nearby town, had spent much money, time, and effort in rebuilding the cottage as a weekend retreat. The renovation was almost completed, and now McCaskie was point-blank refusing permission for the Electricity Board to set up power cables across his land to connect the electricity up. The Pole, in a fury, was threatening to sue; McCaskie, in his misanthropic perversity, enjoyed nothing better than engaging in litigious dispute, and remained intractable, providing the whole glen with the sort of outrageous scandal they enjoyed more than anything television could provide.

"You should have haird the buzzing outside the kirk on Sunday—there hasn't been such a stew in the glen since the time old Geordie stopped his son's wedding," Donny mused over his third cup of tea. "Did you ever hear that one?" He leaned back comfortably in his chair, stirred the sugar in. "He started out in the glen, you ken, with a wife and two bairns. As soon as the bairns were old enough to take care of themselves, his wife ran away, back to her family up in the Black Isle; she couldna' thole another day with that man. So he got in a housekeeper, Mrs. McWheedy, who matches him for illtemper, and even so he has to pay her well, for she's threatening to leave him these fifteen years. Then the younger lad, Charlie, ran away after the old man thrashed him for now't, and no one's haird of him since, though some think the puir laddie's in Canada.

"But Alistair, the older McCaskie boy—he's been working the farm for his father since the old man took him out of school when he was fifteen and told him "You'll work here on the ferm for me or get out and fend for yer sel' (he broke that one's spirit airly)—well, Alistair got engaged to a nice lass from Perth, and the engagement went on and on for I don't know how many years; they say the old man refused to give permission for the marriage. But at last the gairl put her foot down, and the day was set for the wedding. The banns were read out in the kirk, the bride's dress was all ready, the presents had all been sent, the food prepared. And what d'you think the auld devil did then? The night before the wedding he comes into Alistair's room. They say Alistair was looking at himself in the glass, trying on the tail-coat and striped breeks he'd rented for the occasion. And the old man tells him that if the wedding takes place, he's cutting him out of his will, kicking him off the ferm. He'll have a wife, alright—but no job, no house, no inheritance; he'll be left, the auld devil tells him, as nekkid in the world as the day he came into it. And the gormless fellow—he just bowed down to the old man's wicked will, and called the wedding off! Friday night it was; the wedding was set for next day; the flowers had all been arranged in the kirk; even Tottie had bought a new frock for the occasion. That was a scandal if ever there was one. The lad should have gone ahead and called Geordie's bluff. There was no one else could run the farm—no one else would stand his evil-spirited ways—and there's no one else he could leave the money to, seeing all the rest of his loved ones had all run away from him just as fast as their legs could carry them. Mind you, he has enough spite in him to leave the money to a cats' home, even though he doesn't like cats."

We sometimes encountered Alistair McCaskie on our hill walks: a burly, handsome man driving a tractor and yelling at the sheep. He didn't strike us as gormless. "So he's never married?" we asked.

"Worse than that," Donny said, his church-elder's rigid righteousness replacing his expression of malicious pleasure. "*Far worse.* Drove him to sin, the old man did. A father driving his own flesh and blood to sinfulness." He lowered his voice so that the pots and pans on the shelves should not hear what he told us. "He's taken a gairl in to live with him! That Yorkshire lass who's in charge of the pony trekking at the hotel. Living together in sin, they are."

She was a familiar figure in the glen, with her long fair hair, her boots and jodhpurs, currying and grooming the horses in the hotel stables, or graceful on her pony as she led a string of hotel residents, clumsily astride their rented steeds, over the hills and along the drove roads we hiked. "But doesn't Geordie object to that?" we asked.

"Och, he couldn't care less," Donny said with scorn. "He hasn't set foot in the kirk himself these twenty years I've been in the glen. He moved (after his wife left him) to that bungalow he built on the main road; he doesn't give a hoot what scandalous goings on are happening in the farmhouse, just so long as Alistair doesn't wed." He stood up to leave. "That puir Polish grocer's going to have to drag him through the law courts before he gets that electricity into his fine new house. He was planning to move in this August, but he'd best buy some oil lamps and tell his missus to start learning to cook over a stick fire. Och, is that the time already! Tottie will be wondering what's hindering me from my tea." As he went out, along the terrace, we saw through the kitchen window his face aglow with enjoyment at his contemplation of the grocer's plight and Geordie McCaskie's contentious ways.

Year after year, the blessing of the stranger on the train held fast, and the locals could not recall such a succession of warm summers, with the mercury hovering around seventy for weeks on end. We would light the living room fire at night only for the coziness of its mumbling as the tongues of flame licked away at the coals, and because we liked the idea of the smoke rising from the chimney as a sign of human habitation in an isolated landscape, its reassuring quality as elemental for us as it must have been to the early Neolithic people who inhabited these hills. Robbie Kirkbride, in his work as a forestryman, had unearthed a flint axe on the slopes of Dalrioch, to the gratification of the archeologists at the Perth Museum, who until then had had no proof of early civilization in our hills; the find had been named for him, and the axe, wrapped in cotton in a toffee tin, was treasured by the Kirkbrides and displayed with pride to visitors.

On soft warm nights, in the lingering dusk, the bats swooped about the stableyard, looping and diving under the eaves of the stable and the byre; moths battered their winged furriness against our lit windowpanes as we read late into the night, drawn by the lure of the only source of light in the hills. In late August, a harvest moon would swing up, bobbing light and orange over the top of Dalrioch, rimming the hills' edge with pale fire, growing white and brilliant the higher it rose until the loch was brimming with silver and the slopes were transformed to a luminous blue. We would all be afflicted with a sort of moon-madness; it was as though the small stone house

was adrift in a sea of luminescence; the moonlight would not
let us be, and we were drawn out in the way one is drawn
onto the deck of a ship. One after another we would leave the
house to drift about on the banks of the loch as if we were
waiting for something to happen. There was no containing
such luminousness, such absence of substance, the bulk of the
hills without solidity, their composition a mere difference of
quality of effulgence from the flat silver of the water and the
transparent blue of the sky, the brown trout under the water
themselves reduced to silvered flickers of insubstantiality. The
beams would gather into a mercurial, almost solid silver path
across the water, which was black now where no radiance
touched it.

There was a sense of awe, as if we waited, watching, while
some force was building up, something vast and nameless, the
hushed expectation making everyone a little crazy. Even the
sheep on the hillside, their pelts showing blue-white on the
moonlit grass, would shift uneasily, the ewes bleating to the
lambs to move in a little closer, as if the landscape might dissolve in the silent wash of silver. The children would make
crazy jokes, think of wild things to do like stripping and
swimming the length of the silvered path to the far shore of
the loch, dipping their arms in it, expecting to lift them dripping with silver, hurling stones into it, watching it shatter and
re-form. No one could get to bed until, in its slow, majestic
course, the setting moon descended at last behind Ben Shawe,
casting us into soft darkness, and turning the heavens over the
next valley a pearly blue that tipped the tops of the loch's
black wavelets when a small pre-dawn wind ruffled its surface.

When there was no moon, night in the glen would be so
black you could put a fist through it. Late one night, Neil
and I walked home up the hill road. We had been visiting Miss
Kirstie Aird; the dark was so dense we could scarcely see each
other and tried to keep to the humped crown of the unpaved
road to avoid falling into ditches. Suddenly, in the valley to
our left, along the slopes of Dalrioch, a long, tailed comet of
brilliant white light whooshed soundlessly past us like a high-

speed, fully lit, celestial express train that we could not hear, though we could feel the rush of it on our eardrums, and disappeared beyond the black, invisible loch. We stood still, speechless in the pitch-darkness. "Did you see that?" I asked finally.

"*Yes.*"

I felt relieved that there was another witness: if only I had seen it, I would have begun to suspect that the solitude was beginning to affect my perception. Whatever it was—a falling star in horizontal trajectory over the earth, a meteorite, some spectacle wrought by who knows what ancient potency inhabiting these hills from bygone occupations of pagan people closer in touch with the forces of nature than we—we accepted it as part of the wonder of this place. We ploughed our way uphill through the dense blackness, which thinned out where the beam from our lighted cottage window penetrated it at the top of the road.

When the days were too warm and close for walking, we would take towels and swimming suits and drive to the coast. There is nowhere in Scotland where one is far from the sea, and since the late eighteenth century fishing has been an important national industry. Helen is descended from generations of fisherfolk whose fleet sailed out of a small seaport in the border country—hardy, self-contained people who put out to sea in all weathers to net the catch from the cold North Sea waters. Her old mother still lives in the house where Helen was born in the blustery, stony village; whenever she was inclined to be critical of modern-day youth, particularly as manifested by her own grandsons, she would remind Helen, "When my grandfather was only nineteen years old, he was already captain of his own herring fleet—you wouldna' have found him asleep in his bed at eleven in the morning, nor slouching, gormless, picking away at a guitar in broad daylight when there was work to be done!"

In this village, on a certain date every year, all the window-shades in all the windows of the houses are drawn, to commemorate a terrible disaster in the nineteenth century when the entire fishing fleet went down in a fierce North Sea gale. Scarcely a family in the community was untouched by this tragedy, and a whole generation of children grew up without fathers, uncles, older brothers; the women were left widows and there were no young men for the girls to marry. The ceremony recalling the great disaster is an act of homage to the courage of men who daily face, for their livelihood, danger and the possibility of death by drowning. But it seems to be, as well, a propitiatory act, in deference to the absoluteness of the ocean.

Heading for a place to swim, we would drive eastward through the rich farmland of the Kingdom of Fife, until we came to a sea road that links a string of ancient little fishing villages and seaports along the East Neuk of Fife; ruins of medieval castles crumble imperceptibly on top of cliffs that drop sheer to small stone harbors where fishing fleets shelter. There are villages of narrow cobbled streets running between fishermen's houses with pantiled roofs, color-washed pink, yellow, gray, many of them restored by the National Trust, and housing painters, potters, weavers, poets, or university professors who use them as second homes; the locals prefer, if possible, the modern convenience of bright little boxlike council houses to the damp and drafts of poky quaintness. In these villages one can loiter in a boat shed to watch wooden fishing craft being constructed in much the same fashion as Noah must have built his ark; and there are long, pungent-smelling sheds where fisher lassies kipper herring to golden smokiness over smoldering oak-chips, not far from a sixteenth-century tower or toll-booth, or a thirteenth-century church, or a golf-links where retired admirals and colonels and slender, well-preserved ladies in tweeds putt and swing and drive on smooth greensward overlooking the sea.

We would make our way to one or another sandy cove, where we would swim and watch small children digging and splashing or waiting patiently on line for a donkey ride or an ice-cream cone.

On a very warm day in August, when even the bees in our garden moved with torpor from one bloom to the next, their buzzing muted, we decided to take a houseguest, and our young son and the Hunters' daughter, for a picnic on a beach. There was an early harvest that year, and in the barley fields and cornfields the combines were at work, cutting great swathes, threshing, pouring out ripe grain in steady gushes of gold; and on narrow country roads traffic was slowed by tractors lumbering along pulling wagons piled high with straw.

The coastline was misty as we drove along the shore road. We left the car in the village and parked near the Old Men's Club, which had a sign saying exactly that—not "Senior Citizens' Club" or "Golden Age Club." As we carried our picnic down a steep little cobbled street to the sea, we saw that the ocean had become entirely obscured by a great blanket of dense fog which had rolled landward from the horizon. The beach was damp, chilly, and almost deserted, and it was hard to believe that we had taken refuge from the heat just a short while ago. There would be no swimming, but we decided we would have our picnic anyway. The children went for a stroll along the sands while we laid out the lunch on a flat rock.

They walked away a few yards and disappeared from view, swallowed up, in a matter of moments, by the fog. A few minutes later the beach became invisible, and the village, with its houses and crowstepped gables and chimneys and steeples, no longer existed. The three of us, and our lunch on the rock, were merely darker emanations of the fog. It felt eerie, as if we were the last people on earth preparing to eat the last meal. "E-liz-a-beth," we called out. "Ne-il. . . ." There was no an-swer; it was as though the sound of our voices was hitting im-penetrable substance and falling to the damp sands. We assured each other that they were not far and could come to no harm, but felt uneasy in some other way—as if they had been spirited away while we, weighted down and immobilized in dense, slow-swirling nothingness, were destined to stumble and flail about, barely visible to each other, calling out ineffectually in voices audible only to ourselves. After a time of fog-filled silence, the children's voices, strangely muted and muffled and 'echoless, floated through: "Cooeee . . . where . . . are . . . you?" We called back, hallooing, and their ears led them toward us; they materialized out of vapor, laughing and excited and a little scared, declaring they were starving, and insisting upon eating there and then. So we had our ghostly picnic, swallowing mouthfuls of brumous thickened gray-yellow sea air with our sandwiches and hard-boiled eggs and apples, the tea from our thermos flask tasting of salt as the brine-laden vapors swirled into our cups, hands seeming to float to mouths in the fuliginous medium in which we were suspended out of time and place and the familiar. "The *haar* is often pretty bad at this time of the year," Elizabeth told us, matter-of-factly peeling and munching a banana.

We made our way back to the High Street and the car, driving with difficulty out of the village, the full beam of our headlights smacking flat against the fog and providing no illumination, the lights of approaching traffic visible only when we were practically in collision. Yet, less than a quarter of a mile inland, we emerged into a land of grain-yellow fields and blue sky and harvest activity, a transformation out of the mists of a dream into bright daylight.

In the evening, on the phone, I described to Helen our strange picnic. "Aye," she said, "the haar was so thick here this morning that Bob and the men couldn't get out to work on the harvest until the afternoon. That's how it is when you farm near the sea."

There are some smells that give reassurance—a feeling that for the moment at least, life is orderly and pleasant and safe. The smell of bread baking in the oven is one of these, and that of clothes and linen blowing on a washline in sun and wind is another. We would bury our faces in the drying laundry when we passed through the garden, as if it were flowers, inhaling its clean, sunshiny freshness, its happy combination of man-made orderliness and nature's benign elements.

But the very freshness of the wind tunneling between the hills and over the water of the loch, blowing constantly from the same direction so that the trees around the house bowed permanently to its will, kept the climbing rose from blooming until early August; then, long after the roses had filled every cottage garden in the village, the pale pink blooms would open at last, awakening like some sleeping princess. "Pink Dawn" it was named, the bloomy petals just flushed with the mildest pink of early dawn; it went up the wall of the house and around the front door's small stone porch. Donny would always stop to sniff the creamy, faintly apricot scent, his phlegmatic manner giving way to garden flowers. "Och, it's fine to smell an old-fashioned rose that hasn't had the scent of it bred out to keep it hardy. My roses are bonny but there's no' one of them has a pair-fume like this."

Around the corner of the house, bunches of dark pink honeysuckle twining themselves over the gray stone hung as if burdened by their heavy fragrance, their sweet headiness pervading the garden on a warm evening. The deep orange poppies by the kitchen window swayed under the impact of the bees landing to forage in their pollen-heavy centers; on still afternoons, when the only discernible movement was the faint plop on the water's surface as the trout lazily sent up floating rings that expanded and expired under the day's inertia, we would learn to distinguish between the low monotone of the bees' buzz as they collected nectar, the zigzag sound as they hovered, and the higher, intensified note as they flew from one poppy to the next. We lived in a "bee-loud glade."

Year by year, we learned the rhythm of the summer, the steady, reliable timing that sets off the blooming of each species in its season. In late June, when we arrived from New York, the forget-me-nots still showed blue and starry in the ditches and beside springs trickling down the hill. In the early summer the banks of the loch were japanned with pink and white clover, violas (the miniature wild pansies colored purple and yellow), daisies, and buttercups. By mid-July, we knew to be on the lookout for early bluebells; they would appear, shyly at first, rare, a solitary five-pointed corolla delicately drooping in modest seclusion, each bell holding at the center tiny, pale-yellow, triple-tongued clappers, increasing to form drifts of blue as the summer settled in, so that we could gather a handful in a short while. We would carry them home to fill a small pitcher on the kitchen mantel; indoors, they gave pleasure for only a day or two before wilting.

In the same way as we came to know and feel at ease among the glen folk, we acquainted ourselves, each passing summer, with the local wild flowers—neither ever becoming commonplace with familiarity. The tangled yellow mass and balmy perfume of lady's bedstraw (whose ancient name was "cheese-rennet" when the flowers were used to curdle milk) foamed around our hiking boots as we trudged over the hills. Rosebay willow herb's lance-shaped flowers on tall stems lined the forestry road, among yellow ragwort, known as "stinking willie"; creeping meadow vetchling, whose tiny, bright-yellow sweet pea–like flowers and miniature pea pod seed-cases look like play vegetables for a dollhouse; prickly needle-whins; bright purple foxgloves, showing their inner speckled trumpets; white and yellow yarrow; blue field scabious; goldenrod; evil-smelling fool's parsley; ragged robins, whose pink petals emerge from dark red purple-veined calyxes; and yellow mimulus, or monkey-flowers, thick along the banks of our small river.

Later in the season, the tough, wiry heather would open tiny, tight-closed pink buds, which would deepen in color until, by September, great washes of purple shadowed the hillsides and moors. The shrubby, cross-leaved heath, with pale rose drooping flowers, would appear in boggy places, nectar-filled, beloved of bees and beekeepers. The old gardener at Gleneagles kept a few hives whose bees feasted on heather, and we would buy his honey—in jars or on the comb—at our grocer, its tawny sweetness flavored with the scent of heather.

The eye grows sharper living in the country, and the more one saw, the more there was to be seen. Looking out of the windows of the house, the hillside was deceptively mono-chromatic—verdant, with darker patches of bracken; in late summer, the pink of the rosebay willow herb and the purple of the heather tinged the unrelieved green. But we knew that at close quarters the landscape was enameled with exquisite touches, dabs, flecks, points, splashes, and streaks of color. We would bring specimens home to identify in our handy little *Observer's Book of Wild Flowers*. The wild flowers, in their modesty and lack of flamboyance, their understated charm, their hardiness, persistence, and harmony with a cool northern climate, assumed for us the elements of the temperament of the Scottish people who inhabited the glen along with them.

* * *

If it sometimes happened that the Kirkbrides had no eggs to spare, we would get them from Mrs. Kirkland, the wife of the ruddy-cheeked farmer on the other side of the glen, who kept a large brood of laying hens—a pleasant three-mile walk each way, which fitted in nicely between teatime and dinner.

Down the hill road we would go, past browsing sheep who would dash nervously off if we approached too close; past the shed where the Camerons' two sheep dogs, locked up after the day's work, would bark ferociously as if they wanted to harry us back into the mass—the sight of any straying creatures exciting their inbred herding instinct. We would pass the chickens scratching and clucking in the barnyard. Mrs. Cameron complained always of the difficulty of collecting the eggs they laid in hidden places. But once, keeping them all in the barn to make the egg collecting easier, she had found, she said, that the eggs lost their sweet taste and bright color; so she set the chickens free to forage and peck where they fancied.

Usually, Miss Kirstie Aird's blue Mini was parked in the yard, not a day passing that she did not visit her older sister, the two of them as close as when they were the two small Victorian girls in the sepia photograph in the sitting room. We would come to the humpbacked bridge and stand for a while to watch the clear water of the little river slide over the smooth-washed pebbles as it coursed down to the sea. Sometimes we would encounter a hedgehog there, who would roll himself into a ball of bristles at our approach but could be wooed with offerings of food; hedgehogs are friendly, trusting creatures, as well they might be with their bristly exteriors. Elizabeth, the Hunters' daughter, had had one for a pet once, keeping it in the kitchen where it lived contentedly, feeding on bread and milk.

At the bridge we would take a small sheep path that led across a stile into the Camerons' pasture, and follow it along the riverbank to the caravan site, where we would strike up over the hill on the opposite side of the glen road and climb the steep drive to the Kirklands' farm.

After we had bought our eggs, Mrs. Kirkland would invite us into the parlor, which was formally furnished and hung with family photographs and the ubiquitous watercolors of

Highland scenes, the piano piled with sheet music for voice accompaniment: Bach and Handel, Scottish folk songs, Beatle songs. One of the children would be dispatched to call their father in. When we were all seated, Mrs. Kirkland would say to her husband, "Alistair, do what's needful." Mr. Kirkland would rise, remove bottles and glasses from the sideboard, and ritually offer and pour sherry for the ladies, whiskey for the men. The ceremony was unvarying, both in its formality and its charm.

Once, on a Saturday afternoon, we were fortunate enough to be taken care of by Mrs. Kirkland's eighty-one-year-old father, a tall, thin, sprightly old man who was the only one at home. He fetched our eggs and declined our money, saying we would have to settle the financial side of things with his daughter, and as we stood admiring the view of our hills from his side of the glen, he fell into reminiscing about his boyhood. He told us how he had had his first job at a neighboring farm when he "was a lad just fourteen; so many bairns in the family there were, so many hungry mouths wanting their bit porridge and meat and 'tatties, that our mither had to send us all out to earn our own bread just as soon as we were auld enough to be useful. My brothers and me, we were sent to work on ferms, and the girls went into service. I started off as a general ferm worker—long hours, hard work, but they gave me my room and board and a few shullings a week. But I ended up as head shepherd on Lord Dougdale's estate. Twenty-five year I was with him, with never a day off for sickness. I was blessed with a strong physique and good health, and he gave me a pension for good service when I retired five years ago." He leaned on the stone wall of the yard and gazed out over the hills. "I mind, when I was a lad in the glen, there would be up to fifty brace of grouse bagged in a shoot up on the hills around the loch. Now they're lucky if they get half a dozen in a day. Aye, there's been great changes in the glen."

He was interrupted by a car that came tearing into the yard, braking suddenly in a cloud of flying dust and scattered pebbles. All four doors opened to spill out five young persons. "Is my mum home, Grandpa?" a fat young woman called out. She was dressed in tight jeans and sweater that cut where she bulged, face clownish with makeup and hair elaborately styled. Three youths in close-fitted blue denims and black leather jackets, hair lank and greasy, leaned against the car, smoking, looking sallow and ill-nourished, their stance a Glaswegian caricature of John Wayne lounging, pistol in hand, against the bar of a Wild West saloon; a girl, excessively thin and overly made up, with the fragility of a wasting consumptive, her sweatshirt emblazoned with the letters "Michigan State U," removed the cigarette from between the lips of the nearest youth and inhaled hungrily.

"They'll be back in time for their tea, Morag," the old man answered. "You're to set the table and put the kettle on and start frying the bacon, your mither said."

"Tell her we're going for fish and chips and then to the pictures after," she shouted back, never coming near him. They piled back into the car, which reversed like a bucking bronco and sped away, tires screeching, down the steep incline of the road.

"That's Morag, my wee granddaughter," the old man said. "She's no' very interested in what things was like when I was a lad." This was said without rancor, with the philosophical acceptance of one who has reached a hale old age after a full life.

Walking home with our eggs, it seemed to us that the grandchildren's lack of interest in the past meant the end of that past; yet, the old hills endured still, and so long as they remained inhabited the past would no doubt continue to exert a shape on the present.

"Been having a crack with old Mr. Campbell?" Jenny came over to the gate as we crossed the stile where the forestry road abutted on her garden. "He's a rum old one. You should have seen him at the farmers' dance in Auchterbraehead last winter. He's eighty-one and he outwaltzed all the young men—gave me such a twirl that I was reeling—and he keeps on dancing long after everyone else because he's deaf, and he doesn't hear when the music has stopped playing."

CHAPTER 14

Rowan Trees and Standing Stones

The rowan trees, trained to form arches over the three picket gates in our garden, sprouted in all directions, needing pruning to restore their shape. By late August, their clusters of berries were starting to flush, but we never got to see them in the bright orange of their autumn brilliance.

"Better trim them or the witches will get in," Bob advised.

We accepted the necessity of keeping witches away. There is a story of a famous physicist who is known to wear a rabbit's foot around his neck. When he was asked why a person so grounded in scientific principles would submit to a super-stitious belief, he replied, "They say it helps." Like him, we preferred not to take any chances.

Bob lent us a long-handled pruner, and Harl and the boys cut away the offending branches. But as the pruning and clear-ing went along, we began to wonder about the connection be-tween witches and rowan trees. There was not a garden in the glen without its rowan tree, but no one could tell us the origin of the belief; handed down through the generations, it was ac-cepted without question.

Poking about in the library, we came across an old book, *Darker Superstitions of Scotland*, written in 1834 by J. G.

Dalyell. We learned that the rowan tree was a plant "esteemed mystical in Scotland . . . an antidote to sorcery, precluding the access of sorcerers, or defeating their art. . . . The rown tree, or mountain ash, is observed to be frequent in the neighborhood of those monuments of antiquity . . . known as Druidical Circles." Its name is supposed to have been derived from runic characters. The runic form of writing was used extensively throughout northern Europe until it was reviled as pagan by the upholders of Christianity, which meant that we had come upon a system of beliefs so ancient it was no wonder the neighbors did not think to examine it. Elsewhere, we read that the rowan had been venerated by a May Day worship cult that was later displaced by an invasion of solstice worshipers from Greece and Egypt in prehistoric times.

Belief in the rowan's powers seems to have persisted, uninterrupted, and in the sixteenth century its counter-magic was commonly employed in the dairy; when butter would not come, it was presumed that the cream was bewitched, and the remedy was to stir the cream with a rowan twig, or to bind a rowan chaplet around the churn. The rowan tree was also considered beneficial to cattle, "for the dairy-maid will not forget to drive them to the shealing or summer-pasture," Dalyell writes, "with a rod of the rowan tree, which she carefully lays up against the door of the sheal-booth or summer house, and drives them home again with the same."

The glen folk, influenced by these ancient folk memories of whose origin they were not aware, made sure to have their rowan trees in their gardens, in the same way that they made sure their television antennas were securely attached to the chimney pots of their houses so that their color reception would come through clear and steady. It has been observed by the archeologist Cyril Fox that in Britain there is a greater *unity* of culture in the lowlands, but a greater *continuity* of culture in the Highlands, which, because of their remoteness, tend to sustain unique characteristics. Here was a continuity arising, it seems, out of pagan times, its ancient power enduring still, beneath the tumult of contemporary life.

* * *

Learning about the rowan trees, we now became curious about the witches against whom their magic was employed. In a book written about the district in 1899 by Alexander Reid, we found out that our parish had been the scene of some of the most gruesome exhibitions of the mystic cults, and that there had been a witches' coven practicing "unholy arts" right in our glen. Thirteen persons were brought to trial: one warlock and twelve witches, thirteen forming a "covin or de'il's dozen."

The proceedings against three local women in 1662—Agnes Murie, Bessie Henderson, and Isabel Rutherford—are recorded. We would encounter these same surnames in farms, shops, and cottages all over the glen. The indictment is a chilling document to read:

> Ye all three are indyted and accusit forasmuckle as by the Divine law of the Almighty God set down in his sacred word, especially in the 18 chap. of Deut. and the 20 chap. of Levit. made against the useres and practisers of witchcraft, sorcery, charming, soothsaying, and against the seekers of help or responser of them, and in the 22 chap. of Exodus, the 18 verse, *Thou shalt not suffer a witch to live*, threatening and denouncing to the committers of such devilishe practices the punishment of death. . . .
>
> . . . Notwithstanding whereof ye, the said Agnes Murie (for evil and sinful ends) having received instructions and devilish informations from the devil, your covenanted master, how to practise the devilish trade of witchcraft and sorcerie . . . that ye, being coming from the Crook Mill, about Martinmas last, 1661, Sathan did appear to you . . . he desired you to be his servant, whilk you willingly condescended unto . . . and you declared that Sathan was in likeness of a man with grey cloathes and ane blue bonnet, having ane beard. . . .
>
> Ye, the said Bessie Henderson, are indyted and accused of the sin and crime of witchcraft. Ye confessed ye had been forty years in the devil's service, since the time ye milked the old Balie of Kinross his kye before the calf-

ing . . . ye freely confessed that the devil appeared to you in the likeness of ane bonnie young lad at Trufhills, aboon Kinross, with ane blue bonnet, and asked you gif you would be his servant, promising that you should want nothing, whilk ye freely and instantly accepted and granted thereto.

To all of them, Satan seems to have appeared as a young man, in gray or dun-colored clothes, wearing a blue bonnet, his hand cold, offering beguilements: "and he said he would give you a braw gown . . . and said you would never want but would have enough . . . and Sathan shook hands with you to continue his servant, and did all dance and ane piper play."

All three found guilty, their sentencing was simple and grim: "For the whilk cause the Justice General Depute gives sentence, and ordains all three be taken away to the place called the Laumlaires, bewest the Cruik Miln, the place of their execution tomorrow . . . betwixt one and two in the afternoon, and there to be stranglit to death by the hand of the hangman, and thereafter their bodies to be burnt to ashes for their trespass."

Among the crimes for which they were executed there seemed to be the sorts of services for which we would now go to doctors or veterinarians. One of them was accused of curing a young boy of the falling sickness, while John Brugh, a local warlock of renown, in 1643 was accused of curing people's cattle of the murrain, and advising them thereafter to clean out their byres, stables, and houses; also, for "threttie sax zeirs," it was charged, he made people believe "that he was able to give thame health of bodies for the quilk he took from thame dyvers great sowmes of money, victualls, butter, cheese and other commodeteis, impoverishing them thereby."

A shame that he should have been executed after practicing successfully in the district for thirty-six years. Perhaps, like us, the people of the time resented paying their doctor's fee once they were cured—or had he made enemies by becoming too powerful? Among the charms he used was the putting of an "enchatit stane" into the drink of his patient or the cattle he was curing. The use of enchanted stones, sanctioned in Scotland by the Church previous to the Reformation, appears to have been innocent in itself, but, accompanied by incantations, it became sorcery.

There are no records of judicial proceedings against witches until the enactment of a statute of 1563, in the reign of Mary, Queen of Scots. In the access of righteousness following the Reformation in Scotland, where in 1559 the authority of the Pope was abolished, and the celebration of the mass made punishable by a series of penalties culminating in death, it was asserted that truth could be established from the Bible. The ministers were handed the power to interpret the Word of God. This gave people the opportunity to make accusations of witchcraft against others for reasons of personal vengeance, or to incriminate political enemies.

Clandestine information would be sought by placing "an empty box in church, to receive a billet with the sorcerer's name, and the date and description of his deeds. Too many readily assented," Dalyell tells us. The members of the presbytery acted like inquisitors, and the laws themselves were stacked against the victims. The witch hunts were "conducted on a scale of unexampled magnitude, like huntsmen beating up extensive coverts for the dislodging of beasts of prey."

The presbytery admitted to the burning of four thousand witches. Public accusation was invited; if the victims sought to flee, they were pursued, and those taking pity on them and providing shelter "rendered themselves obnoxious to the rigour of the law. That horrid malevolence so deeply incorporated in human nature," Dalyell comments, "found gratification of awful iniquity when threatening the life of the innocent."

Throughout Scotland and all Europe, women were more often accused of witchcraft than men. The cruelty of the torture was limited only by Scotland's backward technology in the construction of devices. To extract confessions, the pilliewinks or thumbscrews were used, and the iron boots; the victims' legs were crushed in the stocks and their fingernails pulled out with pincers; they were pricked and flogged and deprived of sleep for prolonged periods, kept naked on a cold

stone slab for weeks at a time. Torturers appear to do their
work with the same unchanging, monotonous brutality from
ancient times into our own.

Suspected witches were also subjected to the "watery ordeal." The thumb of the right hand would be bound to the
large toe of the left foot, the left thumb bound to the right
toe; the victim was then cast into the water. "If she sincke she
is counted innocent; if she fleet and sincke not, she is taken
for a witch." A no-win situation if ever there was one, since
whoever floated was presumed to be sustained in the water by
Satan.

People found to have falsely, or unsuccessfully, accused
someone of witchcraft were pilloried, or fined, or made to ask
pardon of the accused publicly on the High Street of Edinburgh.

The convicted witches were first strangled and then burned.
Their inquisitors and torturers claimed with self-righteousness
that they were working against the devil when they carried out
their dark and unholy work; but every witch-burning was a
triumph for the prince of darkness rather than the glory of
their God.

On our hikes, we would sometimes pass the Cruik Miln, the
site of the witch burnings. The millstream still brawls noisily
over the pebbles; it is believed that it has been used to power
a grinding mill since Pictish times. But now the massive stone
wheel stands still; a pleasant family lives in the mill; there is a
garden filled with flowers, and the woods are dark green and
leafy all around.

"Betwixt one and two in the afternoon"—the hour of the
three witches' execution—is a quiet time in midsummer.
Dragonflies hover over the millstream with rainbow wings, and
sunlight filters down through the branches, dropping yellow
coins on the water's surface. A crowd would have gathered
here, on that afternoon, to witness the execution of their
neighbors. The awed, excited murmur of their voices would
have overwhelmed the babbling of the water; a baby in its
mother's arms wailed, perhaps, and was hushed and soothed; the
executioner would have been testing the firmness of the knots
of his rope, while those responsible for the fire fed faggots and

small branches to the blaze. The women—Agnes, Bessie, and Isabel—crushed, beyond despair after the terrible ordeal they had already endured, would have been led, then, submissive, to the final infamy. A groan of horror must have arisen from the assembled glen folk as the strangled bodies were flung onto the flames. Later in the afternoon, the crowd would have drifted off, back to their crofts and cottages, their looms and their sheep-tending, some of them gratified in that "horrid malevolence"; others, the families and friends of the tortured and destroyed women, in despair over the conduct of human affairs.

Probably a few of the men would have had to remain behind to keep adding logs to the fire; a pall of black, greasy smoke would hang over the old mill through the twilight evening, a smell of charring wafting along lanes and into cottage doorways in the surrounding glen. And when only a pile of cooling gray ashes remained, the stillness would return to the mill. The miller and his wife and the bairns, asleep in their beds, would dream uneasily, perhaps, as the night breeze stirred the light ashes of the cold fire. In the fresh morning, someone from a nearby farm would have come whistling across the bridge we forded when we left the mill; bowed with a sack of grain slung over his shoulder, he would pass the site of the immolation, and, as he approached the mill, he would call out to the miller to bestir himself to grind his wheat into flour so that his wife could bake her loaves. The hill air would lie once more as still and tranquil as we experienced it on a summer's hike.

The summers passed by, each one adding a richness, a variety, new experiences that would arouse our curiosity and send us questioning, searching, exploring, to gain a firmer understanding of this pocket of human culture in which we found ourselves immersed. Each year, when we returned, it was with a greater vocabulary of understanding.

In the early years, when we had first come into the glen, Britain was going through a relatively prosperous period; the pound stood high against the dollar, unemployment figures were down. Air travel had become cheap, and working-class people were taking their holidays abroad; they had found out that the sun shines with more heat and light in France and Greece and Spain, and that wine drunk on the hot sands of a Mediterranean beach gives more comfort than a thermos of scalding tea on a windy, pebbly North Sea beach.

But Britain's steadily declining condition became more evident as the decade went along. Each year, in the shops on the High Street in the village, everything cost a little more. Bob said that a sports jacket at Marks and Spencer now cost as much as Harl had paid to have one made at the tailor. Donny complained constantly about the high taxes and the decline of services, and Mrs. Cameron, down at the farm, was worried about the rising prices of petrol, electricity, sheep-dip, spare parts for the tractor, wire fencing. In the newspapers we read of rising unemployment, the shortage of housing, manufacturing plants going bankrupt, mindless vandalism by teenagers, Pakistanis and West Indians being beaten up by gangs in slum areas of industrial towns. The homogeneity of British society was being broken down by new waves of migration from the former colonies: The Africans and Indians, whose land and labor had been the basis of the British Empire's wealth and glory, were now claiming the privilege of citizenship, and at a time when everything was running meager and threadbare.

Bored youths caused small havoc in the glen by turning all the signposts on the minor roads so that they pointed in the wrong direction. On our walks, there seemed to be more empty beer cans and cigarette wrappers strewn about the hills, and we were appalled one Sunday, in Auchterbraehead, to see a family in a caravan empty all their garbage onto the curbside of the immaculately clean High Street and drive off; Mr. Beggie of the newspaper shop shook his head gravely at the outrage. "They're no' even English, nor foreigners," he observed. "I haired them; they're as Scottish as I am. Och, things is changing in this country, believe me."

A stained-glass window at the church was smashed by what Donny called a bunch of yobs; as deacon of the church, he went about the glen collecting contributions to a fund for restoration of the window, the cost of which was going to run to several thousand pounds. Jenny Kirkbride, down at the forestryman's cottage, who always worked part-time at the hotel in summer, took a full-time job because Robbie's wages could not keep pace with rising costs.

But the green hills all around our cottage were still quiet and peaceful, and able to dispel the sense of disquiet that was beginning to make us wonder about jetting over from New York to summer so cozily in a community where the neighbors were struggling to make ends meet. Where there was a scarcity of housing for the locals, did we have the right to use, for our leisure, a good house where a family could comfortably live?

Change, however, slow and undramatic, shows itself in small ways, casually perceived, mounting up unnoticed like grains of sand silting up until a flowing stream is seen to have altered its course.

One day, we stopped off in the village to shop; we were on the way back from a visit to a very old church where there was a ring of standing stones on a nearby hill. At the butcher's, while Mr. McKenzie was cutting a steak for us off a fine side of Scottish beef, an old lady dressed in good tweeds came in with a quarter-pound package of tea and two bananas in her shopping basket; she asked for ten pence worth of mince. I felt uneasy as I paid for the slab of red bloody meat, and left feeling a little as if I were some stomping Roman invader among these quiet, modestly contriving natives.

We were receiving intimations that our idyll in the glen would not go on forever. But that is, after all, the nature of an idyll; it is separated off from the everyday—a pastoral episode.

The Hunters were having dinner with us that evening, and when I told them about the uneasiness I had felt in the butcher's shop, Bob laughed. "Scotland's whole history and people are the result of a succession of foreign invaders. I'm descended from Germanic invaders, and Helen from Vikings. We can stand a few Yanks. Anyway, your dollars are good for the economy. Go and buy lots of cashmere jerseys, or order another sports jacket at the tailor, if you've a need to make amends for the falling buying power of sterling."

Though he was unable to dispel the disquiet we felt, we had, by this time, come to appreciate that this tight, xenophobic little country was indeed a melting pot, over millennia, of a rich variety of foreigners, invaders, immigrants. Our expedition that very day, to a fourteenth-century church standing hard by a Neolithic stone circle, had provided abundant evidence of this.

We made this expedition every year. It was a half-hour drive from our cottage. We would be drawn compellingly from the green graveyard of the church up to the hilltop where the stones stood stark and mysterious against the sky. It was as though we could step back, away from the limits the present imposed on the view, into a tract of successive systems of beliefs and ways of being—the rich tilth of the civilizations that had continued here in an unbroken progression of days, since the first people stepped out of their coracles and canoes onto these shores.

The tiny stone church was cool and musty with age. It had been built in the thirteenth century on the site where a church was first erected by an early Christian saint who is known to have died in the year 750. Christianity had come to Scotland in the sixth century, brought by Saint Columba, who left Ireland in 563 and settled on the island of Iona, which became the center for the Celtic Christian church.

The founding saint of this little church, who came also from Ireland, saw the standing stones and started to preach the Gospel here in order to eradicate the dark pagan practices associated with the stones. Carved into the headstone over the gate—a copy of an earlier stone, which is in the vestry—is the Hebrew word for God, *Jahweh*, with a text from Ecclesiastes: "Keep thy foot when thou enterest the hows of God." A Pictish symbol stone in the vestry, discovered in the course of renovation, shows Jonah being swallowed by the whale. In the side of the chancel, there is a small low window, called a "leper squint," through which the lepers—of whom there were many in Scotland—were allowed to watch the celebration of the mass without coming in contact with the other worshipers.

From the church, it was a short walk past the single shop

and few laborers' cottages that make up the village to the stones at the top of the adjacent hill—a short walk that was a journey back a few thousand years in time. The stones never failed to exert a clutch of awe; standing within their circumference, one felt the force of that divine perplexity that had moved men, some four thousand years earlier, to lug these massive hewn slabs to this hilltop, and to raise them up in acknowledgment of it.

They overlooked a panorama of cultivated plain rising up to a further range of hills high against the horizon. Spread out below us were tracts of farmland; fields of barley and wheat, potatoes and kale. Archeologists have pointed out that the proximity of modern croft to ancient monument shows that good land, once found, is utilized in an unbroken line for thousands of years.

Who were the stone circle builders? we wondered; out of what rock-vein of time are they? To locate their stratum in the past, we had to dig our way deep into prehistory, where the only clues are bits of bone and stone, grains of pollen that are resistant to decay, shards of clay pottery, and the evidence yielded up from the ways in which they buried their dead— a characteristic uniquely human, which has to do with a fundamental awe, or fear, of the unknown.

About twenty thousand years ago, Britain was a barren tundra on the northern coast of western Europe, beyond which lay the frozen wastes of the ice sheet. At this time, Stuart Piggot writes in his lively and lucid book, *Scotland Before History*, man was already established in Europe: a fire maker; a craftsman in stone, bone, and wood; a migratory hunter following herds of reindeer. Man was a rare animal, though, and there were probably no more than two hundred fifty people in the habitable areas of England at the end of the Upper Paleolithic or Old Stone Age.

As the ice sheet receded, ten thousand years ago, and our present postglacial age came in, the climate became more temperate, more food became available, and population increased; the zone where it was possible for human communities to settle spread northward toward what is now Scotland. This process was spread out over ten millennia, and man appeared on the Scottish landscape only five thousand years ago. Until then, there had been settlement only as far as Yorkshire. As the climate became milder, there was an increase in grassland; the birch trees came, followed by pine, and then the mixed oak forests that are still the glory of the British countryside.

Around 6000 B.C. the melting ice sheet caused the North Sea to flood and break through to the English Channel; the land connection between Britain and western Europe was severed, and Britain was turned into an island. Food gatherers, fishers, and fowlers settled the new coastline to eke out an existence in the still damp and chilly land.

Early stone-tool-using migrants, spreading across Europe from the Mediterranean, landed in Britain around 2500 B.C. They were seafarers, with a tradition of stock breeding and agriculture that had arisen out of western Asia, where the warm climate favored the domestication of the wild ancestors of farmyard animals and the cultivation of cereals—wheat and barley—that are cultured strains of wild grasses. The migrants brought with them grain to sow, and sheep and cattle to breed, along with their knowledge of farming; they knew the use of fire, made pottery, and mined flint for axe manufacture.

These people are known by their chambered cairns: great communal sepulchral monuments that bespoke a reverence for their dead and a belief in another world, an underworld, to which the dead journeyed.

These first farmers represent the Neolithic period, the New Stone Age, which linked the barbarians of the European continent to the developing civilizations of the ancient East, forming the beginnings of the settled life, the spread of technological development, and the foundation of medieval and modern Europe.

Soon agricultural communities were establishing themselves up the East Coast of Scotland; perhaps, Piggot speculates, a group in dugout canoes coasted up from Yorkshire in a season of good summer weather, landed, and decided to settle there. Immigration took place largely by waterways, along the sea-rivers, estuaries, and freshwater lochs that carve a way through the land mass. It is assumed that the migrants used skin-covered coracles or canoes. In Perthshire, not too far from our cottage, a dugout canoe about five thousand years old has been found. Craft of this type, hollowed out by burning and scraping a tree trunk, were still used as ferryboats in the Highlands as late as the eighteenth century.

The new agricultural economy was mixed farming; they raised wheat and barley, kept sheep, pigs, goats, and dogs, and lived in settlements of stone or wood dwellings. Since there was not much flint available for axes in Scotland, they must have acquired theirs by trading; the variety of pottery types found by archeologists also suggests they were involved in barter and trade. They enclosed their fields and pastures in earthen walls, the remains of which are still visible in many places; on our hill walks we frequently saw the marks of these ancient fields—rectangular enclosures raised like green scars, on hillsides where sheep still placidly graze after three to four thousand years of agricultural life that remains basically unchanged, with wheat and barley still the principal crops raised today.

In the course of their expansion northward in Scotland, the "chambered cairn" people came in contact with, and seem to have fused with, another group known as the "beaker people." The latter had come from northern Europe to natural harbors along the East Coast, settling as far north as Aberdeen. They knew the use of bronze, which had spread from the ancient Orient, where it already had been mastered with the skill and artistry acquired much later by the craftsmen of medieval and Renaissance Europe. With the smelting of bronze came the need for raw materials; since copper, tin, and gold occurred in natural deposits in Britain, the British Isles early became important in the technological development of Bronze Age Europe. Prospectors and traders came, and immigrants bringing new metallurgical skills. Copper was found in the hills where our cottage stands, and one of our walks took us past the remains of an ancient copper mine.

The beaker people, with their distinctive type of pottery, brought with them one special religious practice: the burial of single bodies under round mounds of earth—individually

rather than in collective tombs—together with personal possessions: necklaces, daggers, and small tools. Their burial rite
represented a more individualistic view of the journey to the
other world. It is these beaker people who are often associated
with the tradition of the building of standing stone circles,
though Evan Hadingham tells us, in his book *Circles and
Standing Stones*, that as far back as 4200 B.C. men probably
gathered on prominent hilltops—dramatic sites with sweeping
views over the countryside; these must have been Neolithic
temple sites, where fairs or festivals or some kind of unifying
social interest brought people together. On these hilltops,
sacred enclosures of standing stones were erected.

We would stand within the circle, dwarfed, all of us, by
the gaunt upright pillars framing the panoramic view of distant valleys and hills, and would wonder aloud: How were
those people, with their rudimentary technology, able to drag
these massive stones up the hill? How did they have the engineering skill to set them up in the ground so true and right
that they still stand after thousands of years have swept across
this windy hilltop?

Archeologists have been intrigued by this problem for a
long time. It is conjectured that the erection of these stones
must have been a communal project similar to the building of
a parish church or even a cathedral, involving much organization and the efficient uses of manpower. By calculation, induc-
tion, and even actual demonstration, it has been surmised that
in a period when there were no pack animals and man was the
only beast of burden, two teams of workmen must have been
employed. One team would haul a stone upward using thick
ropes of plaited hide thongs (a type of rope that was still in
use up to the nineteenth century), and logs would be used as
rollers to reduce the friction; the second team, meanwhile,
would be employed to prevent the stone from slipping back
down the incline. When the hilltop was, at last, laboriously
reached, each stone would be positioned beside a prepared
hole, on rollers, and then tipped into the hole. (A previously
computed calculation, involving precise engineering judgment, would have been essential to gauge the exact point of

balance, which has held the stones upright for millennia.) The
stones would then be hauled into position with ropes by brute
force, and the hole tight-packed with rubble, boulders, and
clay.

Radiocarbon dating indicates that the spread and continuation of the tradition of stone circles extends roughly from
3300 B.C. to 1500 B.C. The ordnance survey map of our area is
scattered with standing stones and stone circles marked in
Gothic lettering. Their meaning and function continues to
fascinate archeologists, astronomers, mathematicians, and mys-
tics. They are associated with a megalithic ruling aristocracy
or priesthood, but they seem to have had a scientific as well as
a religious function; it is thought that they were used as ob-
servatories by which the calendar could be calculated, a technique that would have been important for domestic and
farming activities, and for the forecasting of seasonal cycles.

The sites on which the stones are set are usually in relation
to some prominent topographical landmark such as a distant
hill or a mountain peak, so that an alignment to the sun's or
moon's position—the rising moon or the midsummer sunset,
the moon's waxing or waning—could be observed. Any change
in the moon's path, a lunar wobble or an eclipse or the seasonal solstices, could be charted from the standing stones. The
ability to predict solar or lunar eclipses would have been very
useful to a ruling caste; to be able to proclaim to the assembled
multitude that the sun or the moon would be obscured on a
certain day or night in the future, would have been a great
source of priestly power, which the community would have
held in awe.

These megalithic people, then, must have been capable of
abstract theorizing and geometrical calculation. Professor
A. A. Thom analyzed the diameters of over one hundred and
fifty stone circles throughout Britain, and concluded that there
was one standard unit of length from the north of Scotland to
the south of England—the most ancient measurement we
know—exactly 2.72 feet long, the "megalithic yard." Thom's
researches have shown that the megalithic and Bronze Age
people of Britain had considerable intellectual capabilities; he

rescues them from the barbarian image: "almost as savage as the Beasts whose skins were their only raiment," as John Aubrey depicted them in 1659.

Throughout history, a rich accumulation of lore and superstition has gathered about the megalithic sites. There has been a belief that the Druids inherited the religion, magic, and astronomy the stones represented. There are stories that the stones are youths and maidens turned to rock for misdeeds; that at certain times of the year they go down to the water to wash and drink; powers of fertility and healing have been attributed to them; and they were thought to have been raised by giants.

Until the last century, certain families on one of the islands in the Hebrides, Hadingham tells us, were held in secret esteem as "belonging to the stones," though no one knew exactly why; and until a few generations ago, people still congregated there, at the megalithic sites, on May Day and on the morning of Midsummer Day, when it was believed that a deity of some kind manifested itself, heralded by a cuckoo.

The folklore associated with the megaliths is a record of the power of community feeling these monuments once evoked. In Gaelic, a phrase used to ask people if they were going to church translates as "Are you going to the stones?" As late as the fourteenth century, courts were still being held at stone circle sites in Perthshire and Aberdeen; and an oath or marriage was rendered binding by the clasping of hands through a stone with a hole in it. Paganism and witchcraft have been connected with the stones as late as the seventeenth century, when a man was brought before the kirk committee and charged with idolatry for setting up a stone and doffing his hat to it. Dalyell, writing about the magic power of the rowan tree, noted that it was observed to be frequent in the neighborhood of those monuments of antiquity known as Druidical circles.

Christianity absorbed many pagan beliefs, and, as with our little kirk in Perthshire, the early founders of Christianity frequently built their churches close to standing stones, as though acknowledging the mystical forces in which the sites were steeped over thousands of year of religious worship, and ensuring a continuity between the ancient pagan beliefs and the Gospel.

The Bronze Age world was one of trading and voyaging. At the same time that small communities in Scotland were growing barley in roughly hoed patches, breeding animals, making pottery and ornaments, and working and trading in copper, bronze, and gold, the Minoan civilization was already old, and the Greeks were building their civilization to make the world of the *Iliad* and the *Odyssey*.

Cremation replaced burial in their religious practices; immigrants from across the channel introduced the use of the horse for riding and for driving chariots—another tradition out of the ancient Orient. In the late Bronze Age, archeologists find, more bronze seems to have been used for weapons than for tools.

The first few centuries B.C. were a time of much movement and migration of displaced persons and refugees from Roman rule or internecine war. Celts arrived in Scotland before the first century B.C., fleeing from southwest Britain. They brought iron tools, and a system of mixed farming based on the single steading or isolated farmhouse. They built timber-laced hilltop fortifications, to protect people and stock from the intertribal warfare and cattle raiding that characterized Celtic life.

What sort of people and land would Agricola have encountered in A.D. 80? According to Stuart Piggot, great tracts of landscape would have been wooded, with enough cleared parkland for chariots. There must have been much clearance for grazing, and for cultivation. A class of craftsmen with special skills had developed, so that there were carpenters, wheelwrights, blacksmiths, potters, thatchers, and metallurgists. Although there was a ruling class of Celts by the first century A.D. they coexisted alongside the original inhabitants of the land—the fishers and boatmen and the descendants of those who had raised the standing stones; many different tongues were spoken.

The priestly cast of Druids were of great importance in the Celtic area of society: bards, shamans, and magicians were a privileged class entitled to special concessions of land. Intertribal skirmishes were waged constantly; some warriors fought naked in accordance with religious sanctions, some painted or tattooed their bodies, and they went in for head hunting. Cattle raiding was an occupation for a gentleman, and beer and mead were his drink.

Calgacus, who spoke so eloquently against Roman rule in the battle against Julius Agricola at Mons Craupius, is the first named Scotsman in the historical literature. The Celts he led were described by a Roman writer as "sparing of words and enigmatical," though "boastful, threatening and braggarts by nature." He might have been describing the wild grandsons down at the Camerons' farm.

After the Romans left, the Scotti arrived from Ulster; and the Angles, from their kingdom of Northumbria in England, assailed, and then settled in, southeast Scotland. Historical Scotland, its mixture of prehistoric peoples and traditions mingling with tribes of immigrants and invaders—Picts, Scots, Britons, and Angles—began to take shape.

The basic shape of agrarian life as it was up to the Industrial Revolution had been formed by the beginning of the Christian era. No wonder, then, that in the still-isolated pocket of culture in our glen we sensed something abiding, which had endured out of what was fundamental to human life; which had to do with the earliest strivings of our species to make itself civilized—turning its mysterious ingenuity to impose order on the chaos of the primeval landscape, where it first became aware of itself in the early dawnings of its consciousness.

The sheep that grazed our hills, though bred with other strains, may well go back to the breeds first brought to Scotland by Stone Age farmers. A sense of the Old Testament in this still-pastoral corner of the world, which we responded to as soon as we settled into the glen, comes, in an unbroken succession of mornings, afternoons, and twilit evenings, out of our very beginnings.

In the oral tradition that preceded recorded history and later lived alongside it, the tales recounted around the hearth, cave, hut, roundhouse, homestead, or croft are the images and symbols in abundant variety, from pagan times to Judeo-Christian, that all, one way or another, tell the same story; the tradition that we encountered all around in the glen has its roots in the prehistoric times out of which the people of this secluded green wilderness have arisen.

It is believed that the pentatonic scale of the traditional music of the Hebrides, which is associated with voice music rather than instrumental, may have its origin in early prehistoric times. The distribution of this scale, still surviving in remote areas of the world, suggests that it is a remnant of an ancient tradition surviving out of earliest times; so that when "Auld Lang Syne" is sung, it is thought, it might possibly be a perpetuation of the melodic conventions of the circumpolar Stone Age.

We would come down the hill from the bleak site where the stones stood dark and weighted with their own meaning against the sky, their power still immanent thousands of years after they had been raised up. As we passed through the small green churchyard, it was possible to understand why that early Christian saint had caused a church to be erected here to challenge the ascendancy of the stones. The underused kirk looked benign—its medieval architecture symbolizing order, aesthetic sensibility, devoutness. But when we looked back, up the hill, the stones, implacable, even brutal, seemed still to dominate it.

One afternoon in late summer, we found ourselves at the very far end of the village, where the High Street peters out into a country road running between fields of barley. We rarely came to this part of the village as it was out of the way of the shops and postoffice; it was mostly residential, with small, two-storied, eighteenth-century row houses, trim and neat, their front doors opening directly onto the narrow sidewalk, windowboxes spilling over with lobelia, alyssum, nasturtium.

One of the houses had a dim shop front on its ground floor; we peered through, and saw there an array of finely made antique woodworking tools. There was no name displayed; inside, we could see an old, white-haired man pottering about.

Harl has a great liking for old carpentry tools and is always drawn to them. "Let's go inside," he said.

The thin, stooped old man, wearing a carpenter's apron, fine-featured, with a gentle expression, bade us good-afternoon.

"Those tools in the window—could we take a look at them?" Harl asked.

"Aye; they're all antique. They were my father's tools, but I'm closing down the shop and needing to get rid of everything. Those things in the window are all sold already, to a collector, but you're welcome to look at them; you'll no' see a like set of such tools very often, these days."

The workshop was immaculately tidy and clean; tables and workbenches were covered with canvas drop cloths, and bulky equipment bulged underneath. The old man displayed the tools, pointing out their heft, balance, the excellence of their construction.

"Have you worked with them?" Harl wanted to know.

"Och, aye, when I was a lad. My father trained me as a cabinetmaker and wood carver, teaching me with these very tools."

Wood carver. Harl and I looked at each other, both recalling in the same instant that odd young American who had wanted to rent Glenauchen Cottage, those many summers ago when we had first come to the glen; he had come to Auchterbraehead to try to take lessons with a master wood carver. Alexander Shillinglaw—the name came back. "Are you Mr. Shillinglaw?" I asked.

He seemed surprised that strangers should know of him. We reminded him of the young man who had wanted to become his apprentice, told him how he had tried to rent our place.

"Oh, you're the people who have the old waterman's house up at Glenauchen. I used to go fishing there when I was a lad."

"Did you take him on as an apprentice?" Harl wanted to know.

"I mind him well—an odd lad. He went back to the States after a wee while; couldn't get a work permit. Wanted to learn everything in a couple of months that had taken me a lifetime to acquire. And I have not been enjoying good health in recent years, and I told him I could not take on any pupils;

but he wouldna' take no for an answer, so I let him work here two days a week, though my wife was against it."

"Was he a good wood carver?"

"Och, no' bad, no' bad. The problem with training young people today is that they have no patience. Patience is a lost art, and there's no substitute for it. There is no way to learn a trade—any trade—without patience; you have to spend long, tedious, painstaking hours, for years on end. No shortcuts. The experience I've accumulated can only be absorbed by steady, persevering industry, and this laddie wanted it all in a few months. He was keen and willing, but I had to explain to him it was not only what I had learned from my father that he needed to learn—it's a whole tradition of right-making, developed over hundreds of years. He kept on blethering away about 'self-expression,' but he couldna' understand that freedom to express what you're after—the ease of the craftsman—can emerge only out of a rigorous discipline. That must come first."

"He'd read in a book, he told us, that you are one of the finest wood carvers in the world," I said.

"I'm known in this country," he answered, "but I'm no' sure about the rest of the world."

We asked him about his work, and he told us of the restorations and original wood carvings he had done in some of Britain's great historical buildings and churches. "I've never needed to seek commissions; there's always been more than I could handle. It's slow, time-consuming work."

"Are there enough young people being trained so that the craft doesn't die out?" Harl asked.

"Oh, aye—there are places in this country, and in Europe and the States, where one can get a fine training. But I'm no' sure if there's the patience any longer, amongst modern youth —the capacity to endure the drudgery, and tedium, and the long years of practice it takes to achieve the high standard that was expected of us. And of course it's power tools being used these days; that's why all these old things of my father's are considered to be antiques."

"How do you feel about power tools?"

"I've used them a long while now; wouldn't make sense not

to. But your product will still only be as good as you are.
Power machinery cannot make you a better craftsman if
you've not had the right training, nor if you lack the skill."

"That young man told us you were an artist," I said.

"Och . . . there is an endless subject for discussion in that.
Will you no' take a seat?" He sat down on a bench, and
propped his long, spare frame against the wall. "Artist . . .
craftsman. . . . In medieval times, they made no such distinc-
tion. There were only craftsmen: manual workers plying and
learning their trade. Even the great painters went to work as
apprentices in a master's workshop—just as a lad would do if
he was wanting to be a stonemason or a metalworker or a
cabinetmaker. They learned their trade from the bottom up,
by being allowed to sweep the master's floor.

"I've always considered myself a craftsman. Woodworking
is a humble craft. Then I've heard them talking, and they've
written about the *artistry* of my work. But I cannot really
comprehend what it means, beyond the fact that I have a certain skill, and a lifetime of experience."

A door at the back of the shop opened and a woman came
in. He introduced his wife. "These are the folk who have the
old waterman's house up at the loch," he told her. A bustling,
plump woman in an apron, with pink cheeks and white hair,
she stayed to chat only for a moment. "Now dinna' go over-
tiring yoursel', Alexander," she said. "I'll be getting back to
my scones, then, before they scorch."

He was frail-looking, pale. When she had shut the door behind her, he lowered his voice and said, "I'm no' doing much
anymore. I have a serious illness, and I haven't too long left
to live. I don't come into the shop anymore, but I'm straighten-
ing things up today; I want to leave everything right for the
wife when I die. There'll be enough for her to thole without
needing to sort through all this. There's a mannie from Perth
coming to take all this heavy machinery, and the fellow from
the antique shop on the High Street is taking the hand-tools."
He looked around, his glance serene, at the order he had managed to find.

Before we left, he said he would like to give us a small present. He took from a shelf a plaster cast: a head of a child, or

a cherub, with an expression of mild sweetness on its features. "This is a cast I took from the first head I ever carved; it was part of a panel for a church in Derbyshire." He looked at it with interest. "It was one of the first things I did that came close to what I had had in mind when I sat down to carve it, and I cast it in plaster so that I should always have it by me. Here—you have it now."

When we protested, he was insistent. "Take it, now. The wife won't want it; it will be one more thing for her to dust; or it will break and have to be swept away. If you would like to have it, I would be pleased to give it to you."

Grateful, we accepted it.

"Now, I'd best be getting on with my work before the wife calls me in for my tea."

The following winter, Jenny Kirkbride sent us a little clipping from the local paper, announcing the death of Alexander Shillinglaw, wood carver, of Auchterbraehead.

CHAPTER
15

Harvest

Every summer I would precede the family to Scotland by a few days, in order to have the house spring-cleaned by Jessie and her sister, the larder stocked up, and things put in order before they descended on the glen. One year, everyone seemed to have commitments that delayed them in New York, and I found myself alone at Glenauchen for four weeks.

Having since childhood shared a bedroom with my sisters, and marrying young, I had never before lived alone. I thought it might be an interesting experience. Helen was worried. The place was so isolated; wouldn't I rather stay with them at the farm until the family arrived? No, I would try it out; if I found I was uneasy or bored or lonely I would move my cowardly self to the farm. To increase my isolation, something cracked in the innards of our old car, and it was towed away to the village to await the delivery of a scarce spare part.

So I was put to an even more stringent test of my self-sufficiency. As far as subsistence went, the situation was manageable: Mr. McWhirter, the grocer, made rounds through the glen on Wednesday with his well-stocked mobile shop, calling on the most remote farmhouses and isolated cottages. I could buy all the butter, honey, bacon, fruit and vegetables, fish, poultry, and canned goods I needed right in the stableyard, where he would park and position himself behind the counter in the van, wearing his crisp white apron and dispensing his stock as if he were in the bustle of the High Street. The baker's van called once a week; milk could be had at the caravan site (an easy hike); and Meg Cameron would pick up my butcher's order when she went in to the village to her part-time "wee job at the boutique." Donny left the newspaper each morning, and I had a telephone. I was by no means cut off from the outside world. "I feel quite safe," I assured the Hunters. "I'm not afraid of intruders; it's only bats—and ghosts—that I'm worried about." But so far, none of the dusk-swooping bats had ever come indoors, and the spectre of Gray Jane had not been perceived beyond the precincts of the churchyard and Glencorrie House; so I would probably be alright.

The first thing I discovered about being entirely on my own was that I was accountable to no one or no thing not of my choosing. Family life ties one down to the needs and demands of others, so that to find myself free of them was a heady experience, bringing to mind the occasion of first learning to ride a bicycle and finding myself careening along in such wild and precarious freedom that I was forced to forestall fate by crashing down to the ground. I would be taken suddenly by an apprehension prodding me to—to what? There was nothing I was required to be doing, I would remind myself.

After the few days it took to become accustomed to this new state of affairs, I floated like a balloon trailing a string that had come untied from all responsibilities and demands. I could read until two or three in the morning, decide at six in the evening (a time when for two decades now I had been in thrall to stove, pots, knives, meat, and vegetables) that I had a whim to climb to the top of Dalrioch to watch the afternoon give way to the twilight.

The anxiety of family life, another fetter, slipped away. Not knowing where Harl or any of the children were at any given moment, there was no point to which I could fix my concern, no post to hitch my chain to, no sense in worrying about their safety, their welfare, the dimension of the space between what they intended and what they were achieving. Even the larger world—with its terrors and threats and horrors daily enacted and cause for daily despair—for those four weeks had no reality, existing as it did beyond the rolling old hills, which seemed to confer a historic perspective on all events, so that the quotidian took on the same complexion as the past. Reading in the newspaper of an insurgent coup against intolerable repression on another continent, and the spilling and spending of blood and passionate fervor, my usual response of righteous wrath and despair for the victims would have another quality, more as if I were reading of an uprising by ancient Britons against the Roman legionaries: a reflective and philosophical response.

I was never bored nor lonely. The days had a wide spaciousness and moved by with slow-moving grace; yet I was always surprised to find it was already two or three in the morning and time to turn out the lights. There was nothing to do but read, walk, eat, sleep; yet time never hung heavy. With so much time and space at my disposal, I knew the necessity of keeping the days well regulated; I set the alarm clock for eight no matter how late I went to sleep, ate three meals every day, and attended to household chores, the commonplace keeping me firmly footed, in circumstances where there was always the danger of losing touch with reality among all the silence and beauty.

The weather was perfect, stately blue and golden days following one on the next. June is the time of the longest days, and it was almost never dark; twilight merely deepened until two or three in the morning, when the early dawn washed it over with morning light, sunset and dawn blurring into one another. Looking out at the still-bright sky at ten in the evening, I would wonder how mothers enticed small children to bed without the aid of the dark.

As though conforming to a religious ritual, I fell into a custom every evening, around six o'clock, of going up to the top of the hill that rose from the left bank of the loch—one of the highest in the county and affording a sweeping view for miles around. A great, simple quietness overpowered the countryside at this hour, the slanting light running along the flanks of the hills, flooding their smooth green with soft brightness, casting folds and escarpments into mauve shadow, softening and rounding all outlines. In the early evening light an affinity between flesh and earth becomes evident, as all part of the same act of creation; there is something very female about the hills, their swelling roundness, undulating curves, like splendid female torsos and limbs sprawling in abandon; the stream running out of the earth forms a green cleft like a verdant pubis of some great goddess.

On the hilltop, the eye is drawn up, powerfully, to the blue flying buttresses of the domed firmament, and one begins to understand what inspired the architecture of the great cathedrals, which compel the eye, the mind, the spirit, upward in contemplation of majesty and mystery beyond our grasp.

One evening I remained up there in that great open-air cathedral, watching massive cloud formations accumulate over the hill on the opposite side of the loch, great banks of pure white marble mounting up until all the blue was obliterated except for one patch, on the side of the green summit, a patch no bigger than a fist, which, in its plain, blameless blueness, seemed to open up into the infinite. I felt, contemplating that scrap of blue, an awe—a sense of intimidation that reduced one's self to insignificance, so that one's own consequence was no more than an ant's; but gradually, as I reflected, my awareness itself merged with the irreducibility of that blue opening into the eternal, so that I was no longer a separate consciousness, but was part of whatever it was.

Later, as I made my way down the hill, and our stone cottage came into view beside the loch, I felt that if I could only hold onto what I had experienced up on the hill, my life down in the valley would be transformed. However, matter prevailed, hunger gnawed, and I came into the kitchen and peeled potatoes and shelled peas and cooked lambchops—the ribs of wooly little creatures who had gamboled outside my gates. But when I sat down to my meal, I found myself wanting to improvise a sort of grace to utter over the food, aware of it now as something for which thanks and praise ought to be given.

Later that evening, browsing in the Book of Psalms, I found appropriate words in Psalm 104:

> "He causeth the grass to grow for the cattle,
>   and herbs for the service of man;
>   that he may bring forth food out of the earth."

We kept a paperback edition of the Dartmouth Bible in the living room to be resorted to should we ever run out of reading matter. On that long, twilit night, alone in the hills, the loch shimmering with a silver leaden light beyond the windows, a great hush fallen over everything, the poetry of the psalms seemed a suitable way to contemplate God's handiwork:

> "Who shall ascend into the hill of the Lord?
>   Or who shall stand in his holy place?"

> "... We are the people of his pasture
>   and the sheep of his hand."

The telephone rings—the Hunters calling to check up on me. "Reading the Book of Psalms, did you say!" Bob is highly amused. "I'll be right over to fetch you away before it gets any worse. I knew we shouldn't trust you to be all on your own up there; next thing you'll be turning into some kind of religious nut. Wander about in the hills with not enough food in your stomach, and before you know what's hit you you'll be having a religious experience. Helen, come and talk to the puir mad thing; she's gone bonkers from too much solitude."

Helen comes to the phone; she was well grounded in girlhood in the Old Testament by her fanatically religious mother. "Well . . . if that's what you're 'into,'" she says, "you'd best make sure that you have clean hands and a pure heart."

And then she goes on to tell me that Joe, their tractorman, has run off with the wife of the dairyman on the farm next to theirs. "And Bob's been having to drive the tractor all day, while I attempted to calm Joe's enraged wifie and the four greetin' bairns. Though I must confess that I felt a sneaking sympathy for Joe; he's a good worker and likes things neat and orderly, and the mess and dirt and squalor in that cottage would have been enough to drive any man to seek solace in the arms of another."

"Clean hands and an *impure* heart—that's our Joe," Bob calls out.

Now I was more clearly able to understand the significance of the inscribed stone we had found on one of the lower peaks overlooking the glen. On a walk some summers ago, Philippa, our daughter, who was taking a geology course at her college, and who tended to view the landscape now in geological terms —seeing rock strata, sedimentation, mineral composition, and Ice Age formations where we saw only rolling hill country— noticed carvings on a flat stone slab. It lay against the slope of the hill, as random as any stone, unmarked by any cairn. The carvings turned out to be words:

> "I to the hills will lift mine eyes
> from whence doth come mine aid."

We were intrigued, mystified, and asked around the glen; no one else had come across it or could even hazard a guess as to how it had got there. The stone was weathered, the carving crude, its age indeterminate. Jenny Kirkbride, with her keen intelligence and curiosity, determined to trace its origin, and a few years later wrote to us in New York to let us know she had solved the mystery. She had run into a young man whose parents had kept a cottage in the glen to use whenever they were home on leave from the father's engineering job in Saudi Arabia; the young man's childhood had been spent either in the parched Middle East or the chill and gloom of Scottish boarding schools, and the times spent in the glen had been idyllic for him. "I ran into him in the village," Jenny wrote, "and remembered he had always been a great hill walker, and I asked him if he had ever seen the stone. Aye, he said, he had carved it and placed it there when he was a schoolboy! They had come home for the holidays from Saudi, he told me, and he was that happy to be back in the glen, and the hills were so bonny, that it just came on him to do it out of gratitude. And he's not one of your weedy, pale religious types either; he's a muckle six-footer and plays soccer and goes in for rock climbing. He was pleased to hear that you had found it. He lives in Canada now, and his parents are still out somewhere in Arabia."

The source of his impulse was comprehensible now to me.

In the pervading silence to which I became accustomed during that time alone, when sometimes days would pass in which I would not hear even the sound of my own voice, my hearing became more acute. I became aware of the flies' buzz on the kitchen windowpane, the wind stirring the trees before dawn, the mumble of the tongues of flame consuming the logs, ash whispering as it fell through the grate, the plop on the water as the trout's breath surfaced, the sound of the short grass being torn by the browsing sheep, the gargling noise made by the ewes calling their lambs—sounds that go unperceived in the clash and stir of family life.

Alone in the hills I learned to distinguish the different sounds of the water as it ran downhill: the thin fast babble of a spring sounding a treble note that deepened where it joined up with a fuller stream and tumbled into a dark pool; music in a minor key where it meandered slow and smooth over stones; playful and charming where it cascaded over rock faces, whispering where it trickled through boggy places in among the ooze and the wild flowers. It was possible to unravel the sounds, to isolate the most rudimentary elements, like trying to hear, separately, what the violin and flute and piano are each singing in the music of a trio.

In the silence one becomes conscious, as well, of the activity of small-animal life in the heather and bracken, each species with its own laws and necessities—birth, the fight for survival, sudden violent death all dramatically enacted out of sight, day and night, in the undergrowth: the swish and whisper in the long grass, the rustle and scurry of the sudden white scut of a fleeing rabbit, the thin scream of a vole, the whirr and rattle as grouse rise up disturbed from their nests in the heather, the fox loping away over the hill, the eagle, hovering motionless, waiting to pounce on the terrified prey.

If I went walking after dinner, I would stoke up the fire before I left, leaving it flickering behind the wire mesh screen, so that I would have the pleasure of the smoke rising up from the chimney when I looked down from the slopes, the sweet smell of woodsmoke as I returned. "Long may your lum reek" is a Scottish blessing that means "Long may your chimney smoke," invoking a sufficiency of fuel, warmth, ongoing life. That solitary house beside a lake, with its "lum reekin'," had the effect of taming the wild landscape. It held the primal elements of myth and fairy tale: the prince riding on his steed for so many days and so many nights in a land of endless hills, or the lost girl coming, at last, upon a small stone cottage beside an enchanted lake, the chimney smoking.

In fairy tales this is usually not the end of the quest, but a further step toward the acquisition of the golden key, the talisman, the magic word, or whatever it is that brings about the transition to the next stage of the journey—leading then to the freeing of the captive from the dragon, or the winning of the hand of the son or daughter of the king; or the crown itself; the required rites of passage, according to interpreters of mythology—the quest, the battle with dangers and evil, the acquisition of wisdom; then the ultimate deliverance—the flowering of the fully conscious individuality.

One sojourns a while in the enchanted cottage, then one is required to move on.

Jung's autobiography, *Memories, Dreams, Reflections*, was one of the books I read that illuminated June, and in it I found something that came to mind whenever I caught a view of our solitary little dwelling with the smoke drifting away over the slate-tiled roof:

> . . . the cosmic meaning of consciousness became over-whelmingly clear to me. . . . that Man is indispensable for the completion of creation; that, in fact, he himself is the second creator of the world, who alone has given to the world its objective existence—without which, un-heard, unseen, silently eating, giving birth, dying, heads

nodding through hundreds of millions of years, it would have gone on in the profoundest night of non-being down to its unknown end. Human consciousness created objective existence and meaning, and man found his indispensable place in the great process of being.

And it would seem to me, as I came home down the hill, that our small dwelling, with its fire lit, was essential for the completion of that glen, which would have been only the wilderness without it.

Living on my own in such deep solitude, I learned the value of orderliness; in the breadth and depth of those slow days and nights under huge skies, there was the possibility of losing track of time and one's self, so domestic order became the form for the hours to shape themselves around. Outdoors, I became aware of the pleasure that order and pattern imposed on a landscape where the green undulating hills are as perpetual as the sea.

On the sheep track outside our hedge, the voice of the shepherd calls out what sounds like "wurra, wurra, wurra— forebye," and hundreds of sheep come pouring down the hill, the sun glancing along their creamy backs and rumps composing a richly satisfying design: thick-textured, plaited, filleted. As they are siphoned off the slopes onto the narrowness of the track by the harrowing of the sheep dogs, the sheep fall into a single file and run, equidistant from each other, forming a pattern like even-spaced running stitches embroidered in white wool on a green background. A flight of birds in arrowhead formation, switches direction suddenly as a hawk appears out of nowhere to hang ominously in the sky, and the light striking the changed geometrical design formed by their wings shows a richly ornamented monochrome composition. A school of small fish in the clear water of the burn alter course to skirt an obstructing stone or water weed, flick their gray opalescent forms, and slide past, the shoal maintaining the regularity of its rainbowed surface intact. The birds, the beasts, and the fish: each flight, flock, shoal, responds like a single organism powered by its own nervous system, the parts maintaining the harmony of the whole in a manner pleasing to the observing eye, satisfying what must be a deep-seated human yearning for order, pattern, harmony, which compelled the maker of the earliest artifacts to embellish a simple tool or vessel with dots, striations, geometrical ornamentation.

My four weeks of solitude came to an end, and one bright morning in early July I drove to Gleneagles Station to pick up the family. In the clamor and excitement of their return to the glen—their delight in rediscovering that everything was as they remembered it, the exchange of news and gossip—the sense of distance from the world that had accumulated around me in those long, serene days and nights alone dissolved, in the way the increasing warmth of the sun dispersed the early morning mists from the water of the loch.

We stopped off in the village to stock up the larder, and the friendly tradesmen expressed satisfaction to see the family complete. "The doctor is looking a little wearied," Mrs. McWhirter, the grocer's mother, confided as she weighed and wrapped my purchases, "but a few days in the hills will blow all that bad New York air out of his system."

The children did not always come to Glenauchen with us every year. As they grew up and started to go to college, their own pursuits sometimes kept them away. But, generally, one or two of the three were either with us or working for Bob on the farm and coming for weekends to the glen.

Friends from New York or England would visit, and sometimes family from Africa came to stay. If the house was full, the hotel in the glen accommodated our overflow. But no matter who it was who came, or from where, the hills wrought their magic; tense, anxious, and tired guests succumbed to the peace and the green silence.

Driving home past the hotel one day, we saw a group of men with surveyors' instruments taking readings along the ridge of the deep wooded valley that dropped away from the road. Later we asked Donny if he knew why they were there.

"Aye, I do," he said. "The plain fact is that the water supply from your loch and mine together is not sufficient to meet the demand. They're going to be damming up the river down there, and constructing a gigantic new reservoir alongside the glen road."

"Do you mean they're going to flood that whole valley!"

"Aye, that they are," he said gravely. "You'd best take as many walks as you can there this summer; you'll not get the chance again."

An ancient arched stone bridge forded the river at the bottom of the valley; some said it was a Roman bridge; it was named for an early Christian saint who was said to have performed miracles.

"And the bridge?" we asked Donny.

"Not even a miracle could save it; it will go under the water, like everything else down there."

The gray stone of our cottage, the blue of sky and loch, the green of hills—all lines simple, colors pure—formed a childlike composition to the eye of anyone looking down from one of the hilltops. A summer came when, standing high up on a rocky outcrop on Dalrioch, out of the blue I had an urge to attempt to make a painting of our place.

In the village of Douleur (more sophisticated than our own) there was a tiny art gallery that sold artist's supplies. I bought a canvas board, five tubes of color, and a sketch-pad.

I had no idea how to do it. I was unschooled in drawing and knew nothing about acrylic paints, but I wanted to transfer that aspect—so familiar now to my eye—to a square of canvas. For hours at a time, I sat on a flat rock halfway up the hill and stared, and tried to reduce the broad landscape with the small house to the dimension of a page of the sketch-pad. It was difficult and frustrating, trying to put down in pencil, and then in color, what I held with such clarity in my vision.

It took a good part of the summer. I moved, when the scene was penciled at last onto my canvas, down to the terrace above our lawn. Whoever came by—Donny, the postman, fishers, or lost hikers—took an interest in my project. The house was simple enough to do, like the child's drawing it resembled; the water of the loch lapped in front of it, the color of my tube of blue, and the trees bowed to the direction of the wind. The difficulty was in suggesting the breadth of the rolling hills, and the way they seemed to shelter the cottage with their girth. I was forced to stare with such intensity at the scene, to strain after it in an effort to get it from my mind's eye onto the paint on my brush—to breach that space between what is known and felt and the finished piece of work—that it became imbued, indelibly, on the retina or brain. I have now just to glance at the small painting that hangs on the wall of our kitchen in New York for that whole sweep of landscape to come back.

The sheep browsing on the slopes were beyond my ability; the family said they looked like mushrooms; but then, scattered sheep, seen from a distance, I assured my detractors, don't look all that different from mushrooms.

In the stable at Glenauchen there was a paint can with a drop of yellow paint in it, left over from the previous year, when we had repainted the front door a shade of lichen-yellow that goes so well with gray stone. I used that drop of paint to color the front door of the house in my picture; it makes it easy to push the door open, and look in.

What moved me to make the painting that summer, which turned out to be our last summer in the glen, I cannot say. We had no idea that it was to be the last. Perhaps it was an impulse, similar to the one that moved Alexander Shillinglaw, the wood carver, to put his workshop in order. He had his intimations of necessary change; we must have been receiving ours, as well, without consciously heeding them.

At summer's end, as always, we rambled along the banks of the burn, where young ash and hazel saplings flourished; the hazelnuts were hard and green yet, but Jenny would harvest them in the fall after she had gathered the wild brambleberries and made them into jam. The wild raspberries ripened when the caravaners went back to their lives in chilly, windy cities; we would walk on the hill above the deserted caravan site—a dreary place without the sunbathers and transistor radios and flapping laundry lines—picking and eating the raspberries, their tart sweetness tasting of the melancholy we felt at having to pack up and leave at the end of another summer of full, quiet pleasure.

On a Sunday morning, we walked over the hill to a hamlet at the crossroads where they sold the Sunday papers; Donny, as deacon of the kirk, made no delivery on the Sabbath. It was a five-mile walk by the winding road, shorter if one went directly through the hills. We came back past the church, just as the service had ended and the congregation were coming out into the churchyard. The minister stood in the little porch and shook hands with each person who emerged, a courtesy that did not take up much of his time since his flock was a small one.

Outside the churchyard, where the grave of Miss Jane Honeyman, Gray Jane, extended beyond the wall, the glen folk gathered to pass the time of day with one another before going home to the Sunday roast joint. Donny, severe in a dark suit, positively glowed with cleanliness and godliness; Meg Cameron, who was the church organist, and her aunt, Miss Kirstie Aird, were chatting with the couple who owned the newspaper and sweetie shop in the village. "Have you haird?" Miss Kirstie Aird drew us into the circle. "The Manse has been sold."

We had not heard. Social contact with Shuna Balfour-Kinnear had resolved into annual eleven o'clock coffees taken at each other's houses, and occasional encounters over her garden wall. We had never gotten to meet Husband, nor caught even a glimpse of him. Through the gate of the Manse, we could see an Arab mare and her foal cropping grass in the glebe, but no sign of family life.

"Who's bought it?" we asked.

The lady from the sweetie shop looked suspiciously about to make sure there were no eavesdroppers; lowering her voice, she said, "I've haird it's some people from Glasgow who own woolen mills. *They're Catholics*," she hissed. "I always knew that the Catholics were just *waiting* their chance to get back in the glen."

Harl and I looked at each other, amazed; but the rest of the group, joined now by Tottie and Donny, chatted on, discussing the great wealth supposed to have been amassed by these new owners of the Manse. The fresh wind stirred the boughs of the four yew trees that stood at the corners of the grave of Miss Jane Honeyman. We had never seen the ghost of Gray Jane moving through the churchyard, gliding up the hill and over the lawn to the house where she had lived and died. But four hundred years after the Reformation, the spirit of John Knox still haunted the glen.

In early September, we cleaned up the house as usual, and packed our things away in the storeroom under the stairs, out of the way of the tenants.

In the afternoon, on the day before we were leaving, we made our rounds in the glen, taking leave of our neighbors. Miss Kirstie Aird said, "Och, your going means that the hard long winter is on its way; I'm afraid of driving on icy roads, and my puir niece Meg has to do all my shopping for me." She embraced us. "But I'll know it's surely summer when I see you two driving into the glen next year."

At Glencorrie House, Mrs. MacFadyen was taking afternoon tea under the oak tree on the lawn. Mrs. Darroch, her trusty, overworked household minion, appeared without having been summoned, bearing extra teacups, hot water, and a dish of tea-cakes. The late summer sunshine bathed the house and lawns in mellow light, and Jessie MacFadyen poured tea from Georgian silver into fine china as if her needs were tended by a household of butlers, cooks, maids, and gardeners, instead of the chronically harassed Mrs. Darroch, who scurried off to fulfill another one of her many roles. While Mrs. MacFadyen sipped and nibbled, and inhaled at her long jet cigarette holder, she gave us a detailed briefing on how she would like our American president to conduct his foreign policy; when we stood up to go, she said, "Till next year, then," and shook hands with us firmly and briskly, like a general dispatching officers into the field.

At the MacIvers', we were plied with more tea, and scones and tarts and buns; and Tottie and Donny stood at their gate calling, "Goodbye . . . safe journey . . . see you next summer," until we were out of sight. We managed to convince the Kirk-

brides that we had already had tea twice; and they and the
two children, and Spot, the dog, and their two pet lambs—
now fully grown, their trip to the butcher postponed year
after year—walked with us down the hill to where we had
left the car. At the farm, Mrs. Cameron sent Meg to the kitchen
to pack a tin of her famous shortbread for us to take back to
New York.

They would, all of them, in the New Year, send us picture
calendars with scenes of Scotland: green mountains and blue
lochs and streams of unlikely hue, gray castles of such romantic
aspect as to seem unreal. We knew they existed.

We always spent our last night with the Hunters at the farm.
We locked the front door of Glenauchen Cottage, took a long,
lingering look at the water, the hills. "D'you think we'll be
back here next year?" I asked Harl.

"Why do you say that?"

"I just wondered. Do you?"

"Who knows?" he said.

I opened the gate for him to drive out of the stableyard,
closed it, and we drove off.

The weather had been fine for weeks, and there was an early
harvest that year. All through the countryside combines were
at work cutting through ripe fields of grain. At the farm, we
parked our car in the small barn where it would stand through
the winter and spring, with starlings and barn swallows swooping in and out and spattering it with their droppings.

In the early evening Bob and the men were still out in the
fields; as long as the days were dry they worked until the light
faded. We went with Helen up to the field that was being
harvested. Bob and his tractorman were finishing off the last
rows on the side of hill. The great whirring blades of the
harvesting machine glinted in the slanting rays of the westering
sun; the standing crops fell before it, to be gathered up, the
seeds threshed from the stem, and the chaff separated. The
seeds collected up, filling the hopper, and the stripped straw

was returned to the ground, where it matted the sloping field the color of pale brass. Bob came up beside the combine in a tractor with a trailer container attached to it, and a stream of glistening grain was disgorged from the hopper, pouring, until the trailer was piled high and full.

Beyond the yellow fields, the sea fell away, blue and flat. Great cawing crows hopped about among the fallen stalks of straw, pecking at the gleanings, quarreling with flapping wings over disputed grains of barley. "In the village where I grew up," Helen said, "every year, after the harvest, the minister would preach the same sermon: 'The harvest is past, the summer is ended, and yet, O Lord, we are not saved.'"

As we walked back to the farmhouse, a tractor came rumbling along the road pulling a wagon loaded with barley, driven by David, our son, with Tom, the Hunters' son, beside him. David was remaining in Scotland to spend a full year working on the farm for Bob. Both of them had sunburned faces, necks, and forearms—a farmer's suntan, Bob calls it— and both were covered in a layer of dust from the chaff.

"Are you coming in for your supper when you've unloaded that?" Helen called out.

"After we've stopped at the pub for a couple of pints," Tom answered above the noise of the tractor. "This is thirsty work."

David would be the only member of the family who would know the other three seasons in the glen; we never were to see the rowan berries brighten to flame-orange on the trees, or the loch turn a chill gray with the snow-powdered hills reflected in it; we never saw the snowdrops and daffodils that carpeted the sloping lawn of the cottage; never got to hear the sound of the lark.

We had a late supper when the men came in, tired and dusty from the fields. "A heavy harvest this year," Bob observed with satisfaction. In the walled garden beyond the long windows, dahlias and chrysanthemums burned with color in the dusk. Before we went to bed, Helen wedged every spare bit of space in our luggage with jars of her raspberry and black-currant jam—enough to see us through the winter.

Early in the morning, Bob drove us to Edinburgh airport to get the shuttle to London, where we would pick up our plane to New York. The fields were swathed in milky mists. "We won't be able to get on with the harvesting till midday if this haar doesn't start to lift soon," Bob said.

At the airport, businessmen, pin-striped and gray-flanneled, clutching briefcases and newspapers, headed for the shuttle as if wound up and programmed with executive impulse; among them, Bob, in corduroy pants and baggy sweater, his face strong and weatherbeaten beneath the mass of white hair, exuded vigor, earthy vitality.

We said our goodbyes. "Hope the harvest goes well," Harl said.

"Aye—so long as the weather holds, it will." A jet flew overhead, drowning out our voices; we waited for it to pass. When it was quiet again, Bob said, "A good harvest, the summer is ended, and yet we are not saved. I'll be getting along, then; see you next year." He waved, and went off. We joined the line for our plane.

In the autumn, Helen wrote to let us know that Miss Waterman had been offered a teaching post at a university, and she and her consort and their small dog, reluctantly, would be ending their tenancy at Glenauchen.

The Hunters found a pair of divinity students to rent the cottage, but they turned out to be disorderly and unreliable. "Dissolute divinity students—whoever would have thought it possible?" Bob wrote. "Lived like coarse tinks, they did, then did a moonlight flit without paying the rent; while our couthy Miss Waterman, living in sinfulness, was as excellent a wee wifie as ever kept house."

The cottage stood empty for a few months. We imagined its emptiness, the short winter days, the long cold nights, no smoke coming from its chimney. It seemed to us that it had returned to itself. The cold hearth at Glenauchen was like a reproach to us. A fire should burn there through all the seasons; without its warmth and glow the glen was a dark, lonely place. Had it really been ours? we wondered. Or was it a place where we had sojourned in the summers for a while?

We began to feel distanced from it. The last few years, perhaps, had been preparing us; there had been signs and signals we had received and put aside. Now we agreed that the children had been coming to Glenauchen less and less as the claims of their own lives took them in other directions; air travel seemed to have become more frenzied; journeys across oceans and continents seemed too draining for the sake of a summer cottage. Harl and I both found ourselves thinking we should give up the place, let go of it. But how could we bear to give up Glenauchen? the children asked, and we asked ourselves the same question. The truth was that it was perfect—and it was no longer for us.

We told the Hunters. Before putting Glenauchen Cottage on the market, we wrote to Mr. Monroe to ask if he would like to buy the house where his father had been born; his letter thanked us, but said his life kept him too much in England for him to have use of the old waterman's house.

In the spring the Hunters put the property in the hands of real-estate agents. It was bought by a Scottish couple with a child, who were expecting a baby in the summer. We liked the idea of children, a family living there year round. They were keen gardeners, hikers, fishers, they told the Hunters, who thought they were well suited to the place.

Helen and Bob, with David to help them, cleared out our personal things. Mr. Menzies, of the saleroom, bought the contents of the house, most of which he had sold us seven years earlier, and carted everything away.

After seven summers, our time in the glen was over.